D1647914

Second Edition

Approaching Macintosh®

A Guide to Learning Macintosh Software

Second Edition
Approaching Macintosh®

A Guide to Learning Macintosh Software

HOWDY DO.!

Michael Tchao
William Berner
Craig Elliott
Albert Chu
Ron Fernandez
David Finkelstein
Cynthia Frost

Apple Computer, Inc.

ADDISON-WESLEY
PUBLISHING COMPANY

Reading, Massachusetts • Menlo Park, California • New York
Don Mills, Ontario • Wokingham, England • Amsterdam • Bonn
Sydney • Singapore • Tokyo • Madrid • San Juan

Library of Congress Cataloging-in-Publication Data

Approaching Macintosh : a guide to learning Macintosh software /
   Michael Tchao ... [et al.]. --2nd ed.
       p. cm.
    ISBN 0-201-52584-4 (soft cover)
    1. Macintosh (Computer)--Programming. 2. Computer software.
  I. Tchao, Michael, 1963-
  QA76.8.M3A67 1991
  004.165--dc20   90-48189
                                                         CIP

Macintosh, Apple, the Apple logo, AppleTalk, Finder, ImageWriter,
LaserWriter, and MultiFinder are registered trademarks of Apple
Computer, Inc.

Claris, FileMaker, and MacPaint are registered trademarks of Claris
Corporation.

HyperCard and HyperTalk are registered trademarks of Apple Computer,
Inc., licensed to Claris Corporation.

Screen shots ©1987–1989 Microsoft®Excel and ©1983–1989 Microsoft®
Word are reprinted with permission from Microsoft Corporation.

Permission for use of the terms in the Glossary is granted by Apple
Computer, Inc.

Copyright ©1991 by Addison-Wesley Publishing Company

All rights reserved. No part of this publication may be reproduced, stored
in a retrieval system, or transmitted, in any form or by any means,
electronic, mechanical, photocopying, recording, or otherwise, without
the prior written permission of the publisher. Printed in the United States of
America.

3 4 5 6 7 8 9 10 AL 9594939291

0 Approaching Macintosh

Preface
Acknowledgements

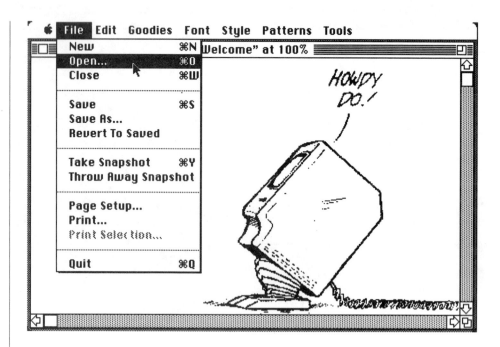

Preface

Some computer books teach their readers about computers by explaining that information can be represented by a series of 0's and 1's. Other computer books teach about computers by teaching their readers how to speak strange languages like BASIC and PL/1. Still other books teach their readers about computers by introducing them to long, complicated terms like complementary metal-oxide-semiconductor.

Approaching Macintosh is not like those books. *Approaching Macintosh* teaches its readers about computers by teaching them how to use one. If learning by doing is the way you like to learn, we're sure you'll enjoy using this book. *Approaching Macintosh* focuses on software for the Apple Macintosh, a computer that has now become a fixture on many college campuses.

This book is the result of two years of class testing on such unsuspecting subjects as Stanford University undergraduates, graduates, faculty, and staff. Using their input, *Approaching Macintosh* was designed to be an effective teaching tool in both self-paced and classroom teaching situations.

Sections

The book is divided into **sections,** each of which treats a general type of personal computer application, such as word processing, database management, and graphics. Each section begins with an overview of the basic terms and concepts you'll be covering in that section. These sections will help you understand what this type of software can do and how it's typically used.

Modules

Every section contains one or more **modules**—the individual exercises that teach you how to use a specific software package. Each module should take about 1 to 1 1/2 hours to complete, and both introductory and advanced modules are provided for many software packages.

Approaching Macintosh was designed so that you can choose to complete the modules that interest you in whatever order you wish. However, it is recommended that you complete the Introduction to Macintosh module first, and that you complete the introductory modules before you start the advanced ones.

Tasks and Reviews

Before you begin a module, be sure to read the paragraphs labeled **The Task** carefully. These paragraphs explain what you're about to do and why. At the end of each module, read the **Review** paragraph to make sure you haven't missed the high points.

Galleries and Exercises

At the end of each section are **Gallery** documents that provide examples of how a software package is used. These gallery ideas should serve as a springboard for your own experimentation. **Exercises** are also provided to test your recall of the most important procedures and concepts of that section.

New in the Second Edition

This new and improved version of Approaching Macintosh is based on the latest versions of the most popular software packages for Macintosh. Here's a list of the software used in each section:

1. Introduction to Macintosh	Macintosh System Software version 6.0
2. Graphics	Claris MacPaint 2.0
3. Word Processing	Microsoft Word 4.0
4. Spreadsheets	Microsoft Excel 2.0
5. Charts	Microsoft Excel 2.0
6. Database Management	Claris FileMaker PRO
7. HyperCard	HyperCard 2.0

We've also increased the number of exercises at the end of each section, and we've included more "do-it-yourself" problems.

The important thing to remember when using *Approaching Macintosh* is that the authors sincerely want you to have fun while you're learning. We've worked long, hard hours (and some legal holidays) to choose examples that will make you smile. Try not to disappoint us.

Michael Tchao

Bill Berner

Craig Elliott

Albert Chu

Dave Finkelstein

Ron Fernandez

Cindy Frost

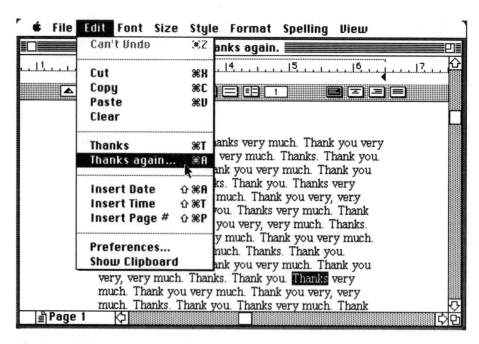

Thanks, again

Thanks to all the people at Stanford University, Apple Computer, and the *real* world for making this book possible.

At Stanford, thanks to all the students, faculty, and staff who took our course "Using the Macintosh at Stanford." You were our unsuspecting guinea pigs. Thanks to all of the CS1c teaching assistants who were our partners in crime.

Thanks to Lynn Takahashi, Dan'l Lewin, the Apple University Team, and the members of the Apple University Consortium for encouraging us to publish this book and for supporting us in our efforts. Thanks to Chris Espinosa, Moira Cullen, Stacey Bressler, and Nicole Kowalski for answering every question we could ask as well as many we would never have thought to ask. Also, thanks to the Macintosh User Education Group, the Apple Support Training Group, and the scores of other folks at Apple who helped us out and cheered us on.

Thanks to our reviewers: Richard Alpert, Boston University; Sheryl Blix, University of Washington; Kelly Callison, U.S. Coast Guard Academy; Shirley Fenton, University of Waterloo; James Gips, Boston College; Sandra Helmick, University of Missouri; Marvin Marcus and Susan Franklin, University of California, Santa Barbara; Joe Marks, Harvard University; Vickie Mullen, Linfield College; Robert L. Oakman, University of South Carolina; Jeff Popyack, Drexel University; and Andrea Butter. Your comments and suggestions kept us on our toes until the very end.

We'd like to extend special thanks to Stuart Reges, Assistant Chairman of the Department of Computer Science at Stanford University. Stuart inspired and supported both the book and the course it came from. He encouraged us to try something new and gave us the charter to do it.

Finally, special thanks to Berke Breathed for illustrating our cover. We think it's terrific.

ACKNOWLEDGEMENTS

Contents

HOWDY DO!

1 Approaching Macintosh

Introduction to Macintosh

Exercises

Before Getting Started

Welcome to the first step. Before you can begin to become a pro at personal computing, you'll need a quick introduction to the Macintosh and how to work with it. If you've never used a Macintosh before—if you've never used a computer before—you'll want to become familiar with the parts of the Macintosh and learn some basic terms and techniques used throughout this book.

In order to complete this module, you'll need:

- A Macintosh computer
- A copy of the Microsoft Word application program
- A blank diskette (to save a copy of your work)
- A copy of Plato's **Republic** (just kidding)

This module assumes that your Macintosh has been unboxed and set up, the system software has been loaded, and the application software or programs that you'll be using have also been loaded. If you haven't done this, or if you have no idea what all this means, you may want to either ask a friend or follow the instructions in the manuals that came with your Macintosh.

This module also assumes that you have the Microsoft Word word processing application. You'll use it to learn the basics of Macintosh applications.

Meet Your Macintosh

Macintosh computers come in a number of different shapes and sizes, but there are two basic types: One-piece or **compact** Macintoshes where the screen and computer are all one box, and two-piece or **modular** Macintoshes where the Macintosh is divided into the screen part or **monitor** and the computer part, or **CPU**. (CPU stands for *Central Processing Unit*—just in case you were wondering.)

Compact Macintoshes have the advantages of being easier to carry (because they come in one piece) and easier to set up (because you don't have to worry about connecting cables between the two pieces). Modular Macintoshes let you choose between different types and sizes of screens.

The diagram on the next page shows the major parts of the Macintosh system and their appropriate names. These parts of the Macintosh (or any computer) that you can see and touch, like the monitor and CPU, are called **hardware**.

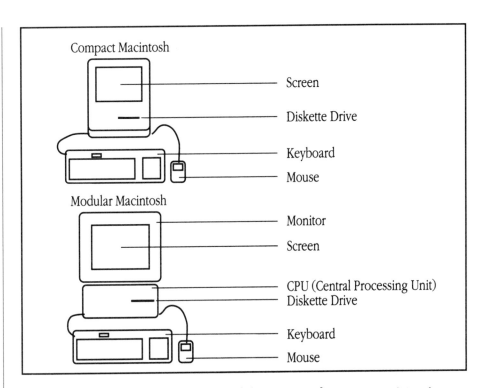

Use the diagram to locate the parts of the Macintosh system you're using. (Yours may look slightly different.)

If you're ever unsure of what a part of your Macintosh is called, or where it's located, you can use this diagram for reference.

Screen

The Macintosh screen is much like the screen on your television set. It's different from screens on many other computers because it can display highly detailed or **high-resolution** pictures or **graphics**. Depending on the type of Macintosh, and the type of monitor, Macintoshes can display black-and-white or color images. Typically, the Macintosh displays black characters on a white background, much like you would see on a typewritten page.

Mouse

The mouse is a small box about the size of a deck of playing cards that's attached to the Macintosh with a thin cord. You'll use the mouse to select and move objects on the Macintosh screen and to choose commands that tell the Macintosh what to do. You'll learn how to use the mouse later.

Diskette

The Macintosh uses 3 1/2-inch diskettes, which hold the documents you create and the **application software** that creates them. Diskettes work a lot like cassette tapes. Inside the plastic shell is a disk coated with magnetic material that your Macintosh can record on much like your tape deck records on cassette tapes. Just like your cassettes, keep your diskettes away from dust, heat, water, and above all, magnets. More about diskettes later.

Diskette Drive

Every Macintosh has at least one built-in diskette drive. The diskette drive records or **writes** information onto the diskette, and plays back or **reads** that information to the computer. In addition to the internal diskette drive, your Macintosh may have an external diskette drive which works just like the internal one.

Hard Disk Drive

In addition to a diskette drive, most Macintoshes these days also have a hard disk drive. It's often built into the computer or CPU, or it could be in a separate box under or beside the computer. The best way of thinking of a hard disk drive (or just "hard disk") is like a very big, very fast diskette drive. If you want to use lots of application software to create and store lots of documents, a hard disk lets you do that without constantly having to swap diskettes.

This book and this module assume that the Macintosh you're using is equipped with a hard disk drive. If you're using a computer with diskette drives only, you can still complete most of the modules in this book, but watch carefully for special instructions. Things may work slightly differently for you.

Keyboard

Just as Macintoshes come in different shapes and sizes, so do Macintosh keyboards. In general, Macintosh keyboards are laid out much like a typewriter keyboard—with a few notable exceptions. Find these special Macintosh keys on your keyboard:

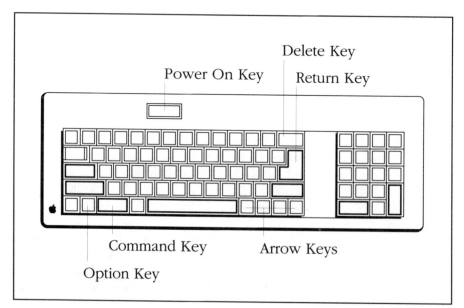

The Return key

The Return key works much like the carriage return on a typewriter. When you're typing, you'll use the Return key to leave blank lines between lines of text and to start new paragraphs.

The Delete (or Backspace) key

The Delete key erases or deletes the previously typed character or the current selection. So if you make a mistake when typing, simply use the Delete key to erase it.

The Command key

The wide key at the bottom left of the keyboard—the key with the symbol on it that looks a little bit like a freeway interchange—is the Command key. Many of the short cuts and special features you'll learn use the Command key in conjunction with another key or keys.

The Option key

The Option key is located to the left of the Command key. Like the Command key, holding down the Option key while typing another key modifies that key to perform a special function or short cut.

Arrow keys

The Arrow keys point up, down, left, or right—and that's the way they help you move when you're within a document.

Power On key

Some Macintoshes (most modular Macintoshes) let you turn them on from the keyboard using the key with the triangle on it. If your keyboard doesn't have one, or it doesn't seem to do anything, don't worry, you can use the power switch on the back of the computer. We'll get to that part next.

Getting Started

Now that you know where everything is on your Macintosh, you're ready to learn how to make it work. The first task is easy—turning it on.

Turning It On

Ask anyone. They'll tell you that a Macintosh works best when it's turned on. So let's get to it.

Turn on the Macintosh by pressing the Power On key (the one with the triangle on it). If nothing happens (or you can't find a key with a triangle on it on your keyboard), flip the switch or press the button on the back of the computer.

The Macintosh will beep softly, a small picture of a smiling Macintosh will appear as the Macintosh loads *system software* from the disk.

System Software

The Macintosh uses special files called **system software** to start up and keep running. System software is what makes a Macintosh work like a Macintosh, and therefore makes possible everything you're about to see and do.

Startup Disks

So, the first disk your Macintosh sees has to be one with those all important system files on them. This disk is called a *startup disk* or *system disk*. If you have a hard disk attached to your Macintosh, that disk is your startup disk. If you're using a system with only diskette drives, the Macintosh will display an icon of a disk with the flashing question mark until you insert a startup diskette into one of the diskette drives. If you haven't created a startup diskette yet, see your Macintosh system software manual to learn how.

Only if you're using a Macintosh without a hard disk drive, insert a startup diskette—label side up and metal end first—into the built-in diskette drive.

After you see the banner welcoming you to Macintosh (these computers are *so* friendly these days), the Macintosh **desktop** will appear.

The Macintosh Desktop

One way to make computers easier to use is to make them more familiar. Macintosh uses the metaphor of a desktop to make the tools you use and the things you do easier to understand. Small pictures, called **icons**, represent objects you already know, such as documents, folders, and even a trash can. Using the mouse, you move these desktop objects and choose commands from the **menu bar** at the top of the screen to tell the Macintosh what to do. You'll learn more about how to do this in just a minute.

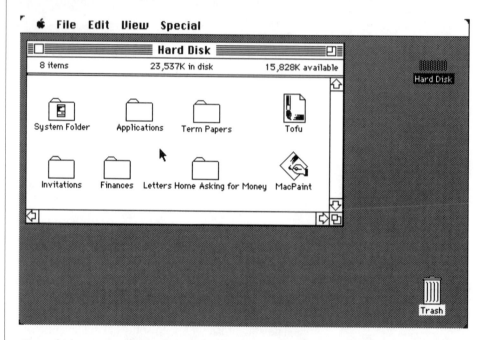

Your desktop may not look exactly like this—it depends on how many disks are attached to your Macintosh, and how things are organized on those disks. Here is a guide to some things you might see.

Hard Disk

The icon in the upper right-hand corner of your desktop represents the disk that you started from. Once again, depending on the type of hard disk you have, your icon may look a little different—and it may have a different name.

Diskette

Just like the hard disk icon, the diskette icon represents a diskette in any diskette drive attached to your Macintosh.

File Server

Application

Document

Folder

System Folder

If your Macintosh is connected to other Macintoshes over a **network,** you may see an icon of a **file server.** You see, aside from connecting a bunch of computers to each other, a network can also connect a bunch of computers to a shared printer or a shared hard disk. That's what a file server is—a hard disk shared over a network. And you work with it just like you would work with a hard disk connected directly to your Macintosh.

Applications or **application programs** are tools used to create and modify documents. For instance, Microsoft Word is a *word processing* application that you can use to create documents like letters to loved ones, term papers on genetic mutations, or textbooks on Macintosh computers. Applications are usually represented by diamond-shaped icons.

Documents are the things that applications create. Documents are usually represented by page icons. Since documents know which application created them, each application's document icons look different so that it will be easy to tell your letters from your spreadsheets.

The way you organize things on your Macintosh disks—whether they be hard disks, diskettes, or file servers—is in folders. Just like the folders you might have on your desk, Macintosh folders are containers for things: documents, applications, or other folders. You'll learn more about working with folders later in this module.

System software is kept in a special folder called (appropriately enough) the **system folder.** It's easy to distinguish the system folder from the other folders because it sports a small picture of a Macintosh on it. You may not be able to see the system folder on your Macintosh, but if your Macintosh is working, trust us, the system folder is there.

Using the Mouse and the Pointer

There are icons to represent everything available for you to use on the Macintosh desktop. The way in which you tell the Macintosh you want to use something is by selecting its icon. You select icons and commands by using the **mouse.** Notice the small black arrow on the screen; this is the **pointer.**

Without lifting it, move the mouse back and forth. (Make sure that the mouse button is at the top.)

Notice that the pointer's movement on the screen follows your movement of the mouse.

Lift up the mouse and look underneath.

Notice the ball on the bottom of the mouse. When you move the mouse, the ball rolls and tells the pointer how to move. If the mouse ball is not touching a flat surface, the pointer doesn't move. Therefore, if you ever run out of room while moving the mouse, all you have to do is pick the mouse up and reposition it on a clear, flat area. Try this.

Move the mouse and watch the pointer move on the screen. Then, pick up the mouse and place it somewhere else on your desk. Note that the pointer doesn't move while the mouse is lifted.

Now try another experiment with the mouse. You may at some point begin to worry that, if you're not careful with the mouse, you could run the pointer off the edge of the screen, never to be seen again. Not so.

Try to move the pointer off the screen.

You can't. Honest. So don't worry about moving the mouse quickly across the desktop. If you should overshoot your target, simply move it back into position.

Mouse Techniques

Now that you've learned how to move the mouse, here are a few basic mouse techniques that you'll need to know before you continue. Don't worry if they seem a bit confusing at first; they'll become clearer once you use them.

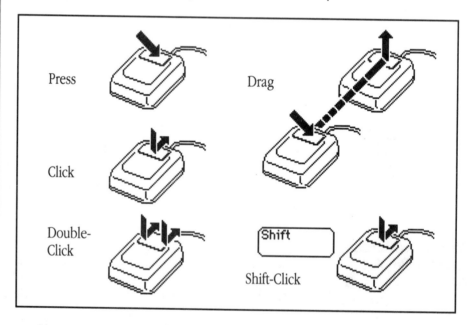

Press
As you might expect, pressing involves depressing the mouse button.

Click
To click an object, use the mouse to position the pointer over the object. Then press and release the mouse button.

Double-Click
You double-click an object by positioning the pointer over the object and clicking the mouse button twice in quick succession. Double-clicking is usually a short cut to perform a specific command.

Drag

To drag, position the pointer at the desired location and press down the mouse button. With the mouse button depressed, move the mouse to drag the pointer accordingly.

Shift-Click

To Shift-click, hold down the Shift key while clicking the mouse button. Shift-clicking usually extends or adds to a selection.

How You Work with a Macintosh

One of the things that makes Macintosh easy to learn is that no matter what you do with a Macintosh, you do it in the same way:

- First, **select an object**, usually by clicking on its icon.
- Then, **choose a command** to act on that object.

For example, if you want to duplicate a document or a folder on the desktop, first you select it and then you choose the command to duplicate it.

Selecting

To select something on the desktop, simply use the mouse to position the pointer above the object that you want to select, then click the mouse button. (Remember, "clicking" means to quickly press and release the button on top of the mouse.) Practice selecting by choosing the trash can.

Select the Trash by positioning the pointer over the trash can icon at the lower right corner of the Macintosh desktop and clicking the mouse button.

Notice that as you select an object, it becomes dark or highlighted. This highlighting helps you to quickly identify the current selection. If the Trash icon was already selected, it would have been highlighted.

Making Another Selection

If you change your mind about your selection—perhaps you decide you'd like to select something else—you need only to move the mouse pointer over the new icon and click the mouse button. Your previous selection becomes "unselected" when the new selection is highlighted.

Move the pointer over the hard disk icon at the upper right of the screen and click the mouse button once.

(Remember that you click by quickly pressing and releasing the mouse button.)

Notice that the disk icon is now highlighted and the Trash icon is unselected.

Choosing Commands

Once you've selected the object you'd like to work with, you'll need to choose a command to act on that selection. In general, you'll choose commands from the **menu bar** that run across the top of the desktop.

To choose a command from a menu:

- First, use the mouse to position the pointer over the appropriate menu.
- Press and hold the mouse button to "pull down" the menu.
- While still holding down the mouse button, drag down until the appropriate command is highlighted.
- Finally, release the mouse button.

You'll "open" the Trash using this technique.

First, click on the Trash icon to select it again.

The Trash icon becomes highlighted, indicating that it's selected.

Position the pointer over the File menu (on top of the word File in the menu bar). Press and hold the mouse button.

A "pull-down" menu of available commands appears from the menu bar.

While holding down the mouse button, drag the mouse downward until the pointer is over the Open command.

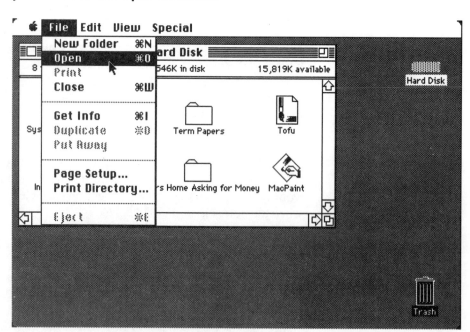

The Open command should be highlighted.

Release the mouse button.

An empty Trash window opens on the desktop. More about windows in a bit. Notice also that the Trash icon is now hollow, indicating that the Trash is now open.

If a window didn't appear, make sure that the Trash icon is selected before you choose Open from the File menu.

Use the technique you just learned to choose Close from the File menu.

Remember: Move the mouse pointer over the word File; press and hold the mouse button; drag down to the word "Close"; and release when Close is highlighted.

Practice opening and closing the Trash until you're comfortable with using menus.

Now that you're familiar with the basics of how a menu works, you might be curious about some other interesting features of menus. If you've already forgotten what a menu looks like, you might want to refer to the pictures of menus on this and the previous page.

Dimmed Commands

You may have noticed that when you pulled down the File menu, some of the commands were dimmed (shown in gray). These are commands that aren't appropriate at this time and can't be selected. (You can't "eject" the trash can, for instance.) By making it impossible to choose inappropriate commands, the Macintosh actually prevents you from making those embarrassing little mistakes.

Command Key Short Cuts

You also may have noticed that to the right of some of the commands listed in the menu is a letter preceded by a special symbol. That symbol corresponds to the symbol on the Command key, located just to the left of the space bar.

By holding down the Command key and typing the letter listed, you can invoke the command without using the mouse to pull down the menu. You may want to use these keyboard short cuts after you've become more familiar with the Macintosh.

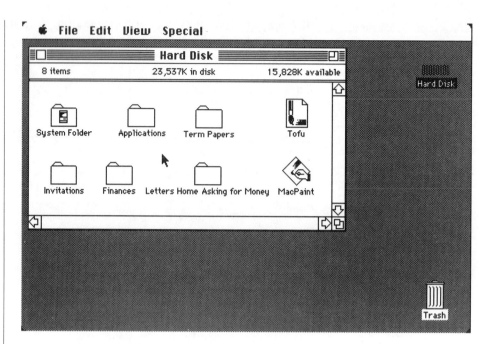

If the hard disk window isn't visible on your desktop, open the disk by selecting the hard disk icon and choosing Open from the File menu.

Working with Windows

A **window** is an area of the Macintosh screen that displays information. The disk window, for instance, displays the contents of the disk. The Trash window that you opened earlier displayed the contents of the Trash (clever, huh?). The parts of a window are shown here.

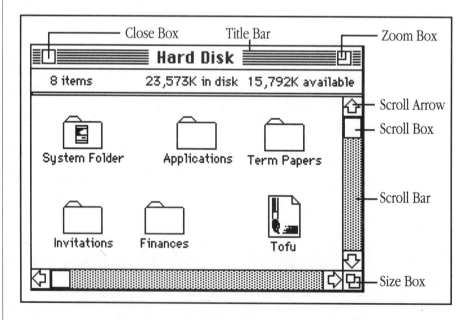

Changing the Size of a Window

There are times when you want to work with a large window, in order to easily see what's inside. Other times, you'll prefer a smaller window, in order to let you see more than one window at a time on the desktop.

Size Box

To change the size of a window, you use the mouse to drag the **size box** in the bottom right corner of the window.

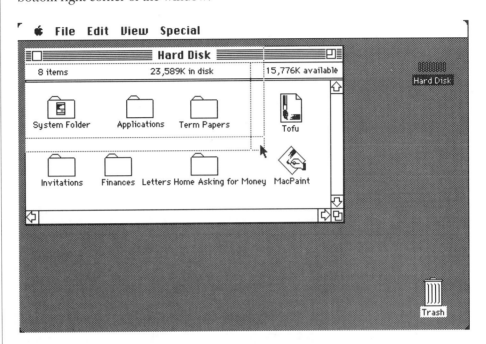

Position the mouse pointer on the size box and drag up and to the left.

As you drag, a dotted outline of the window follows. As you drag up, the window becomes shorter. As you drag to the left, the window becomes narrower. When you release the mouse button, the window changes size.

Experiment with resizing the window until you feel comfortable using the size box.

Zoom Box

When you want to quickly expand a window to its maximum size to get a better view of what's inside it, the **zoom box** in the upper right corner of the title bar is for you.

Click in the zoom box.

The window "zooms" to its maximum size. (If the window was already near its maximum size, not much zooming takes place.)

Click in the zoom box again.

The window "zooms" back to its original size. Pretty nifty, eh? Using the zoom box you can easily zoom up to get a look at the big picture, then zoom down to take up less space on the desktop.

It's important to remember that changing the size of a window doesn't change the window's contents. Even though you may not be able to see everything in the window, its contents are still there.

Scrolling

But, if you can't see everything that's in the window, how can you get at it? A good question.

Whenever a window is too small to show its entire contents, the **scroll bars** along the right edge and bottom of the window will appear gray. By clicking the **scroll arrows** at either end of the scroll bar, you'll be able to scroll through the contents of the window that you can't see.

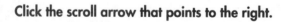

Using the size box, make the disk window small enough so that some of the icons are hidden from view.

Notice that the gray scroll bars indicate that some of the contents of the window is hidden.

Click the scroll arrow that points to the right.

The icons that were hidden should zip by to the left. You can use the other scroll arrows to scroll up, down, or to the left as well.

Using Multiple Windows

As we mentioned earlier, you can have more than one open window on the desktop at a time. With multiple windows open, windows can overlap like pieces of paper lying on top of one another. The frontmost window—the window you're working in—is called the **active window**.

Open the Trash by selecting it and choosing Open from the File menu.

The Trash window is now the active window.

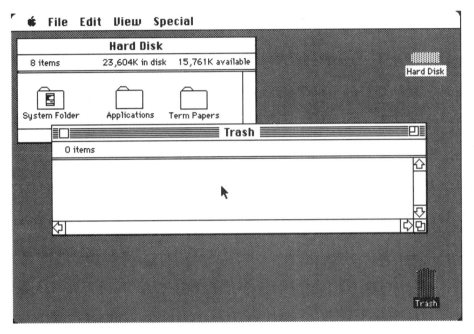

Notice that the active window is the frontmost window and its title bar is highlighted with horizontal lines. This makes the active window easy to identify.

Activating a Window

To activate a window, simply click anywhere inside it.

Click in the hard disk window to activate it.

Note that the disk window now moves to the front and its title bar is highlighted. The Trash window is now behind the disk window.

Moving a Window

In order to work with multiple windows, it may be necessary to move a window around on the desktop. To move a window, simply drag it by its **title bar**—the top part of the window near where the name of the window is.

Move the disk window by dragging it by its title bar.

Remember that to drag, you need to press and hold the mouse button while moving the mouse. A dotted outline of the window follows. When you release the mouse button, the window snaps to its new location in a flash.

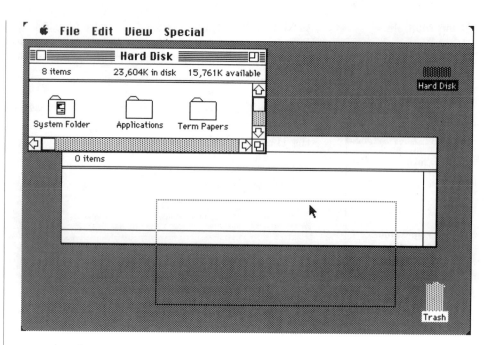

Note that if you move the window, it becomes the active window, whether it was active before or not.

Closing a Window

Earlier, you learned that you could close the active window by choosing Close from the File menu. Another way to close the active window is to click in the small white **close box** at the top left corner of the window.

Close the Trash window by clicking in its close box.

The Trash window closes and the disk window becomes active.

Memory versus Disk Space

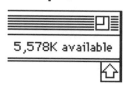

If you look just below the title bar of the hard disk window, you'll see a few mysterious looking numbers. The one on the left tells you how many items (folders, applications, and documents) there are in that particular window. A folder and everything inside it are counted as one item. The number in the center of the window tells you how much space is used by all items in the disk. And the number on the right tells you how much disk space remains available. That last number is one to watch to make sure that it's not approaching zero.

Disk Space

Disk space (also called storage), is measured in **kilobytes** (or "K" for short), or in thousands of kilobytes—called **megabytes** (or "MB" for short). Just to give you an idea of how big a kilobyte is, a one-page text document takes up about 2 to 4K on your disk, so 1MB is enough to store from 250 to 500 pages of your finest work.

Macintosh diskettes store 400K, 800K, or 1.4MB of information. 400K disks are called **single-sided** because they store information on only one side of the disk. 800K disks are **double-sided** and store information on both sides. (You don't have to worry about flipping them; the diskette drive reads and writes on both sides automatically.) Finally, some Macintoshes are equipped with **high-density** diskette drives (also called FD/HD or SuperDrive) which can read and write disks up to 1.4MB.

In each case, you need to make sure you're using the right type of diskette. Diskette drives are **upwardly compatible**—meaning that they can read or write the lower capacity formats, but they can't read or write higher capacity formats. That means that an 800K diskette drive can read and write 400K diskettes, but not 1.4MB diskettes. If you're not sure what type of diskette drive you have in your Macintosh, you can find out in the instruction manual.

System Memory

System memory, the amount of memory inside the Macintosh, is also measured in kilobytes or megabytes. Applications and documents you open are loaded into system memory while you're working with them. Therefore, how much memory you have determines how many applications you can use at once and how many complex documents you can open at once.

The Macintosh you're using probably has somewhere between 1024K (1MB) and 8192K (8MB). If you want to find out how much memory you have, choose About the Finder from the Apple menu. (The Finder is the part of Macintosh system software that organizes folders, documents, and other things inside your disks.)

Choose About the Finder from the Apple or "⌘" menu at the far left of the menu bar.

A small window will appear. Aside from listing the total memory in your Macintosh, this window also tells you what version of the Finder and System files you are using. Some newer applications require the latest version of system software. If you ever need to find out which version you're using, you now know where to look.

Click in the close box of the window to close it.

Using an Application

Next, you'll learn how to manage the documents that you'll create. You'll use the Microsoft Word application to create a sample document that you can save, place in a folder, and throw into the trash—all things you'll want to do with your real documents when that time comes.

Word 4.0

You'll start by opening the Microsoft Word application. Remember that applications are things that create and modify documents. The Word application is represented by the diamond-shaped application icon with the zippy "W" on it.

Double-Clicking

Before you can use an application, you have to open it. Earlier in this module, you learned to open a disk icon by selecting it and choosing Open from the File menu. Opening an application (also called launching) works the same way. However, as a short cut, you can also open any icon (thus any disk, folder, application, or document) by **double-clicking** on it.

Launch the Microsoft Word icon by double-clicking on it.

In case you've forgotten, double-clicking means to click the mouse button twice in quick succession. The pointer will change to the wristwatch to indicate that the Macintosh is busy loading the application into its memory.

Creating a New Document

Don't worry if you don't know how to use Microsoft Word. You'll learn all about Word in the Word Processing section of this book. All you'll need to do to create a new document for this example is type a little text and save it.

But before you start typing, you'll select a typeface or **font** for the text you're about to type.

Choosing Fonts

One of the things that sets Macintosh apart from the rest of the pack is its ability to easily mix different fonts and styles of text throughout a document. So that your documents will look good both on the screen and when they're printed, you'll want to avoid those fonts named after cities. Thus, Helvetica and Times are good choices.

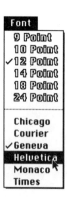

Choose Helvetica from the Font menu.

From now on, everything you type will be displayed in the Helvetica font..

Typing

Now that you've selected a font, you're ready to go. The blinking vertical bar marks the **insertion point**—where the text you type will be inserted. As you type, the insertion point will follow you to show you where the next character will go.

Type your name—or somebody else's name.

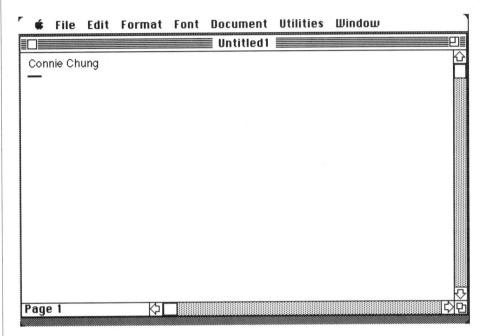

That's it! If you want to type something longer or more inspiring, you may. Use the Delete key to backspace over any mistakes you make.

When you work with a document in most Macintosh applications, you're actually working with a temporary copy stored in the Macintosh's **memory**. The memory of the Macintosh isn't permanent, however, and if you, your pet rabbit, or your local electric company should accidentally turn off the power to your Macintosh, all your work that hasn't been saved will unceremoniously vanish forever. No fun.

Saving a Document

Saving a document places a copy of your work on your disk. Unlike information in the memory of your Macintosh, information stored on a disk doesn't disappear when you turn the power off. It's there for safekeeping. You should save your work by choosing Save from the File menu about every 10 to 15 minutes or so. That way, if the unthinkable should happen, you'll only lose a few minutes of work.

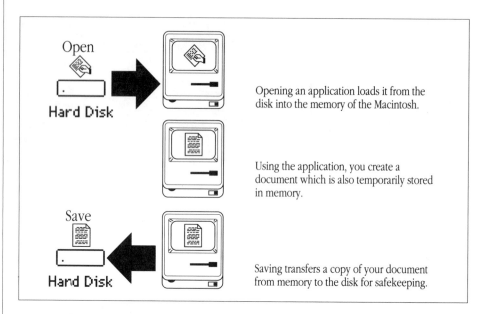

Open

Hard Disk

Opening an application loads it from the disk into the memory of the Macintosh.

Using the application, you create a document which is also temporarily stored in memory.

Save

Hard Disk

Saving transfers a copy of your document from memory to the disk for safekeeping.

Imagine that the work you've just done is part of an important term paper on the fascinating history of asphalt. You'll want to save it using the Save command from the File menu.

Choose Save from the File menu.

A **dialog box** appears asking you to name the document you are saving. Dialog boxes are a standard part of the way you work with Macintosh. Whenever the Macintosh system or a particular application needs to tell you or ask you something important, it puts up a small box like this one to get your attention.

File	
New	⌘N
Open...	⌘O
Close	⌘W
Save	⌘S
Save As...	
Print Preview...	⌘I
Print Merge...	
Page Setup...	
Print...	⌘P
Quit	⌘Q

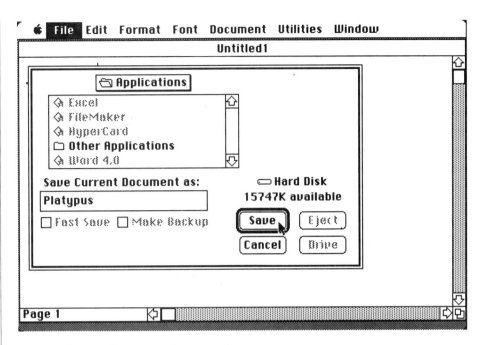

Type an interesting name for your document.

Click Save.

In a few seconds, your document is safely stored on the disk.

Printing a Document

You've just learned how to commit your documents to electronic storage. But you'll probably also want to learn how to commit them to paper.

Before you can print your literary masterpiece, you have to tell the Macintosh what kind of printer (and if you're on a network, which printer) you want to print to. To do that, you'll use the Chooser. The Chooser is a **desk accessory** that lives under the Apple menu at the leftmost edge of the menu bar. Desk accessories are like little application programs that live in the Apple menu and can be opened at any time—either at the desktop or when you're using another application.

In this case, the Chooser is a desk accessory that lets you choose the printer you want to use. It's possible, even likely, that the correct printer will have already been chosen. But just in case, let's check the Chooser now.

First, make sure your printer is connected and switched on.

If you don't know how to do this, check your printer's owner's guide.

Choose Chooser from the Apple menu.

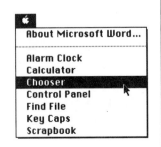

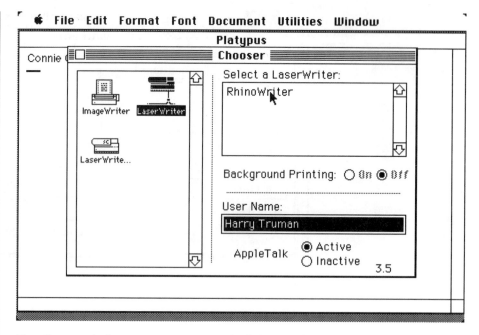

The Chooser desk accessory appears. The left side of the Chooser lists the types of printers that your Macintosh is ready to print to. Each type of printer requires a piece of software called a *printer driver* in order for the Macintosh to know how to print to it. You may have more, fewer, or different icons in your Chooser, depending on which printer drivers were loaded on your system.

If it's not already highlighted, click on the icon of the printer you'll be using.

Different types of printers print differently, so if you're switching between different printer types, the Macintosh reminds you to check the Page Setup dialog box of the application that you're using. You'll learn more about Page Setup in the later modules.

If you're printing to a LaserWriter printer, select the name of your printer by clicking on it.

If you're printing to an ImageWriter printer, select the port that your printer is connected to by clicking on the appropriate icon.

You've finished with the Chooser and you can put it away.

Close the Chooser by clicking in its close box.

You're ready to print.

Choose Print... from the File menu.

A dialog box appears, letting you change various parameters for printing. You just need one copy of this masterpiece, so you'll confirm the **default** settings (the ones "prechosen" by the system).

Click the OK button in the print dialog box.

The print dialog box disappears and your document begins printing. Depending on the type of printer you're using, in a few seconds or minutes, your document will be ready to pick up from the printer. Hey, it's not the Magna Carta, but it's a start.

Choose Quit from the File menu to close the Microsoft Word application.

In a few seconds, the desktop will appear with an icon of your new document in the same folder window as the application was. If you can't see it, use the scroll arrows to find it. The icon of the document is specific to the application that created it—in this case Microsoft Word—and it's labeled with the name you gave it. If you wanted to open the document to print it or make changes, you'd simply open its icon; the application that created it would be opened automatically.

Using Folders

After working with the Macintosh for a while, you'll accumulate a number of documents on your disk. Folders help you organize related documents into groups so that they'll be easier to find on the desktop. To create a new folder, use the New Folder command in the File menu, but first, make sure that the window in which your document is stored is the active window.

Make sure that the folder or disk window in which your document is stored is active by clicking on it.

Choose New Folder from the File menu.

A folder named Empty Folder will appear on the desktop. Before you put anything in the folder, you'll type your own name for it.

When you create a new folder, it is already highlighted, ready for you to type a new name. If you've clicked elsewhere and deselected the Empty Folder, simply click on the empty folder icon to select it again.

Type "Biology Papers" as the name of your folder.

To place your document in the folder, drag the document icon over the icon of the folder. When the icon of the folder is highlighted, release the mouse button.

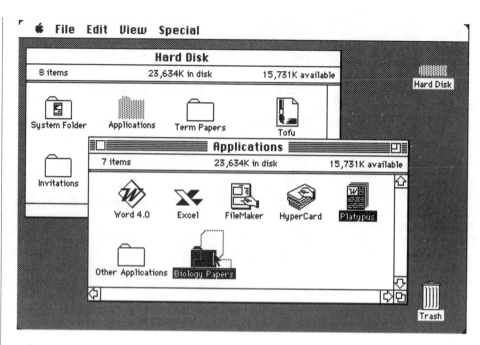

When you release the mouse button with the folder icon highlighted, the document disappears into the folder.

Double-click on the folder to open it.

A folder window opens on the desktop with your document inside. When you create other similar documents, you can group them in this folder to keep them organized.

Click in the close box of the folder window to close it.

Folders in Folders

The great thing about folders is that when you get too many of them, you can organize groups of folders inside folders. So your "Biology Papers" folder, "History Papers" folder, and "English Papers" folder can all be stored in a folder called, well..."Papers."

Choose New Folder from the File menu.

Another empty folder appears.

Type "Papers" as the name of your folder.

Place the "Biology Papers" folder in the "Papers" folder.

Remember, to place something inside a folder, drag its icon over the icon of the folder. When the icon of the folder is highlighted, release the mouse button.

Navigating Folders

Word 4.0

To open a document, you know that you can just double-click on its icon. But what if you're already inside an application and you want to open a document that's hidden somewhere in some folder within a folder? Let's find out.

Open the Microsoft Word application by double-clicking on its icon.

Microsoft Word lets you work with two documents at once so you can easily **copy** from one document and **paste** into another one. In this case we don't need the Untitled1 document that Word opens for us automatically.

Close the Untitled1 window by clicking in its close box.

Choose Open... from the File menu.

You'll see a list of the folders or documents that are in the same folder as the Microsoft Word application. This is called a **directory.** Yours will look different depending on what's on your disk and how it's organized. At the top of the list is a small box with the name of the folder (or if Word wasn't in a folder, the name of the disk). Remember that in the disk there are folders, and some folders containing other folders, and so on. These layers of folders are what's called a **hierarchy.** The box at the top of the list helps you navigate through the hierarchy.

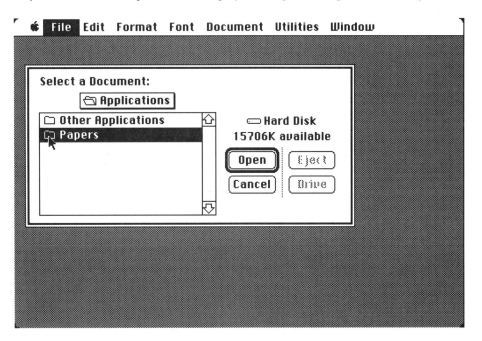

Find the "Papers" folder on the list and double-click on its name to open it.

The name of the "Papers" folder should now appear in the box at the top of the list to indicate that you're now in the "Papers" folder. You should see the name "Biology Papers" in the list now. You'll need to open it to get to your document.

Double-click on the "Biology Papers" folder to open it.

"Biology Papers" should now be at the top of the list. Because your document is the only Word document in this folder (and, in fact, it's the only thing of any kind in the folder) it should also be the only thing in the list. You can now double-click the on the document to open it...but wait! We'll get to that in just a minute.

Let's say you decided the document you wanted wasn't in this folder and you wanted to get out of this folder and move back up the hierarchy. The box at the top of the list is a **pop-up** menu that let's you do this easily. A pop-up menu works much like the menus in the menu bar. The only difference is that pop-up menus can appear anywhere, not just at the top of the screen.

Press and hold down the mouse button in the "Biology Papers" folder box at the top of the list.

A list of the folders you've traversed should appear under your mouse pointer with the name of the disk that contains all of these folders at the very bottom. To get to any of these folders, all you have to do is drag to their name, and release the mouse button.

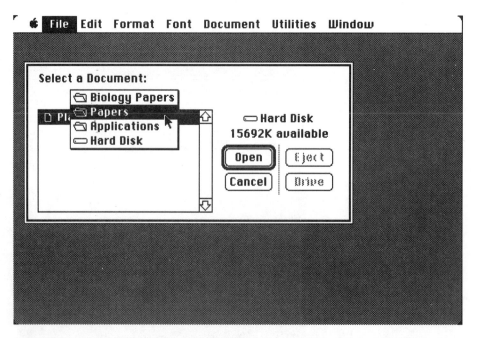

Select the "Papers" folder by dragging to down to its name and releasing the mouse button.

You're now in the "Papers" folder again. If you wanted to go all the way up to the top level—to find the documents on the disk that aren't in any folders—all you need to do is go back up to the pop-up directory menu and select the hard disk name. You don't have to do it—but you could.

For now, let's get back to your document.

Double-click on the "Biology Papers" folder to get back to your document.

Double-click on your document to open it.

In a few seconds, your document is loaded from the disk.

Make a few changes—either type some new text or use the delete key to erase some text.

Saving Changes

One of the great things about using a computer—especially a Macintosh—is the ease with which you can make changes. Once you've saved a document, you can easily experiment with how things would look if you made them a little different. As long as you don't save the changes, none of your new work is saved on the disk. But what if you forget to save after you've made changes that you do want to keep?

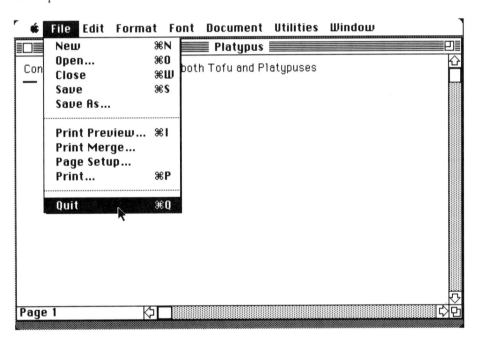

Choose Quit from the File menu.

A dialog box appears asking if you want to save the changes you've made. If you say yes, the changes you made will become a part of your document. If you say no, the document will remain exactly as it was before you made the changes.

Save As...

But what if you want to save this document as a separate document—a different version of your document that you want to keep along with your original? The Macintosh can do that, too.

Click on the Cancel button.

The dialog box graciously disappears.

Choose Save As... from the File menu.

A dialog box much like the Save dialog box you've seen before appears.

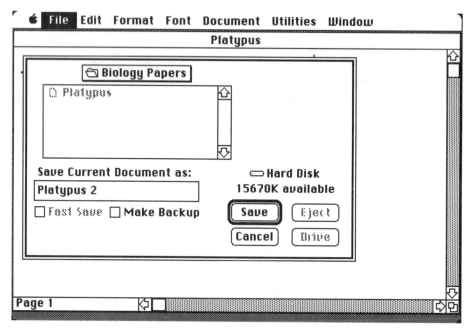

Type a name for your new document.

Notice that when you type a name into this box, the Save button is highlighted with a thick black border. This border indicates that in this case, the application assumes that you'll want to click on the Save button. (Pretty good assumption, eh?) But to provide a short cut, you can do the equivalent of clicking the highlighted button by simply pressing the Return key on the keyboard.

Press the Return key after you finish typing the name.

In a few seconds, the new document is saved.

Choose Quit from the File menu.

Since your changes have been saved, the application doesn't prompt you to save them this time.

In a few seconds, you're back at the desktop—but this time with *two* documents in the "Biology Papers" folder. You don't believe us?

Platypus Platypus 2

Using Find File

Open first the "Papers" folder and then the "Biology Papers" folder by double-clicking them.

There they are: your two documents—and you doubted us.

Close the "Papers" and "Biology Papers" folder windows by clicking in their close boxes.

The Find File desk accessory, as its name aptly suggests, helps you find documents, folders, or other things that you may have difficulty locating.

Choose Find File from the Apple menu.

You'll use Find File to find your document.

Type the name of the document you created into the "Search for:" box and press the Return key.

A list of documents, applications, or folders with that name appear in the window below.

Click on the name of your document in the list.

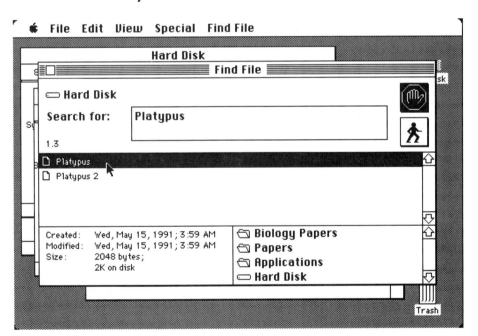

In the lower right, you see the path you need to take to get to your document.

Especially when you have a number of things on your hard disk, you'll find Find File a helpful desk accessory to tell you where things are.

Close the Find File desk accessory by clicking in its close box.

You can experiment with the other desk accessories under the Apple menu.

Copying Things to and from Diskettes

Now that you know how to create and save documents to your heart's content, you'll want to learn how to copy the documents you've created from the hard disk to a diskette either to use on another Macintosh, make a backup copy for safekeeping, or to pass off to a friend or co-worker. For this part of the module, you'll need—you guessed it— a diskette.

Take a close look at your diskette.

As we mentioned earlier, Macintoshes can use different types of diskettes. How can you tell what kind of diskette you have? It should tell you. Look for markings that say things like "400K," or "Double-sided," or "HD" (which stands for High Density).

To familiarize you with the buzzwords, here's a bit of a field guide to diskettes:

- 400K and single-sided diskettes are the same.
- 800K and double-sided diskettes are the same.
- HD, High Density, and 1.4MB diskettes are the same.

Insert your diskette into any diskette drive in your Macintosh.

Before you can use any blank diskette, you must prepare the diskette to hold the information you'll store on it. This process is called **initializing**. To initialize a blank diskette on the Macintosh, simply insert the blank diskette into a diskette drive.

If your diskette has already been initialized, a diskette icon will appear on the desktop and you can skip these next couple of steps. If your diskette hasn't been initialized, a dialog box will appear indicating that the diskette is unreadable, and asking you if you want to initialize it..

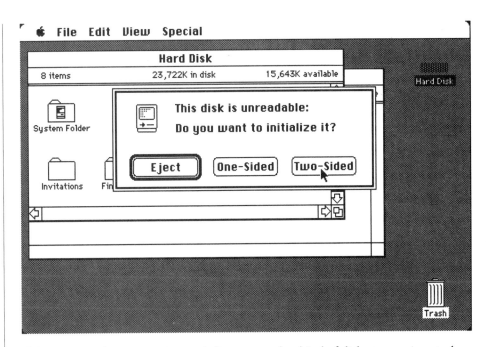

If the Macintosh you're using can't figure out what kind of diskette you inserted, this dialog box will ask you how you want the diskette formatted. Luckily, you know the answer to this question, because you've studied.

Click the appropriate button for the type of diskette you inserted.

A dialog box appears to make sure that you realize that initializing a diskette erases any information on that diskette.

Click Erase.

A dialog box will appear asking you to name your disk.

Type an inspiring name for your disk then press the Return key.

After a minute or so, a diskette icon will appear on the desktop. Next, you'll open the diskette window.

Open the diskette by double-clicking on its icon.

If your diskette was already initialized, the diskette window may already be open.

When you put the document you created into its folder, you learned how to move things from one place to another. Copying things from one disk to another works the same way. Just drag the document, folder, or application on top of the icon of the disk that you want to copy to and release the mouse button when the disk icon is highlighted. In a few short seconds, the copy is completed. But you already know how to do that…that would be too easy. So let's try a new way.

Another way to copy or move files is simply to drag them into the window of the disk or folder where you want them to go.

Rearrange or resize windows so that the "Papers" folder and the diskette window are both visible.

If you've forgotten how to move or resize windows, you might refresh your memory by turning back a few pages.

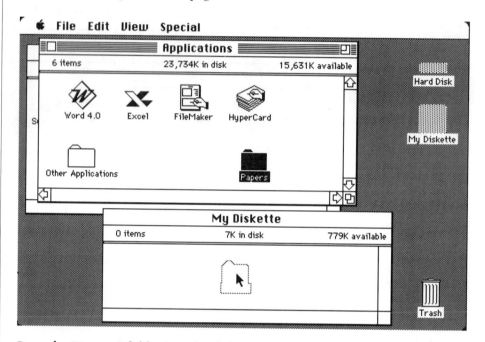

Drag the "Papers" folder into the diskette window and release the mouse button.

A dialog box appears informing you of the progress of the copy operation. In a few seconds it's done, and a copy of the "Papers" folder and everything in it is now on the diskette.

Copying from diskette to hard disk (or from diskette to diskette) works just the same way.

Using the Trash

Now that you know how to copy things to a diskette for safekeeping, it seems only fair that you should learn how to throw things away. Throwing away documents, applications, or folders full of documents and applications on the Macintosh—just like throwing things away in the real world—means using the Trash.

With a safe copy of your document on your diskette, we can throw away the "Papers" folder from the hard disk to make room for someone else to do this module. When you throw away a folder, you throw away everything inside that folder.

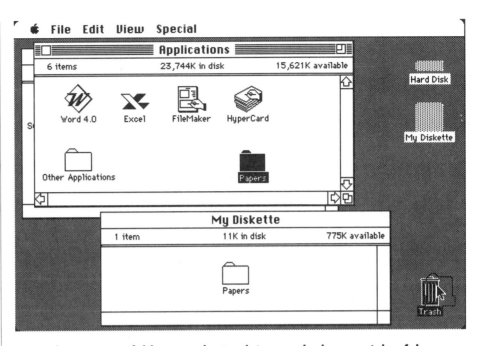

Drag the "Papers" folder over the Trash icon at the bottom right of the screen. When the Trash icon highlights, release the mouse button to drop the folder into the Trash.

The folder, documents and all, disappears into the Trash. The Trash icons "gets fat" to indicate that there's something inside.

Trash

Retrieving Items from the Trash

It's inevitable. Someday, when you're in a hurry or when it's either very late or very early, you'll accidentally throw away something that you really wanted to keep. Don't dismay. If you catch your mistake quickly, you'll be able to retrieve what you've thrown away.

Open the Trash by double-clicking on its icon.

The Trash window contains the folder you just threw away. Inside the folder is your document. (You can check if you'd like.) To retrieve an item from the Trash, simply drag it out of the Trash window back to where it came from, in this case, the hard disk window.

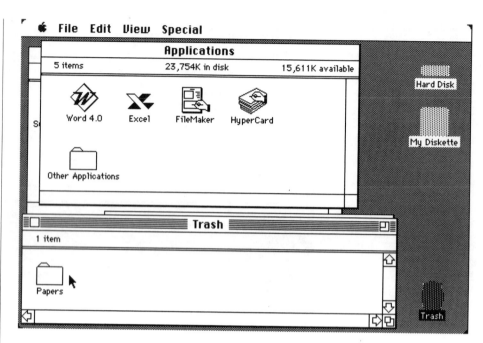

Any document, folder, or application you throw into the Trash remains there until you: (1) eject the disk it came from, (2) open any application, or (3) choose Empty Trash from the Special menu.

You really do want to throw this folder away, so while you could retrieve it now, you won't. In fact, you'll use the Empty Trash command to free up the space on your disk.

Choose Empty Trash from the Special menu.

In a few seconds the folder will disappear from the Trash window.

Close the Trash window by clicking in its close box.

Ejecting a Diskette

Now that you've saved your documents to the diskette, you'll want to eject the diskette. You can do this by selecting its icon and choosing Eject from the File menu, but there is a faster method that both ejects the disk and removes its icon from the desktop.

Find the diskette icon on the desktop.

You may have to move or resize a window that might be covering it up. (Remember, move a window by dragging it by its title bar, and resize a window by dragging the resize box.)

Notice that when the disk window is open, the diskette icon is gray, or **hollow**. Don't worry, that's just to let you know its window is open. You can do almost anything with this icon that you could if its window was closed. Including what we're about to do to eject the diskette...

Trash

Shutting Down

Special
Clean Up Window
Empty Trash
Erase Disk
Set Startup...

Restart
Shut Down

Drag the disk icon into the Trash.

Have no fear, dragging a diskette into the Trash simply ejects it and removes it from the desktop.

You're finished! Honest. Well, there is one more thing.

Whenever you finish working with the Macintosh, you should shut it down properly. To do this, there's a special command in the Special menu (where else?) called Shut Down.

Choose Shut Down from the Special menu.

Any diskettes that are in any of the drives attached to your Macintosh will be ejected as the system cleans up. If you have any documents open with unsaved changes, the Macintosh will ask you if you want to save them before you shut down. Then, depending on the Macintosh you have, it will either turn the power off itself, or put up a dialog box indicating that it is now safe to turn off the power switch on the back.

Always use the Shut Down command before pulling the plug or switching off the power.

Congratulations! You've just completed the first step to becoming a Macintosh expert. If you feel you still need more information or practice, or if you have a quick question not covered here, consult your Macintosh owner's guide.

Now that you've just completed the first module in this book, you should have learned:

- How to identify the parts of a Macintosh system
- How to work with the Macintosh desktop
- How to select objects by clicking on them with the mouse
- How to Press, Click, Double-Click, Drag, and Shift-Click with the mouse
- How to activate, move, resize, and scroll through windows
- How to open an application by double-clicking on its icon and how to close an application by choosing Quit from the File menu
- How to use folders to organize documents
- How to use desk accessories
- How to copy things to and from diskettes
- How to throw away unwanted objects in the Trash and how to retrieve accidentally discarded objects from the Trash
- How to use the Shut Down command to eject all disks and restart the Macintosh

Exercises

1. Collect several articles and advertisements for personal computers. (Skip the ones filled with technical jargon, if you can.) Make a list of the commonly mentioned features in the articles and ads. How does the Macintosh that you're using compare on these points?

2. Visit a computer store or any other place where you can try other computers. Spend a few minutes using a few other computers. Make a list comparing them. What features did you like or dislike? Why? Which computer would you choose to do your daily work?

3. Identify the parts of the Macintosh window displayed below.

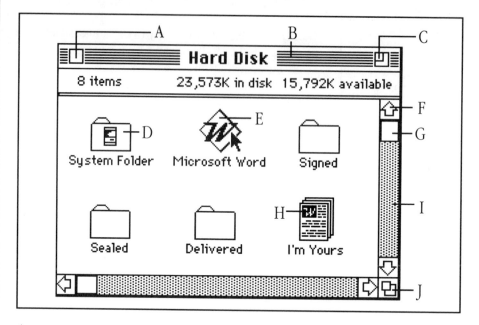

4. Both system memory and disk space are measured in the same units (kilobytes or megabytes). Explain the difference between system memory and disk space.

Let's say you have a hard disk system and that you can have either more system memory, more space on your diskettes, or more hard disk space. Which would you need to accomplish each of the following:

a) Transfer a document from your Macintosh to a friend's

b) Store several documents and applications which you use frequently

c) Create a long complex document with lots of graphics

5. What is the significance of the term "active window"? How do you know which window is the "active window?" How do you make a window the "active window?"

6. Applications, documents, and folders can all be stored on diskettes, hard disks, or file servers. What are the differences between these three storage devices? When would you use each of these devices?

7. A friend calls to tell you that she can't find an important term paper stored on her Macintosh. What steps would you use to find the missing document.?

8. How do you tell if there's something in the Trash? When does the Trash get emptied? What happens when you drag a diskette into the Trash?

9. If a window is too small for you to see the icon you want, name two ways to find it.

10. You're typing a paper. As you finish Chapter 3, you choose Save from the File menu to save your document. You go on to write Chapter 4 and as you finish the last paragraph a massive earthquake cuts power to your Macintosh. When you clear the rubble and restart your trusty Macintosh, how much of the document was stored safely on the disk? How can you soften the blow of such a disaster?

11. Define the following terms and explain how and when they are used:

    a) application
    b) desk accessory
    c) dialog box
    d) dimmed command
    e) Command-key short cut
    f) document
    g) initialize
    h) mouse
    i) zoom box
    j) platypus (just kidding)
    k) Shift-Click
    l) startup disk
    m) system software

12. Describe two ways to open a folder, launch an application, or open a document. **Extra Credit:** Describe a third way.

13. Are you kidding? There is no 13th question. Eeesh.

2 | Graphics

About Graphics
Claris MacPaint
Galleries
Exercises

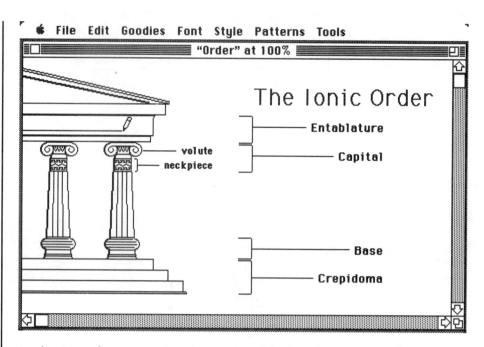

**About
Graphics**

Applications of computers in the area of graphics have become so widespread that the term "computer graphics" can be found attached to everything from motion pictures to medicine. A computer's ability to create and manipulate images quickly and skillfully has made it an indispensable tool in the field of graphics—especially where images must be changed or moved often.

On a personal computer like the Macintosh, drawing programs have been one of the most popular types of graphics applications. These applications, which transform the computer's screen into an electronic canvas, offer a set of computer drawing tools that can be used in much the same way as a pencil and paint brush.

The advantage these electronic drawing tools have over their standard counterparts is that they often make the difficult, cumbersome, and tedious tasks of drawing easier. Straight lines, perfect circles, and scaling are a snap with the appropriate drawing software. But computer drawing tools aren't merely electronic simulations of pencils and pens, nor are they a substitute for artistic skill. By providing electronic design tools that are different from their physical counterparts, computer drawing applications also open up a new medium of artistic expression.

**About Claris
MacPaint 2.0**

Claris MacPaint 2.0 is a drawing application for the Macintosh. But more than that, MacPaint is the drawing application most responsible for the explosion in popularity of this type of application on microcomputers like the Macintosh.

From the day it was released, MacPaint's clever design and remarkable utility instantly made it the target of imitators. MacPaint, more than any other Macintosh application, demonstrates the advantages of the Macintosh's mouse and high-resolution screen. But while some thought of MacPaint as a clever demonstration application, others were busy using it for everything from newsletters to architectural renderings, from X-ray analysis to mapping. The flexibility and features of MacPaint make it particularly well-suited for a number of surprisingly diverse graphics applications.

MacPaint is classified as a "bit mapped" drawing program. When you use MacPaint you control every dot on the screen individually. This gives you a tremendous amount of control over you creation, but you sacrifice the always smooth lines of an "object oriented" program like MacDraw.

MacPaint features a number of tools for drawing lines, ovals, rectangles, polygons and free-form shapes. MacPaint also makes it easy to move, duplicate, invert, or flip any drawing or part of an drawing that you create. A selection of patterns, which can be modified by the user, makes shading and filling areas a snap. Zooming In and Out allows you to make detailed changes with ease and to view the entire drawing at once.

Claris MacPaint 2.0

The Task

Did you ever write a term paper in which you had to try and describe the appearance of something like the wiggly border between two nations or the orientation of atoms in a particular molecule? There must have been times when you've wanted to describe something in pictures, not in words.

Come to think of it, you have that term paper on the history of the Ionic and Doric styles of ancient Greek architecture that's due soon. Since the single most recognizable difference between the two styles is in the design of their *capitals* (the decorative tops of columns), you would like to have a drawing of two different capitals in the term paper. Fine, but how can you produce the drawing with the least effort and the best results, especially if you are not particularly gifted with pencil, pen, ruler, and markers? This is where MacPaint comes in handy.

Simplicity is the key to creating effective explanatory drawings. Both the general designs of the Doric and Ionic capitals can be reduced to a few basic geometric shapes which are easily created with MacPaint's drawing **tools**.

Since each capital must sit atop a column, you will need to make two columns. Or will you? With the **lasso** and **selection rectangle** tools, you will make a single column quickly and easily out of basic shapes. But that's not all. Using the same tools, you'll be able to duplicate that column and thus eliminate the need to draw it a second time.

After both capitals and columns are drawn, you'll choose from MacPaint's many shades and patterns and selectively add them to your drawing with the **paint can**.

In your drawing, you'll use MacPaint's **text** functions. You'll be able to add captions, identify labels, and include historical information. Finally, your drawing will be ready for inclusion in that important term paper.

GRECIAN ORDERS

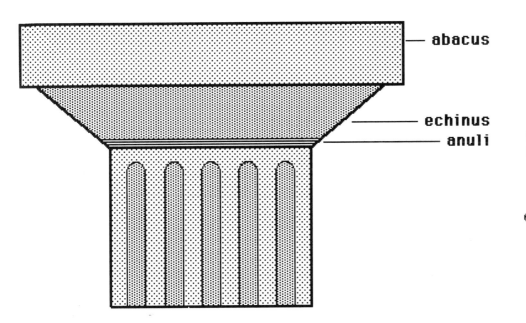

— abacus

— echinus
— anuli

Doric Order

Flourishing between the 6th and 5th centuries B.C., the Doric Order was characterized by its mathematical and exacting demands for proper proportion. For example, the ratio between any two sides of the Parthenon is always 9 to 4.

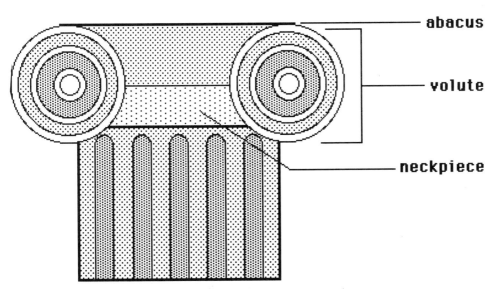

— abacus

— volute

— neckpiece

Ionic Order

Less severe and mathematically rigorous than the Doric Order, the Ionic Order had its heyday between the 5th and 1st centuries B.C. Without the Doric rules for scale and proportion, Ionic architects designed a far wider variety of temples and secular buildings.

Getting Started

This module assumes that you are familiar with the basics of using the Macintosh, how to work with a hard disk and/or diskettes, how to choose menu commands, and so on. If these concepts are not familiar, please review the Approaching Macintosh module.

First, you'll start from the Macintosh desktop.

Turn on the Macintosh. If you're not using a hard disk, insert the system diskette in the internal drive.

You'll see the Macintosh desktop.

MacPaint

Next, you'll open MacPaint.

If you are using a hard disk, find the MacPaint icon and double-click on it to open MacPaint.

If you don't have a hard disk, insert the MacPaint program disk, wait for the icon to appear, and double-click on MacPaint to open the application.

The MacPaint screen will appear in a few seconds.

Getting Acquainted

Before proceeding with the module example, familiarize yourself with the MacPaint screen and some of the functions of the application.

Menu Bar

Close Box

Drawing Window

Scroll Bars

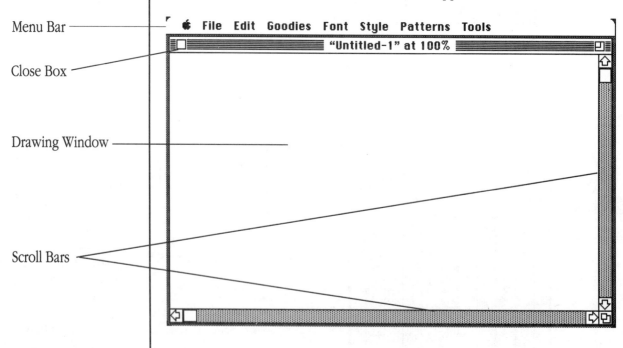

The Menu Bar

As with all Macintosh applications, the **menu bar** is located at the top of the screen. To see a list of the commands or options under any particular menu, press and hold the mouse button on the particular menu name. To choose a command or option, move the pointer to your choice and then release the mouse button. Particular to MacPaint is the **Goodies** menu.

The Drawing Window

Tools and patterns are used in the **drawing window**. The drawing window shows only a small part of the 8- by 10-inch area available to MacPaint users. You'll learn how to move within the drawing window to view more of a MacPaint document.

The Tools Menu

At the far right of the menu bar is the **Tools menu**, a palette of 20 symbols representing the various MacPaint drawing tools and a selection of different line weights. At the top right of the tool menu are six vertical lines which represent the various line thicknesses or "line weights" that you can draw with. The currently selected line weight is indicated by arrowheads above and below it. Whether you draw a circle, box, or whatever, that line weight will be used.

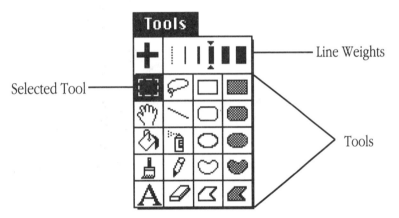

Selected Tool

Line Weights

Tools

The Tools menu can be "torn off" and the palette repositioned on the screen by pulling down the menu and moving the cursor past its edges. The outline of the menu will follow the cursor so you can place it in a convenient place on the screen.

Pull down the Tools menu and drag it to the bottom right corner of the drawing window.

The Patterns Menu

Located to the left of the Tools menu, the **Patterns menu** contains a palette of 38 available shades or simulated textures. This is also a tearoff menu. The currently selected pattern, the one you're currently painting with, is shown in the larger rectangle at the top left of the menu.

Pull down the Patterns menu and drag the Patterns palette to the top right corner of the drawing window. You must position the palettes in the drawing area—not on the menu bar.

By moving the menus to the drawing surface you can now select tools and patterns without having to pulling down menus each time.

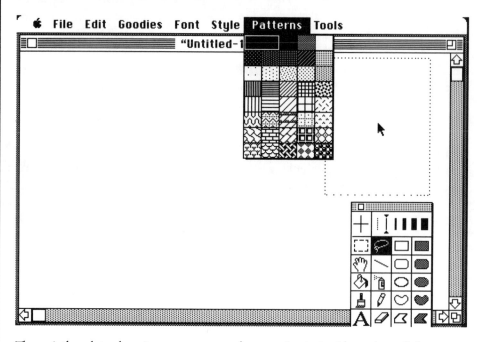

Painting

The paintbrush tool, as its name suggest, lets you "paint" with strokes of electronic paint much like you would with a real paintbrush. The paintbrush tool is ideal for free-form drawing.

Select the paintbrush tool from the Tools palette by clicking on it. Make sure that the pointer is inside the drawing window. It will look like a small black dot.

Press and hold the mouse button while moving the mouse.

As you may recall, this is known as dragging.

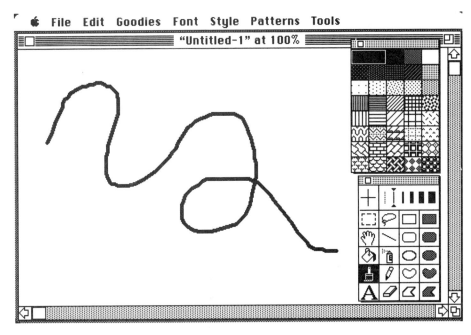

A black line appears. You have just painted in MacPaint.

Erasing

The eraser allows you to remove anything you've drawn. You use it by dragging it over the offending item and the item will vanish.

Select the eraser tool from the Tools palette by clicking on its icon.

Notice that the paintbrush tool is now highlighted to indicate it is selected.

Move the pointer to the drawing window.

The pointer changes from an arrow to an eraser icon.

Press and hold the mouse button as you drag the eraser over your black line.

The eraser removes the paintbrush line from the drawing window.

Using Patterns

Patterns are simulated textures that allow you to paint in shades.

In the Patterns palette, select any pattern you desire by clicking on it.

The pattern you selected now appears in the larger rectangle in the upper left of the Patterns palette.

Select the paintbrush from the Tools palette and draw a new line or two.

The paintbrush now paints with the newly selected pattern.

Clearing the Drawing Window

Before going any further, you should erase any lines in the drawing window that you made while experimenting. A handy way to erase the entire drawing window is to double-click on the eraser icon in the Tools palette.

Double-click the eraser icon.

The drawing window is now clear.

Using Undo

The most obvious way to correct mistakes is to use the eraser. Often, a more effective (and neater) solution is to use the **Undo** command in the Edit menu to undo the last thing you did.

Using the paintbrush, make a horizontal line. Cross it with a vertical line.

Let's assume that you wish to keep the horizontal line, but the vertical line has to go. Since the vertical line is the last thing you did, you can use the Undo command to un-draw it.

From the Edit menu, choose the Undo command.

The vertical line disappears. Remember, Undo only works on your last action.

Double-click the eraser icon to clear the drawing window.

The drawing window is clear again.

Creating Ionic and Doric Columns

Pay some attention to the various parts of the example page. You'll want to make your capitals and columns roughly the same size and position as they are on the example page.

You will begin by creating the column. The Ionic and Doric capitals will be made later. The unfilled rounded rectangle tool will produce the vertical grooves found on the column.

Using the Shapes

The paintbrush is a versatile tool, but it would take an abundance of talent and time to use it to draw shapes such as squares and circles. MacPaint has a variety of different tools for drawing shapes automatically. These tools come in two varieties: filled and unfilled. The filled tools are farthest to the right on the Tools palette and produce shapes filled with whatever pattern you've selected from the Patterns palette. The unfilled shape tools draw shapes that are just an outline with a clear center.

Select the unfilled rounded rectangle icon in the Tools palette. This tool is located in the third column, second from the top.

Select the second line width from the left in the Tools palette.

Make sure that the small arrows are above and below the second line. If not, simply click on the second line width to select it.

Now, move the pointer into the drawing window. Drag the cross-shaped pointer diagonally down and to the right.

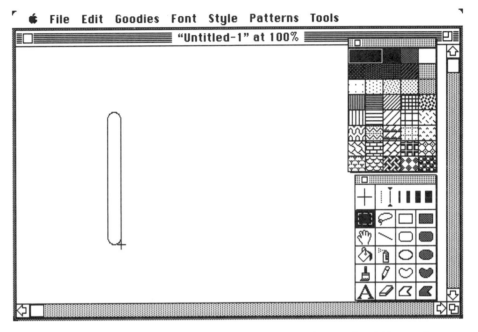

Your goal is to make a tall, thin, rounded rectangle. In fact, it should be so thin that the top and bottom have no flat faces.

If necessary, select the eraser, drag it over the rounded rectangle, and try again.

Next, you'll want to duplicate the rounded rectangle to make the vertical grooves found on Greek columns. When you wish to duplicate or move an object in MacPaint, you must first select the object with either the lasso or the selection rectangle.

The Selection Rectangle

The selection rectangle selects everything within the moving box it creates. This tool is useful in selecting square objects or selecting along the straight edge of an item.

Choose the selection rectangle. Drag the pointer diagonally across the rounded rectangle.

Make sure the entire rounded rectangle is enclosed by the selection rectangle. You can tell when you've drawn using the selection rectangle because the rectangle continues to move after it's drawn, like a marquis.

Once it's selected, you can move whatever is inside the rectangle easily.

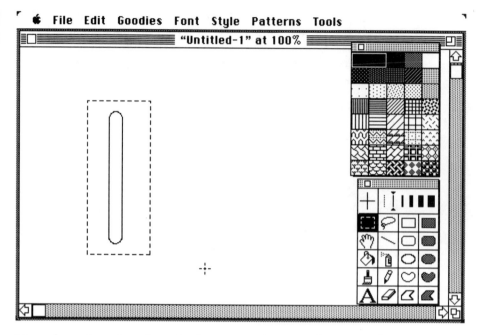

Move the pointer into the selection rectangle, press the mouse button, and drag.

The selection rectangle and its contents will move about the screen in response to movements of the mouse. You can reposition the rounded rectangle at will. The selection rectangle is handy for moving objects that you can easily draw a rectangle around.

Now you will duplicate the rounded rectangle.

First, drag the rounded rectangle to the left side of the drawing window. Release the mouse button.

Remember, to do this, move the mouse pointer inside the selection rectangle, press and hold the mouse button, and drag.

This will be the left-most groove in the column.

Duplicating Objects

Once an object is selected, it's easy to duplicate. To duplicate a selection in MacPaint, you use the Option key and just drag away copies.

Press and hold down the Option key. Now, press and hold the mouse button. Drag a copy of the object away.

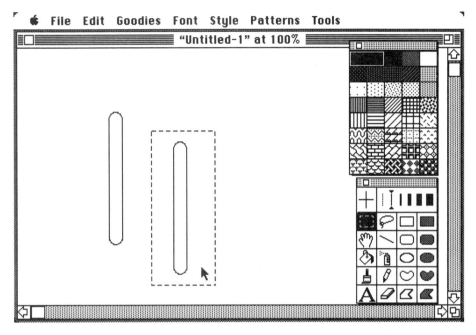

You have just learned a speedy means of duplicating objects in MacPaint. Once a duplicated object is in the position you want, lift up on the mouse button and click anywhere in the drawing window. The duplicate will be unselected and will be fixed in its new position.

If you press the Backspace key while an object is selected, that object will be removed from the drawing window. Since the rounded rectangle is still selected, pressing the Backspace key will delete it.

Press the Backspace key.

The selected object disappears.

The Lasso

The lasso is another selection tool. Instead of selecting a rectangular area like the selection rectangle does, the lasso tightens up around an item's edges and just selects the item itself.

Select the lasso tool.

Position the lasso near the remaining rounded rectangle. While holding down the mouse button, drag the lasso around the rounded rectangle.

As you drag the lasso, a line tracing its path will appear. Be sure that this line completely encircles the rounded rectangle. It isn't necessary to make a perfect circle or oval around the rounded rectangle.

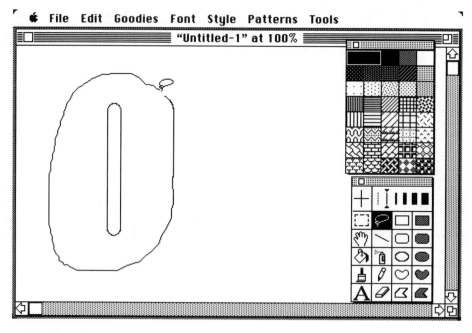

Unlike the selection rectangle, which selects an entire surrounded area (including any white space), the lasso "shrinks" to conform to the contours of an object. The ability to shrink around an object allows you to select an independent part of your drawing without having to carefully outline it. The outside edge of the object will move, indicating that it is selected.

Position the pointer inside the selected area. Drag the rounded rectangle around the drawing window.

Repositioning objects selected with the lasso is very similar to repositioning them with the selection rectangle. As with the selection rectangle, you can duplicate any object selected with the lasso using the Option key.

Look closely again at the completed example. The top and bottom edges of the five column grooves are level. As you duplicate the rounded rectangle to make the other four grooves, you'll need some help keeping them level with one another. If you use the Shift key while duplicating, you will only be able to move the duplicates horizontally or vertically. Once you begin moving in one direction, that is the only direction you can move in. If you accidentally begin moving up, you will only be able to move vertically until you release the mouse button and click on the object again (while still holding down the Shift key).

Position the rounded rectangle slightly to the left in the drawing window.

Press and hold the Option and Shift keys. Drag the duplicate rounded rectangle to the right a distance approximately equal to its width. Release the mouse button.

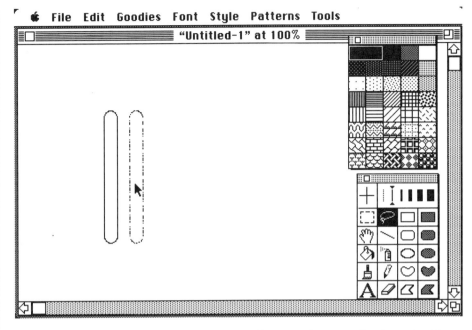

With the Shift key pressed, the duplicates will remain horizontally aligned with each other.

The duplicate rounded rectangle should still be selected.

With the Option and Shift keys, make three more duplicates, all approximately one width from each other.

As long as the Option and Shift keys remain pressed, you can just press the mouse button again and drag. A duplicate will be left behind in the old position, and you can place the next duplicate in a new spot.

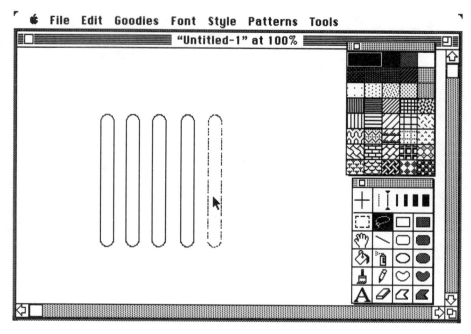

The grooves are now properly positioned. Examine the completed MacPaint document once more. Notice that the grooves are flush with the bottom of the column. From looking at the finished drawing, you should notice that the body of the column is simply a rectangle. Luckily, MacPaint's rectangle tool helps you easily draw perfect squares and rectangles.

Rectangle Tool

Select the unfilled rectangle tool from the Tools palette. Then, select the fourth line width.

You will make a rectangle around the five grooves. If you had chosen the filled rectangle tool just to the right of it, the rectangle that is drawn would be filled solid with the currently selected pattern.

Position the cross-shaped pointer near the bottom and left of the five grooves. Drag diagonally upward and to the right.

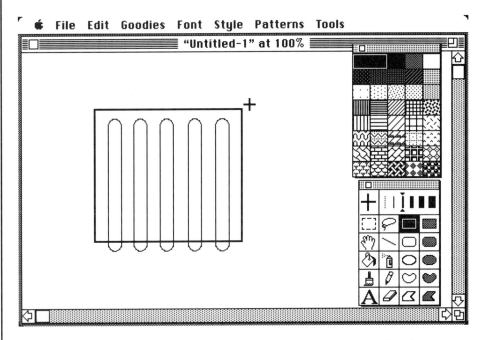

The grooves should be roughly centered horizontally in the rectangle. The bottoms of the grooves should extend beyond the bottom of the rectangle. If the rectangle is not positioned correctly, you can choose Undo from the Edit menu and try again.

When the rectangle is finished you can erase the rounded bottoms of the grooves. To constrain the eraser to a straight line, use the Shift key again.

With the Shift key depressed, use the eraser to remove the bottoms of the grooves.

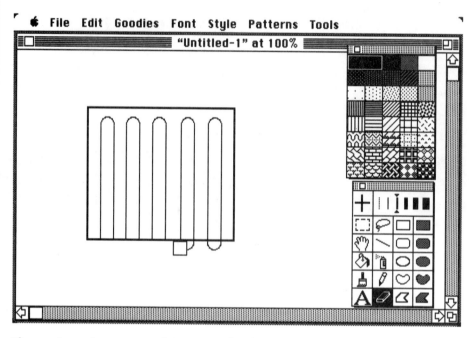

If you miss and erase part of the rectangle, choose Undo and try again. Once the groove bottoms have been erased, the basic column for both Doric and Ionic capitals will be complete.

Saving Your Work

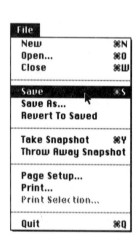

You should get into the habit of saving your work every 10 or 15 minutes. Should the unthinkable happen, you'll only lose a few minutes of your work.

Choose Save from the File menu.

The Save dialog box appears asking you to name your document.

Type the name of your document, "Doric/Ionic".

You can use the Backspace or Delete key to correct any mistakes you might make.

Click Save.

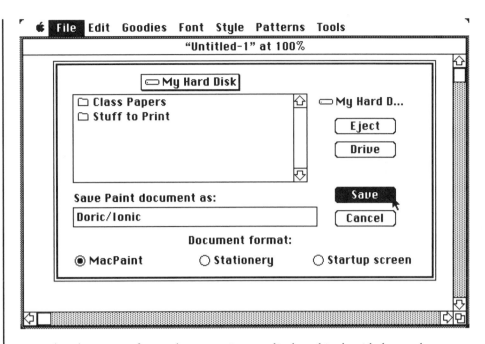

Note that the name of your document is now displayed in the title bar at the top of the drawing window.

Adding to the Scrapbook

You will eventually need a second column to complete the other half of this document. Rather than draw it again later, you'll store a copy in the **Scrapbook** so you can use it again.

The Scrapbook

The Scrapbook is a permanent storage space that can hold often-used text and graphics. You can add or delete items from the Scrapbook as you wish. Since the contents of the Scrapbook are stored in the Scrapbook file in the system folder on the hard disk, you have access to these items whenever you're using that particular hard disk.

Copy

To place a copy of an item in the Scrapbook, the first step is to select and copy it.

Use the lasso to select the column.

Remember, to select an item with the lasso, drag the lasso entirely around the object. The lasso "shrinks" to fit the selected object.

Choose Copy from the Edit menu.

The Copy command places a copy of the current selection on the **Clipboard,** a temporary storage area that can hold the selection as it is being moved or until you need it somewhere else in the drawing.

The Clipboard holds only one selection at a time, and copying another selection would replace the current contents of the Clipboard with the latest selection. That explains why something as important as the column should be kept in a permanent storage space like the Scrapbook.

Also, since the contents of the Clipboard are not stored permanently on the disk, turning off the Macintosh will erase the contents of the Clipboard.

Choose Scrapbook from the Apple menu.

(Note: Because every Scrapbook contains different images, your Scrapbook will probably not look exactly like the one shown above.)

The Scrapbook window displays the first of the stored images. The fraction in the lower left corner provides information about the Scrapbook images. For instance, the fraction "1/11" would mean that you were looking at the first of eleven stored images. (Make note of the current fraction.) If the Scrapbook is empty, there will be an "Empty Scrapbook" message in the window.

The gray bar across the bottom of the Scrapbook window is a **scroll bar.** Clicking within the bar, dragging the scroll box, or clicking the arrows at either end of the scroll bar allows you to look at different items in the Scrapbook. Understandably, you can't scroll through an empty Scrapbook.

You copied the column to the Clipboard just moments ago. Now you'll paste a copy into the Scrapbook.

Paste

While the Scrapbook is open, choose Paste from the Edit menu.

The Paste command inserts the current contents of the Clipboard into the Scrapbook. Under some circumstances, the Scrapbook window may be too small to show the entire image. Nevertheless, the entire image is stored in the Scrapbook.

Note the change in the fraction in the lower left corner of your Scrapbook window.

The new fraction reflects the addition of one more image into the Scrapbook.

To close the Scrapbook, click in the close box in the upper left corner of the Scrapbook window.

The Scrapbook window closes and MacPaint returns to the drawing window.

Completing the Doric Capital

Now that the column is finished, you can complete the Doric capital. Look at the completed Doric capital. You'll begin by making the slanted underside of the Doric capital.

Use the lasso to select the column. Position it in the lower center of the drawing window.

The Rubber Band Tool

If you'd like to stretch a straight line between two points, the rubber band tool is what you should use. You'll use this tool to make a slanted line for your capital.

Select the rubber band tool in the Tools palette. Then, select the third line width. In the drawing window, drag the pointer.

This tool makes a line that's anchored to its starting point and connected with the pointer. The line remains connected to the pointer until the mouse button is clicked.

Drag the pointer to make a line approximately one inch long and angled at about 30° to the horizontal.

You'll now use the selection rectangle to select and duplicate your line.

Select this line with the selection rectangle. Use the Option key and duplicate the line.

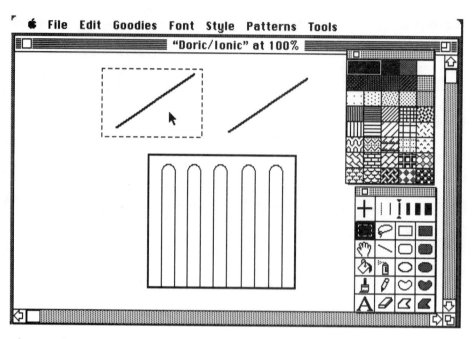

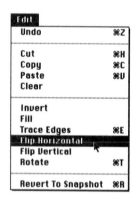

Choose Flip Horizontal from the Edit menu.

The selected line is flipped about its horizontal axis, creating a mirror image of the first line.

Trace Edges, Flip Horizontal, Flip Vertical, and Rotate in the Edit menu only work with the selection rectangle chosen.

With the lasso, select and position both diagonal lines on the upper corners of the column.

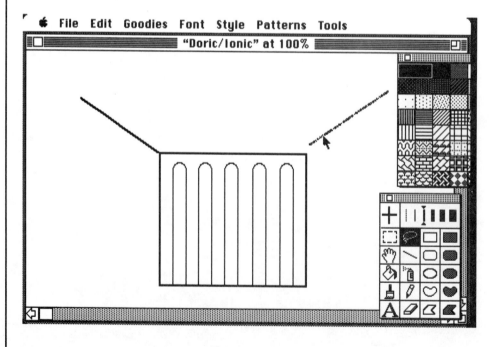

Look at the completed example again. Now, you'll need to make the very top of the Doric capital. This will be represented by a long, thin rectangle.

Use the unfilled Rectangle tool and the third line width in the tools palette to make a long and relatively thin horizontal rectangle.

Select the rectangle with the lasso and maneuver it into position on top of the column.

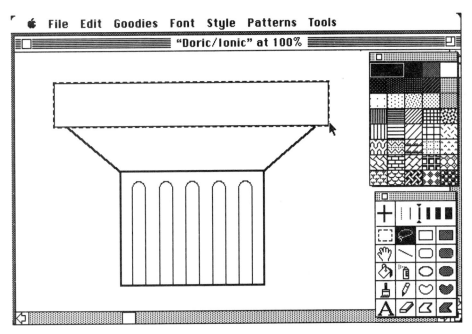

Brush Shapes

You'll need to use the paintbrush to add some detail to the seam between the capital and the column. Look closely at the Doric column in the completed example. The current paintbrush shape is a little too large for that fine work, so you'll need to change the brush shape to a smaller size.

Choose the paintbrush from the Tools palette.

Choose Brush Shape from the Goodies menu.

A selection of all the available brush shapes appears.

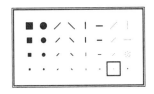

Click on the absolute smallest brush shape (bottom row, second from right).

No matter what the size of the paintbrush, using the Shift key will constrain the brush movements to horizontal and vertical lines only.

Make sure the current pattern is black. While holding down the Shift key, use the paintbrush to add the thin horizontal lines between the column and the capital.

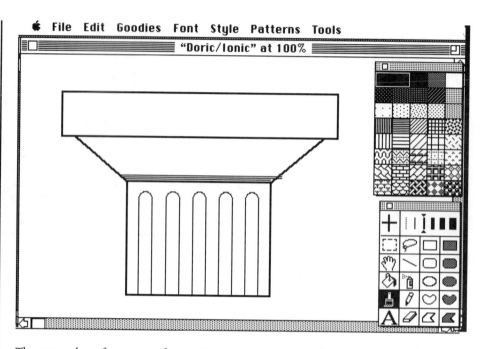

Using Zoom

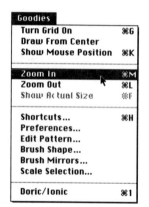

The Grabber

There may be a few parts of your Doric column that could use a little touching up. For instance, the horizontal lines between the column and the capital might need some extending or shortening. There is a way to do that kind of detailed work in MacPaint by zooming in on key details.

Choose Zoom In from the Goodies menu.

Zoom In allows you to alter MacPaint documents dot-by-dot. You can Zoom In more than once to see even more detail. Virtually all MacPaint tools work while zoomed in, though in the enlarged scale, they may require some getting used to. The title bar will indicate the percent enlargement or reduction of the drawing, with 100% indicating actual size.

To see another section of the enlarged MacPaint drawing, you have to move the drawing while zoomed in. This is accomplished with the scroll bars or, more easily, with the **grabber.**

The grabber does just that. It grabs your document and slides it in the direction you drag, just as you would a piece of paper.

Select the hand-shaped grabber tool from the Tools palette and position it in the drawing window. Drag in any direction.

The document moves in the drawing window.

The zoom window, like the drawing window, only shows a portion of the full page. The grabber allows you to push the MacPaint document around.

Position the drawing so that the lines between the column and the capital are visible.

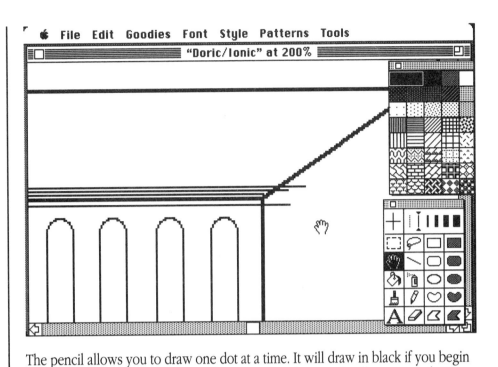

The Pencil

The pencil allows you to draw one dot at a time. It will draw in black if you begin on a white space. If you begin to draw on a dot, the pencil will erase any dot it runs into. You'll use the pencil to clean up details in your drawing.

Select the pencil from the Tools palette.

Look closely at the seam between the capital and the column. If some of the lines are shorter than they should be, extend them with the pencil. If they are too long, carefully erase them with the pencil.

Remember, when you click on black dots with the pencil, they turn white.

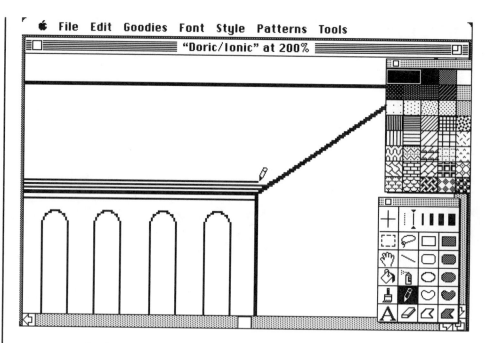

Be sure to check the other side of the capital and column as well. When you are finished, choose Zoom Out from the Goodies menu.

The title of your document should be Doric/Ionic at 100%, indicating that the drawing is back to actual size.

It's about time to save your document once again.

Choose Save from the File menu.

The Paint Can

You now want to paint the whole column gray. Rather than using the paintbrush, you can use the paint can to fill enclosed areas with the selected pattern.

Select the paint can tool from the Tools palette.

This tool fills areas with the currently selected pattern. Place the tip of the dripping paint can within any closed area (such as a closed loop or a solid black region), and then click. That area will be filled with the chosen pattern.

However, if the area you wish to fill has any gaps, the pattern will leak out and fill a much larger area than you expected. If this should happen to you, proceed immediately to the Edit menu and choose Undo. Check your drawing closely and repair any leaks with the pencil while zoomed in before using the paint can again.

It's a good idea to save your document just before using the paint can. If you don't catch a mistake in time to use the Undo command, you can choose Revert to Saved from the File menu. With Revert to Saved, your document (and the mistake) is replaced by the last saved version of the document.

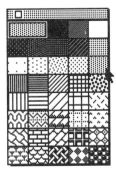

Click on the gray pattern on the third row of the Patterns palette, all the way on the right.

Position the paint can in the area outside of the grooves but still within the column. Click to fill the area.

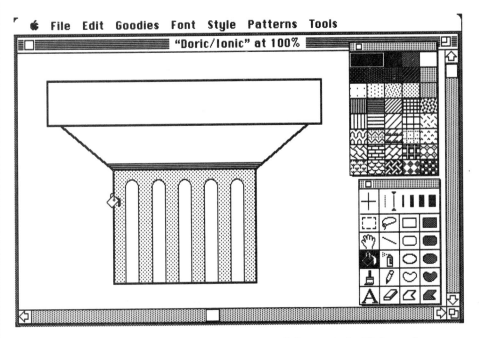

With the same pattern, fill the upper portion of the capital. Click on the next darkest gray and fill the tapered section of the capital. Then, fill the grooves.

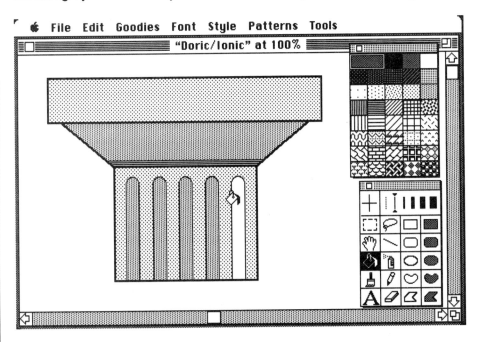

The Doric column and capital are now complete. Before beginning the Ionic column, you'll practice with a few more MacPaint functions you'll need to finish the module.

Working with the Entire Drawing

You have just completed one of the two capitals and columns needed for this document. Unfortunately, there probably isn't much room in the drawing window for the second capital and column. What you need to do is to reposition the drawing on the document page so you'll have room for the second capital and column. Only one-third of the entire page appears in the drawing window at any one time. With either the grabber from the Tools palette or the Zoom Out command in the Goodies menu, you can easily move about the full 8 by 10 inch MacPaint drawing area.

Using Zoom Out

Choose Zoom Out from the Goodies menu.

A reduced view of the entire MacPaint page appears. Now, you can move the drawing around the entire page by using the selection rectangle and lasso. All the standard drawing tools work in this view as well.

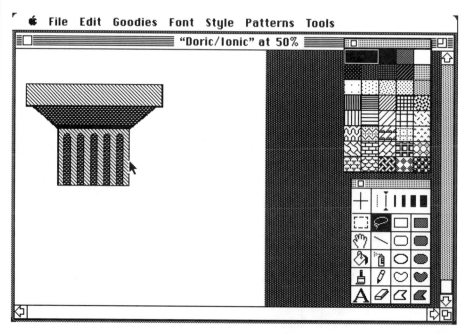

Use the Lasso to select the Doric column and move it close to the top of the document page.

Choose Zoom In from the Goodies menu to return to actual size.

Use the scroll box on the right side of the drawing window to move to the bottom of the window.

Creating the Ionic Capital

You're now ready to begin the Ionic Column.

Many of the techniques used to make the Doric capital are needed to make the Ionic capital. Because much of this should be familiar to you by now, the instructions are going to be in a much shortened form. One suggestion—save your work after each step. Some mistakes are very difficult to correct. If you've saved after every step, you can always choose Revert from the Edit menu to correct such mistakes. While you may lose a few minutes of work by choosing Revert, it can save you more time than you would spend actually correcting those mistakes.

Like the Doric capital, the Ionic capital rests on a column. Remember the column you made for the Doric capital that was saved in the Scrapbook? Now you can reuse it here.

1. Copy the column from the Scrapbook and paste it into the drawing window.

Open the Scrapbook, scroll through until you see the column, and choose Copy from the Edit menu. Close the Scrapbook and choose Paste. Since the column is still selected when it appears in the drawing window, you can drag it to the bottom center of the window. Now you have room to make the capital. Do not try to build the capital directly on top of the column. Make the capital above the column. It can then be selected and repositioned later.

Historically, Ionic capitals had spiral ornamentation. Because of the difficulty in drawing a smooth freehand spiral, the spirals will be approximated by a series of concentric circles. Remember how you duplicated the grooves for the column using the lasso and the Option key? Similarly, you will only make one set of concentric circles, even though the Ionic capital requires two. To make the second set, you'll duplicate the original with the lasso and Option key.

2. Use the Shift key with the unfilled oval tool to make several circles. Use the lasso to position them within one another. Duplicate this set of concentric circles once it is finished.

The Shift key will constrain the unfilled oval tool to produce only perfect circles. The Shift key always acts to constrain drawing tools.

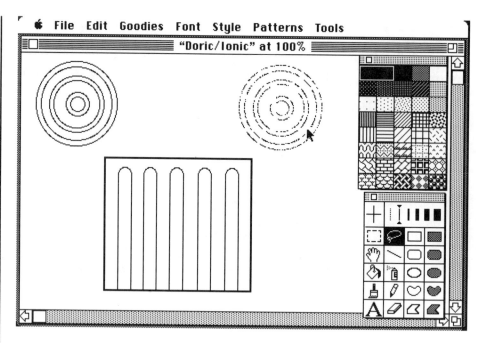

The unfilled oval tool works like the rectangle tool—you simply drag diagonally. By holding the Shift key and dragging, the tool will produce only circles.

Do not try to make the circles within each other. Make them off to the side, select with the lasso and then position them within one another. Once you've made one "spiral," select and duplicate the whole thing with the lasso and the Option and Shift keys. The Shift key will keep the duplicate level with the original.

3. Use the rubber band tool with appropriate line widths to connect the spirals. Use Zoom In, if necessary, to clean up the intersections of the lines and the spirals.

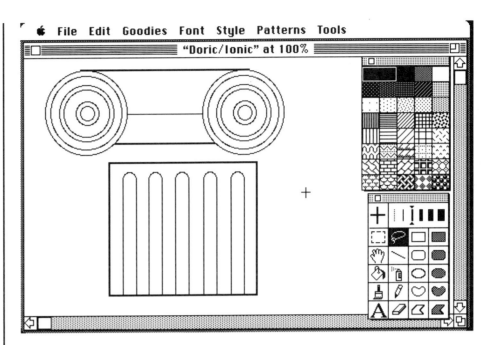

The Shift key will constrain the rubber band tool to horizontal, vertical, or 45°
angle lines.

**4. Now select the entire capital with the lasso and position it on top of the
column.**

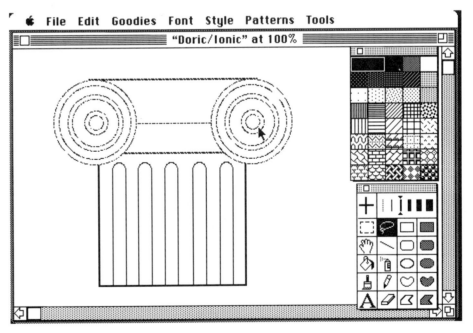

5. Use the paint can to fill the capital and column as shown.

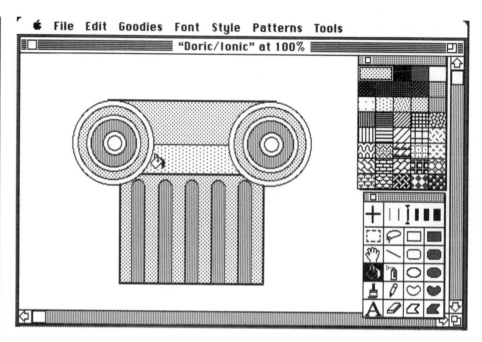

6. Using Zoom Out and the lasso, reposition the two finished column and capital combinations in the lower left corner of the page. Reposition the drawing window as shown. Zoom in to actual size when you are finished.

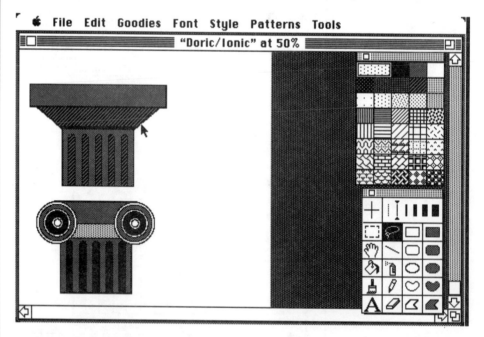

7. Save your work.

In capsule form, you've just learned how to make an Ionic column. To finish the document, you must add some explanatory captions with MacPaint text.

Using MacPaint Text

MacPaint's text function allows you to add words, sentences, and paragraphs to your drawings. Since MacPaint is a bitmapped program, the output of the text will only be as good as you see on the screen—even when printed on an Apple LaserWriter. The Font and Style menus in the MacPaint menu bar are devoted specifically to MacPaint text.

The Font Menu

The **Font** menu allows you to select from a wide range of typefaces. The fonts loaded on your system may be different from the ones that appear in the examples.

The Style Menu

The **Style** menu lets you choose from a variety of type sizes and allows you to emphasize words by creating bold, underlined, and italic text, as well as other options. The alignment commands allow you to align your text against the right edge, left edge, or center of a particular area of your drawing.

Creating Text

Use the grabber to position the drawing window directly to the right of the uppermost (Doric) column.

Close the Patterns palette by clicking on the close box in its upper left corner. This will free up work space.

Select the text tool (the capital "A").

The pointer now looks like an I-bar.

Choose Geneva font from the Font menu. From the Style menu, choose 18 Point and then choose Align Middle.

Position the I-bar in the space between the capital and the edge of the MacPaint page. It should be centered horizontally and about as high as the top edge of the capital but not too close to the edge of the drawing window. Click the mouse button to set the insertion point.

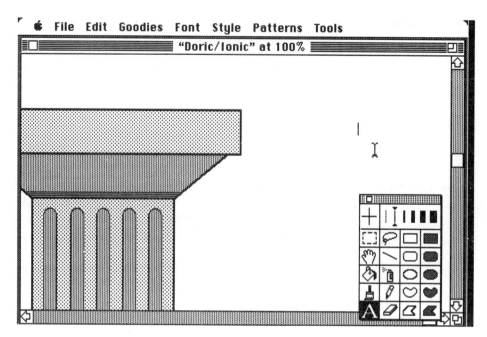

The flashing insertion point will appear.

Type "Doric".

Press the Return key.

Type "Order".

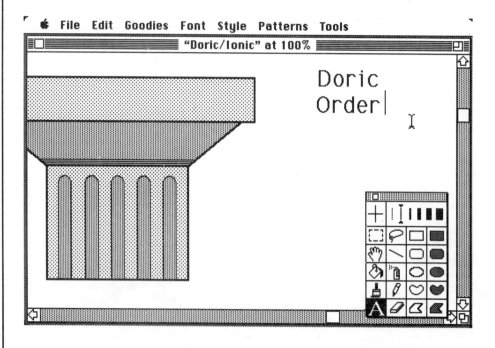

Align Middle will cause the text that you typed to be centered from the initial point that you click. Align Right will cause the text start at the original insertion point and continue to the left. Guess what happens with Align Left? Bingo.

The text menus can be used to alter any text you've just typed. You can continually alter text until you reposition the I-bar and click the mouse button, or until you select another tool. After that, the Font and Style of a particular block of text are fixed. If you decide you want to change the text later on, you have to erase and retype the text.

Close the tool palette to give yourself room to work.

Position the I-bar underneath the "Doric Order" headline. Click the mouse button to set the insertion point. From the appropriate menus, choose Geneva, 12 pt., Plain text, and Align Middle.

Type the following information about the Doric order, remembering to use the Return key to start a new line.

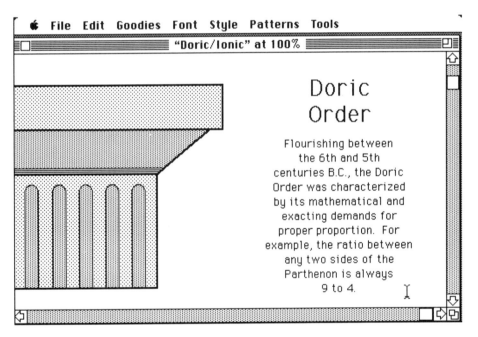

Except for the actual words, the procedures for adding text about the Ionic Order are identical to those used for the Doric Order.

Add the appropriate headline and text about the Ionic Order. Use the same Font and Style commands as you used for the Doric Order text.

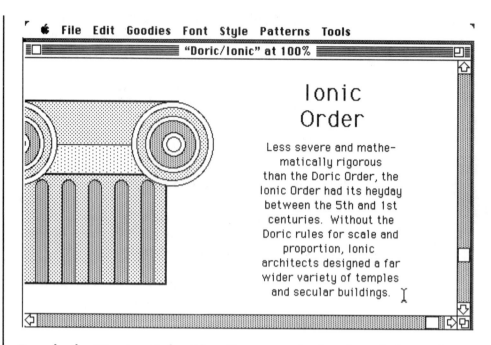

To make the "Grecian Orders" headline, move the drawing window to the top of the document using the scroll bars.

Select the text tool.

Set the I-bar in the middle of the drawing window. Use the following settings from the type menus: Geneva, 24 pt., Bold, and Align Middle. Type "GRECIAN ORDERS".

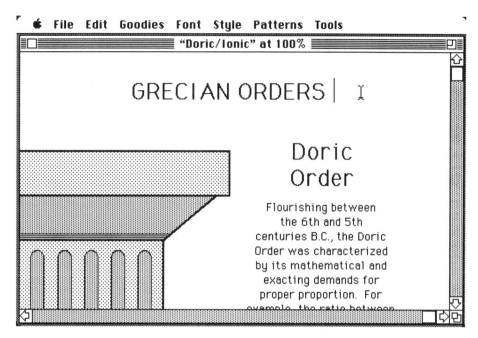

Finally, if there is room between the capitals and the historical information, add further identification labels to the diagrams. Refer to the completed example as needed.

Use the following settings: Geneva, 12 pt. (or smaller), Bold, and Align Right. (With Align Right, you position the insertion point where you want the right margin of the text to be.)

The lasso can be used to circle text and reposition it just like any other object.

Use the rubber band tool to connect the labels with the appropriate part of the capitals.

You can now print your finished MacPaint page, but first, you should save your document.

Choose Save from the File menu.

Make sure your printer is chosen correctly, turned on, and ready to print.

Choose Print from the File menu.

A dialog box appears. If you'd like multiple copies, type the number of copies you want.

Click OK to confirm your print settings.

In a few seconds, your document will begin to print.

Saving and Printing

Choose Quit from the File menu.

You're back at the Macintosh desktop. A computer artist in the making.

If you are in a public Macintosh lab, remember to copy your finished document to your personal data diskette. Then, drag the document that is on the hard disk or application diskette to the Trash.

Review

In this module, you've learned:

- How to use MacPaint's freehand drawing tools, specifically the paintbrush and the pencil
- How to correct mistakes by erasing or using the Undo command
- How to use the shape tools to create rectangles, rounded rectangles, and circles without ruler, compasses, or templates
- How to select, reposition, and duplicate parts of your drawing with the lasso and selection rectangle
- How to Save and name your MacPaint document
- How to Cut, Copy, and Paste to and from the Clipboard and Scrapbook
- How to make straight lines of varying widths with the rubber band tool
- How to use the Shift key to constrain shape tools and the rubber band tool
- How to use Zoom to touch up and add small details to larger drawings
- How to move the drawing window around the page using the grabber and the Zoom Out command
- How to apply MacPaint's wide range of shades and patterns with the paint can
- How to add descriptions and labels to drawings with MacPaint's text functions
- How to print your finished document

What to Turn In

Turn in a copy of the finished document.

The Bean

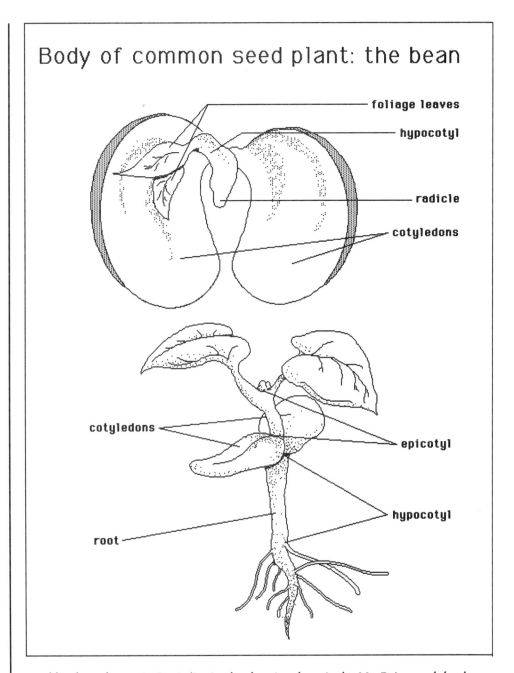

Body of common seed plant: the bean

foliage leaves
hypocotyl
radicle
cotyledons
cotyledons
epicotyl
hypocotyl
root

Description

Unlike the columns in Doric/Ionic, the drawing done in the MacPaint module, the bean was drawn freehand, using the smallest paintbrush and the pencil. MacPaint's duplicating and flipping features helped reduce the time needed to draw the parts of the bean. For example, only the left cotyledon was drawn initially. Then it was duplicated and flipped horizontally. Parts of the duplicate were then erased and redrawn so that the two cotyledons would be slightly different. The same procedure was used to make the leaves of the seedling.

MacPaint's text function produced neat, legible labels, and these were connected to various points on the drawings with the rubber band. Zoom Out and the grabber were frequently used since both drawings are larger than the drawing window.

the EnvironMentalists 23119 beech san francisco, california 94124

Description

The Earth's continental detail was added pixel-by-pixel with the pencil in Zoom In to 200%. The oceans were added with the paint can using a gray from the Patterns palette. The lines to the right of the Earth were made with the rubber band. Two horizontal lines were drawn near each other, selected with the lasso, and then duplicated. The duplicate lines were then positioned underneath the original lines. This procedure was selected with the lasso, the ocean gray was selected from the Patterns palette, and Fill was chosen from the Edit menu. The lines turned gray.

"EarthGram" was typed in Athens, 36 point, and selected with the lasso. The same gray used for the lines and oceans was selected from the Patterns palette. Fill was chosen again. "EarthGram" turned gray. Another "EarthGram" was typed, selected with the lasso, and positioned over the gray letters to create the shadow effect.

Exercises

1. Name the specific MacPaint tool or menu you would use to complete each task listed below. In some cases, a combination of tools and menus may be required. (There are often several ways of completing the same task.)

  a)   Drawing very detailed, fine work
  b)   Drawing a very thick, wavy black line
  c)   Drawing a very thick, wavy gray line
  d)   Erasing (name at least three ways)
  e)   Moving the document around the drawing window
  f)   Drawing a perfect circle
  g)   Filling a screen with perfect circles
  i)   Move an entire drawing within the document margins
  j)   Adding a pattern to an enclosed area

2. The Clipboard and Scrapbook are found in all Macintosh applications and work exactly as they do in MacPaint. Proper use of the Clipboard and Scrapbook often save time and work when using Macintosh applications.

In MacPaint, a drawing can be located in the drawing window, the Clipboard, the Scrapbook, or a combination of all three. For the following procedures, determine where the drawing(s) could be found.

  a) A drawing is selected with the lasso. Copy is chosen from the Edit menu.

  b) A drawing is selected with the lasso. Cut is chosen from the Edit menu.

  c) Drawing A is selected with the selection rectangle. Cut is chosen from the Edit menu. Drawing B is selected with the lasso. Copy is chosen from the Edit menu.

  d) A drawing is on the Clipboard. It is not in the Scrapbook or in the document. The Scrapbook is not open. Paste is chosen from the Edit menu.

  e) A drawing is on the Clipboard. It is not in the Scrapbook or in the document. The Scrapbook is open. Paste is chosen from the Edit menu.

3. "Selecting" is an important action common to all Macintosh applications. You select menus. You select specific commands. You select documents and application icons before moving, duplicating, or opening them.

In MacPaint, drawings can be selected in the drawing window with either the lasso or the selection rectangle. In what ways do these two tools work similarly? In what ways are they different? Which menu commands work with both tools? Are there any menu commands that work only with the lasso? What are they? Are there any menu commands that work only with the selection rectangle? What are they?

4. While MacPaint's uses are as numerous as its users, the application is perhaps most commonly used for making announcement flyers. Make an eye-catching flyer describing an upcoming event. The flyer doesn't have to have any relation to an actual group or event. However, the flyer should include the name and nature of the event (party, debate, movie series, organizational meeting, etc.), the sponsors, date, time, and admission fee (if any). Use a few sizes and styles of text to emphasize important points. For decorative purposes, add an event or organization logo and map to the flyer.

HOWDY DO!

3 Word Processing

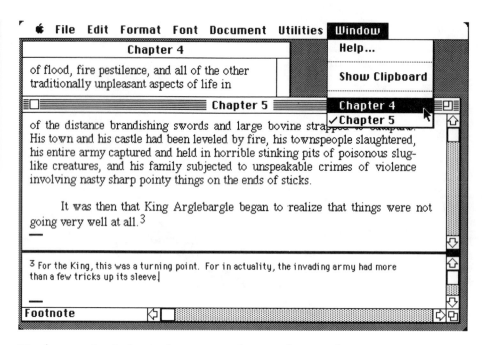

About Word Processing

Word processing is the single most popular use of personal computers today. This is because word processing applications make it easy to compose, recompose, and reformat documents without erasers, correction fluid, and endless retyping.

Word processing features the ability to add, delete, and move words, lines, and paragraphs in a snap, making it easy to make changes and correct errors. Thus, using word processing software significantly reduces the time it takes to create and edit a document. Also, some word processor users feel that the power to easily write, rewrite, and reformat their documents actually increases the quality of their writing.

Word processing involves three closely related functions: typing, editing, and formatting.

Typing

Generally, to create a document, you simply type. The words you type are stored in the memory of the computer, and when you save your work, a copy of those words are stored on your disk.

Editing

The ability to easily edit, or change, the text you've typed is what makes word processing far more powerful than typing on a typewriter. Using a word processing application's editing functions, you can quickly move and change the words electronically without having to retype the entire document.

Formatting

Another job that word processing applications handle well is formatting the text you've typed. When you format a document, you determine what the document will look like when it is finally printed. Formatting involves setting margins, tabs, indentation, and other similar attributes of your document.

To make this kind of formatting easier, the trend has been toward "What You See Is What You Get" (WYSIWYG, pronounced "wizzywig") word processors, where the document appears on the screen of the computer exactly as it will appear when printed. The Macintosh's high resolution screen makes it well suited for WYSIWYG word processing applications.

Integrating information from other applications has recently become an important feature of word processing software. The ability to insert a diagram or graph from a graphics application, a table from a spreadsheet, or even a paragraph from another word processing document can dramatically simplify the production of complex documents. The Macintosh's Cut, Copy, and Paste commands make this type of integration across applications possible.

About Microsoft Word

Microsoft Word version 4.0 is a full-featured word processing application for the Macintosh. It incorporates all of the basic capabilities of a word processor, while adding a number of advanced features that make working with long and complex documents easier. These features include:

Advanced Formatting. Word's advanced formatting features allow for multiple-column documents and other special formats, such as graphics that are surrounded by text, tables that have borders around them, and so on.

Automatic Footnoting. Word automatically numbers your footnotes and makes room for them at the bottom of the page or at the end of a section. If you add or remove footnotes, Word renumbers and repositions them automatically.

Print Merging. Using the Print Merge function, you can print customized versions of form documents, such as personal form letters.

Introduction to Microsoft Word

The Task

Your classmates have honored you by choosing you as coordinator of a festival celebrating the 50th anniversary of the introduction of tofu and other soybean products at your university. Your first step as coordinator of this momentous occasion is to enlist the help of the local merchants. You'll need to draft a short, one-page letter to the merchants asking for their support. Because Microsoft Word is well suited to producing short documents quickly, you'll use Word to create and format your letter.

First, you'll type the bulk of your letter. You'll then use that text to experiment with some of the basic Word editing techniques, including selecting and replacing text and changing fonts.

Next, you'll use other Word formatting techniques to set margins, paragraph indentation, line spacing, and alignment.

You'll use Word's Cut, Copy, and Paste commands to move a block of text around in your document.

When you're finished, you'll save your new document and print a copy. The finished document should look like the one shown on the next page.

August 18, 1990

Dear Local Merchant:

As you know, this year marks the 50th anniversary of the introduction of tofu and other products at this university. To celebrate this special demi-centennial, a number of student groups have joined to plan Tofu Festa 50, a week-long celebration of the spirit of soybean products and their role in university living.

To quote Laura Palmer, head of the Student Soy Council and last year's Tofu Queen:

> *The spirit of soy products has touched all of us on this campus.*
> *Never before has a food group created such feelings of camaraderie*
> *and togetherness. We truly are what we eat. As a result, the theme*
> *of this year's special festivities shall be "Tofu Is You."*

Minutes of preparation have gone into the planning and execution of the "Tofu Is You" campaign. We now need your support as a sponsor of this event to provide whatever money, supplies, or manpower you can donate to make Tofu Festa 50 the success we all want it to be.

Thanks in advance for your generous contributions.

Sincerely,

Dale Cooper
Tofu Festa 50 Coordinator

Getting Started

This module assumes that you are familiar with the basics of using the Macintosh, how to work with a hard disk and/or diskettes, how to choose menu commands, and so on. If these concepts are not familiar to you, please review the Approaching Macintosh module.

First, you'll start from the Macintosh desktop.

Turn on the Macintosh. If you are not using a hard disk, insert the system diskette in the internal diskette drive.

Soon, you'll see the Macintosh desktop.

Next, you'll open Word.

Microsoft Word

If you are using a hard disk, open Word by finding and double-clicking on its icon.

If you do not have a hard disk, insert the Word program disk and double-click on the Word icon.

Word opens a new document named "Untitled1" in the Word document window. If you're familiar with Macintosh windows, you should recognize the **menu bar,** the **title bar,** the **close box,** the **scroll box,** the **size box,** and the **zoom box.** Inside the Word document window there is a blinking vertical line called the **insertion point,** which you'll learn more about later. At the bottom of the screen, the page number is displayed in the list box.

The **menu bar** contains the titles of menus from which you choose commands.

The **close box** lets you close the window.

The blinking vertical bar marks the spot where text appears as you type. That spot is called the **insertion point.**

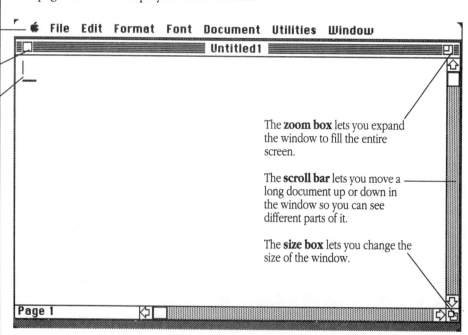

The **zoom box** lets you expand the window to fill the entire screen.

The **scroll bar** lets you move a long document up or down in the window so you can see different parts of it.

The **size box** lets you change the size of the window.

Because Word has many advanced features, it could be a little unwieldy for the beginning user. To overcome this problem, Word lets you hide some of the more

advanced commands if you aren't going to use them. This feature is called **short menus.** Because this is an introductory module, you'll use short menus to keep things simple. To see if you need to turn short menus on, look at the list box at the bottom of your screen. (The list box contains the text "Page 1.") If there is a box to the right of the list box with the word "Normal" in it, you should change to short menus.

If necessary, choose Short Menus from the Edit menu.

If you are already using short menus, the Short Menus command will not appear in the Edit menu. Instead, the command will be **Full Menus.** If you see the Full Menus command, you don't need to do anything.

Now you're ready to begin work.

Typing Text

To create a Word document, whether it be a letter to your first cousin or a marine biology term paper, all you need to do is type.

The Insertion Point

The blinking vertical bar marks the **insertion point,** the place where whatever you type will be inserted.

Type "Dear Sir".

The words you type fill in behind the insertion point as it moves to the right.

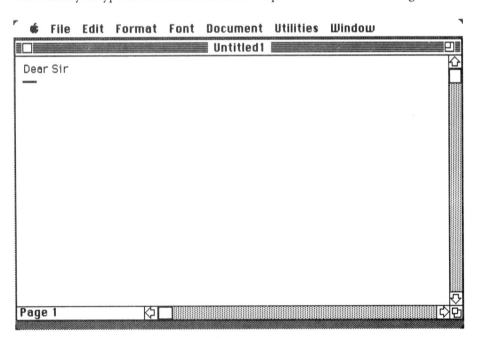

Using the Delete Key

Removing text is as easy as pressing the **Delete key,** (or the **Backspace key** if you are using a Macintosh Plus).

Use the Delete key to remove "Sir" and replace it with "Local Merchant:".

Note that the Delete key moves the insertion point backward, deleting the letters and spaces as it goes. Holding down the Delete key causes it to repeat, successively removing the characters to the left of the insertion point.

Using the Return Key

The **Return key** moves the insertion point down to the beginning of the next line, much like the carriage return key on an electric typewriter. You'll use it twice here to skip a line.

Press the Return key twice.

Word Wraparound

Word wraparound is a Word feature that automatically starts a new line when you reach the right margin of your document. This means that you don't need to press the Return key at the end of each line. Use the Return key only to start a new paragraph or to skip a line.

Type the following text without using the Return key:

As you know, this year marks the 50th anniversary of tofu and other soybean products at this university. To celebrate this special demi-centennial, a number of student groups have joined to plan Tofu Fest 50, a week-long celebration of the spirit of soybean products and their role in university living.

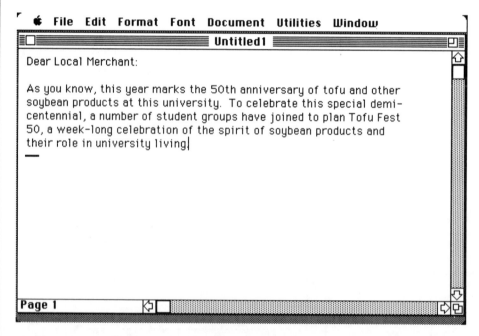

Word wraparound makes it easy to type quickly, because you no longer have to worry about when to press the Return key. It also allows Word to automatically reformat your paragraphs when you add or delete a sentence, change the margins, or change the justification (more about that in a minute).

Inserting Text

Inserting new text in existing text is a simple matter of learning how to position the insertion point (that blinking vertical line that follows you when you type). To set a new insertion point, you'll need to use the mouse.

Position the pointer between the word "anniversary" and the word "of" in the first sentence.

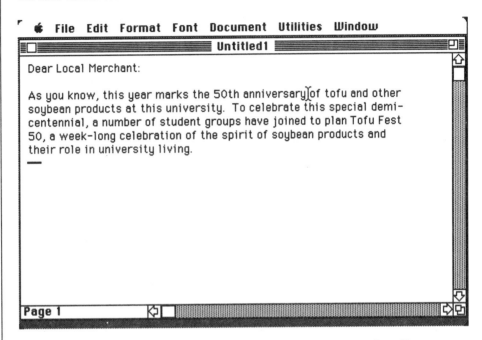

Notice that when you move the pointer inside the document window (for example, from the menu bar or the scroll bar), the pointer changes to an I-bar. You'll use this pointer shape to set the new insertion point.

With the pointer positioned right before the word "of", click the mouse button to set the new insertion point.

The new insertion point is now right before the word "of". That's where you'll insert a few extra words.

Type "of the introduction" and a space.

Note that the inserted text pushes everything in front of it out of its way, but word wraparound keeps things looking neat.

Move the pointer (the I-bar) to the end of the paragraph and click to set the insertion point there.

Creating a New Paragraph

With the convenience of word wraparound, you may be tempted never to touch the Return key at all. Resist that temptation, though—you still need it to start new paragraphs and to skip lines. You'll use the Return key here to start a new paragraph with a blank line separating it from the one you just typed.

Press the Return key twice.

Remember that Return—like most keys on the Macintosh keyboard—repeats if held down. If you get too many Returns, just press the Delete key to remove them.

Type the following:

> Hours of preparation have gone into the planning and execution of the "Tofu Is You" campaign. We now need your support as a sponsor of this event to provide whatever money, supplies, or manpower you can donate to make Tofu Fest 50 the success we all want it to be.

If it turns out that you've made a mistake (no one's perfect), Word, like most Macintosh applications, allows you to undo your last action.

The Undo Command

Choose Undo Typing from the Edit menu.

 File   Edit   Format   Font   Document   Utilities   Window

Untitled1

Dear Local Merchant:

As you know, this year marks the 50th anniversary of the introduction of tofu and other soybean products at this university. To celebrate this special demi-centennial, a number of student groups have joined to plan Tofu Fest 50, a week-long celebration of the spirit of soybean products and their role in university living.

Page 1

The last paragraph you typed is gone. But perhaps you've changed your mind and decided to keep that paragraph. You can undo the Undo command using Redo.

Choose Redo Typing from the Edit menu.

Your words return as quickly as they vanished. So remember that if you make a mistake—or just change your mind—Undo (and Redo) can help save the day.

Editing Text

Now that you've learned how to type text to create your document, you may decide that you want to edit, or change, some of the things you've typed. Editing can be anything from deleting one letter to moving an entire paragraph. The important thing to remember is that no matter what type of editing you do, the general procedure will be the same:

First, you make a selection. Then, you act on that selection.

Selecting Text

When you make a selection, you indicate which part of the document you wish to work with. To select text in Word, **drag across** it. To do this, position the pointer at the beginning of the word, hold the mouse button down, and drag the mouse to the right. When the pointer reaches the end of the word, release the mouse button.

Select the word "anniversary" in the first paragraph by dragging across it.

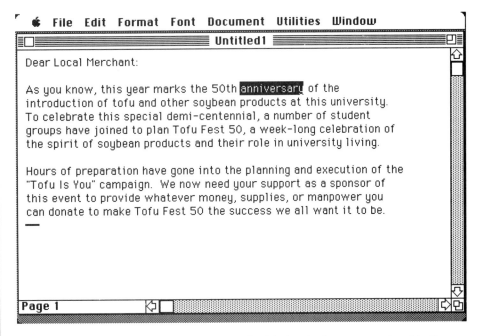

Notice that the word "anniversary" is now highlighted. This is your visual indication that you've selected the right word.

Selecting a Word

A quicker way to select a single word is to **double-click** on it.

Position the I-bar over the word "celebration" and double-click to select it.

Remember: to double-click, click the mouse button twice in rapid succession.

Note that when you selected the word "celebration", the word "anniversary" became unselected. To avoid confusion (yours and Word's), you generally make only one selection at a time. When you make a new selection, it replaces your previous selection. So, if you want to cancel a selection (deselect), just click anywhere in your document.

Click the mouse anywhere in the document to deselect "celebration".

To select more than one word, just drag across them. Dragging the pointer down rather than across selects entire lines at a time.

To select the first paragraph, you would position the I-bar at the beginning of the paragraph, hold the mouse button down, drag down to the last line of the paragraph, and then continue dragging to the right until you reach the end of the line. Release the mouse button when the I-bar reaches the end of the line.

Select the entire first paragraph by dragging down and across.

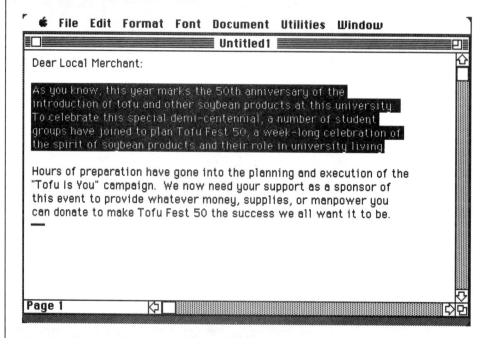

If you move the pointer too far to the left when you are selecting, the pointer may change to a right-pointing arrow. The left edge of the screen where the pointer shifts right is called the **selection bar.** You'll learn more about the selection bar in the intermediate module. For now, just ignore it and move the pointer slightly to the right until it becomes an I-bar again.

Extending a Selection

Another short cut to selecting large blocks of text is by **shift-clicking.** You do this by clicking to mark the start of your selection, moving to the end of the selection, and clicking the mouse button again while holding down the Shift key.

Mark the beginning of your document by clicking the mouse button before the word "Dear".

Clicking the mouse here serves two purposes: it deselects the previous selection and marks the beginning of your next selection.

Move the pointer to the end of the document (after the words "to be.").

Hold down the Shift key while clicking the mouse button.

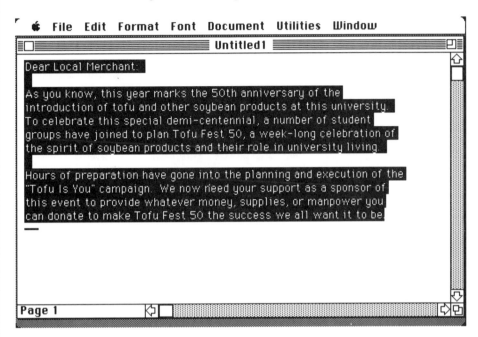

The entire area between your first click and your second is selected. This short cut comes in especially handy when you're selecting a large piece of your document.

Practice selecting parts of your document until you're comfortable with the various techniques you've learned.

Selecting is an important part of using Word. Make sure you know the selecting techniques before you continue.

You've learned the first half of the editing process—making the selection. Now you'll learn the second—how to do something to that selection.

Changing Fonts

The Macintosh can display characters on the screen in different typestyles called **fonts.** When you are creating a document, you can use different fonts to achieve different goals. For example, in *Approaching Macintosh,* a distinct font is used for all of the instructions to make them stand out.

When you are choosing fonts, you should consider the kind of printer you are using. If you are using an Apple LaserWriter, some fonts will look better than others. In this module, you'll use two fonts, **Times** and **Helvetica,** that print well on both Apple ImageWriter and LaserWriter printers.

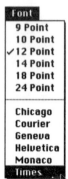

To change a font in Word, you first select the text that you want to change, and then you choose the font you want to use from the Font menu.

Select the entire document. Then, choose Times from the Font menu.

The text in your document changes to the Times font.

You can click anywhere in the document window to deselect the current selection.

Deselecting Text

Click anywhere inside the document to deselect the text you've selected.

Next, you'll change the words "Tofu Fest 50" to make them stand out from the rest of the text.

Select the words "Tofu Fest 50" in the first paragraph by dragging across them. With the words "Tofu Fest 50" selected, choose Helvetica from the Font menu.

The words "Tofu Fest 50" are now in the Helvetica font. The Helvetica selection in the Font menu is checked. This font change nicely sets off these words from the rest of the text.

Replacing a Selection

If you make a selection and type, your new words will replace the old selection.

Select "Hours" from the beginning of the second paragraph.

Remember, to select just double-click on the word.

Type "Minutes".

By typing "Minutes" while "Hours" was selected, you replaced your exaggeration with something a bit more truthful.

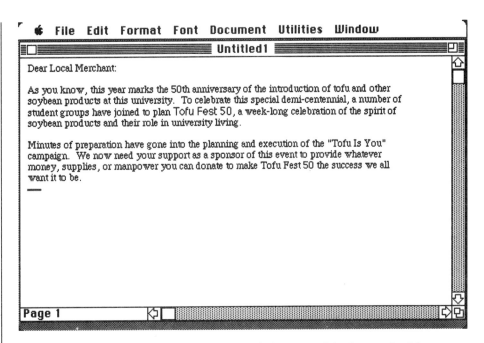

Formatting Techniques

When you format your document, you decide how it will look in its final form. This means setting the margins, tabs, indentations, line spacing, and text alignment that will appear when you print. You can have many different formats all within the same document.

Using Rulers

Word uses **rulers** to set the format. There is a separate ruler for every paragraph in the document, but you won't be able to see them until you use the Show Ruler command. You'll do that now.

Choose Show Ruler from the Format menu.

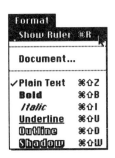

A ruler appears, with settings for the current paragraph.

The parts of a ruler are shown below. Although rulers appear in the document window, they aren't printed when you print your document.

Use the **First Line Indent Marker** to set special indentation for the first line of the paragraph.

The **Left Indent Marker** marks the left edge of the paragraph.

The **Tab Stop Icon** is used to set tab stops for the paragraph.

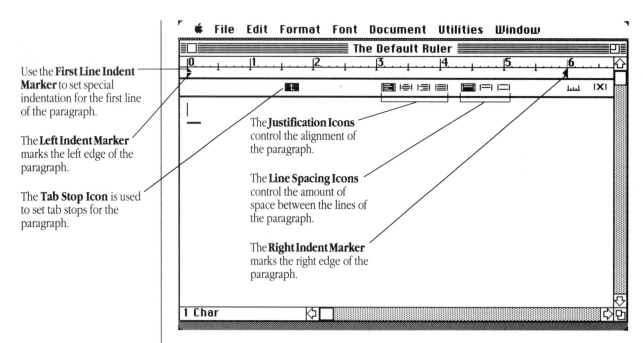

The **Justification Icons** control the alignment of the paragraph.

The **Line Spacing Icons** control the amount of space between the lines of the paragraph.

The **Right Indent Marker** marks the right edge of the paragraph.

When you start with a new (or "Untitled") document, Word provides you with a preset ruler that you can use or change. This preset ruler sets the following format:

- A 1 1/4-inch left margin with no paragraph indentation
- A 1 1/4-inch right margin
- Single spacing
- Left alignment

The information given above should puzzle you. The ruler on your screen shows the left margin at 0, but the text above says it's at 1 1/4 inches. Remember that the ruler shows the left and right margins for the current paragraph. The 0 means that the current paragraph is even with the left margin for the whole document. You access and change document settings with the Document... command. You'll check the current document margins now.

Choose Document... from the Format menu.

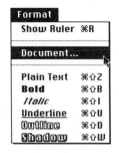

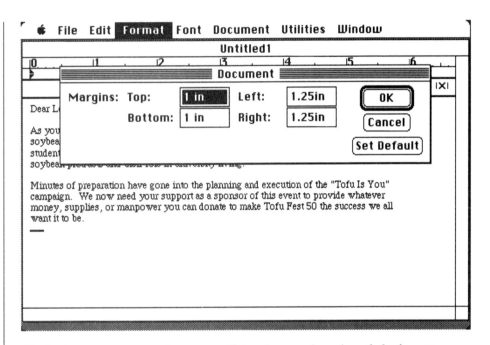

Check the settings to convince yourself that the preselected, or **default,** settings given above are correct.

When you have looked over the settings, click OK.

Though you can see only a small part of the left and right document margins, the full margins will appear when you print your document. Think of yourself as looking through a small window at a standard page.

You can change these preset margins, add and move tabs, or change some other aspect of the preset format. You'll make some of these changes to the next paragraph you type.

Position the insertion point at the end of your document.

Press the Return key twice and then type the following text.

> To quote Laura Palmer, head of the Student Soy Council and last year's Tofu Queen:
>
> The spirit of soy products has touched all of us on this campus. Never before has a food group created such feelings of camaraderie and togetherness. We truly are what we eat. As a result, the theme of this year's special festivities shall be "Tofu Is You."

Changing Margins

You'd like to indent the quote you just typed and change the style of its font to make it stand out from the rest of the document. To indent it, you'll move both margins inward.

To change the margins, you simply drag the the **right indent marker** and the **left indent marker** to the spot on the ruler. If you've been taking advantage of word wraparound, the text should reformat instantly.

To drag a marker, you position the pointer on the marker, press and hold down the mouse button and drag. When you have moved the marker to its new position, release the mouse button.

◀ **Drag the right indent marker to the 5 1/4-inch mark on the ruler.**

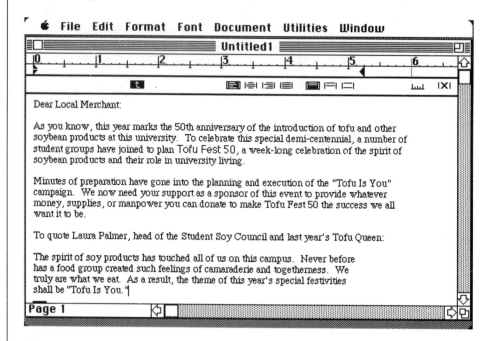

Ruler scale icon ⊔⊔⊔

If you accidentally miss the margin marker and click on the ruler scale icon, the appearance of the ruler will change. Don't worry—just click on the scale icon to change it back, then try again.

The First Line Indent Marker

First line indent marker ▸
Left margin marker ▾

If you look closely at the left margin marker, you'll see that it looks a bit different from the right margin marker. This is because it's actually two different markers aligned vertically. The marker on top is called the **first line indent marker.** You use it to set the indentation of the first line of each paragraph.

Remember that each time you press the Return key, you start a new paragraph. The position of the first line indent marker determines where the first line of the paragraph will start.

▸ **Drag the first line indent marker to the 1/2-inch mark on the ruler.**

It may take a few tries to pick up the first line indent marker while leaving the left indent marker behind. Don't worry, be persistent.

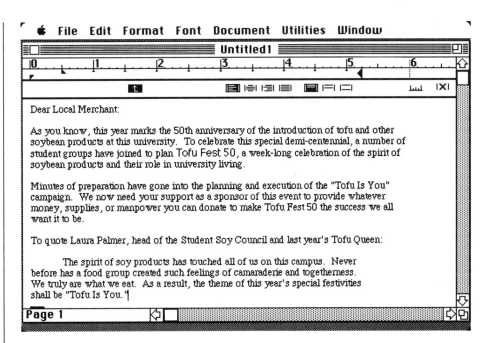

Moving the indentation marker to the right on the ruler indents the first line of the current paragraph. Word copies the current paragraph format when you create a new one. So, from now on, each time you press the Return key to start a new paragraph, Word will move the insertion point where you placed the first line indent marker.

What would happen if you moved the left margin marker *inside* the indentation marker (to the right of it)? You'll do that in a moment, but first some information on how to move the left indent marker. When you click on the left indent marker and drag it to the right, the first line indent marker will move with it. You'll move the left margin marker now.

Move the left indent marker to the 2-inch mark on the ruler.

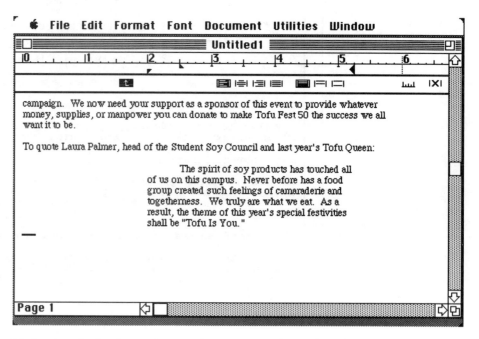

Notice that the first line indent marker moves to the 2 1/2-inch mark on the ruler.

Scrolling

Unless you are using a large-screen monitor, all of the text of your document no longer fits in your document window, and Word automatically scrolls to show the end of the document. To move around in your document, you'll need to know how to use the **scroll bars.** If you don't remember how they work, here's a quick review.

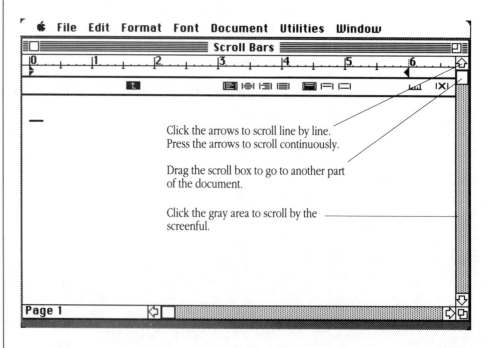

Click the arrows to scroll line by line.
Press the arrows to scroll continuously.

Drag the scroll box to go to another part of the document.

Click the gray area to scroll by the screenful.

Next, you'll move the first line indent marker to the left of the left margin marker.

Move the first line indent marker to the 1-inch mark on the ruler.

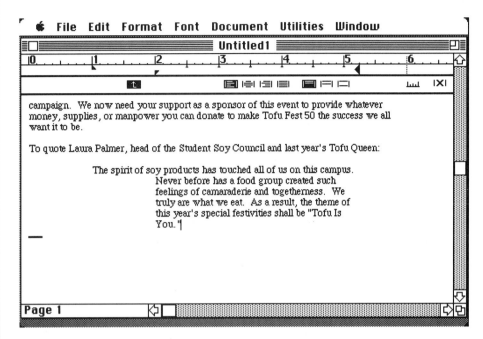

The first line is now "outdented" and the following lines align to the new left margin.

This probably isn't the best format for the quote. You'll set both of these markers correctly now.

Move both the first line indent marker and the left indent marker to the 3/4-inch mark on the ruler by first moving the first line indent marker in line with the left margin marker, and then moving both to the 3/4-inch mark on the ruler.

Remember that moving the left margin marker also moves the first line indent marker. If you try to position the left margin marker first, you'll have trouble.

Now the quote is nicely positioned.

Line Spacing

The line spacing of your paragraph is controlled by the three **line-spacing icons** at the right edge of the ruler between the 4- and 5-inch marks.

The single-spacing icon is highlighted, showing that single-spacing is preselected for this paragraph. To change the spacing, simply click the appropriate icon.

Click the double-space icon.

Single

1-1/2

Double

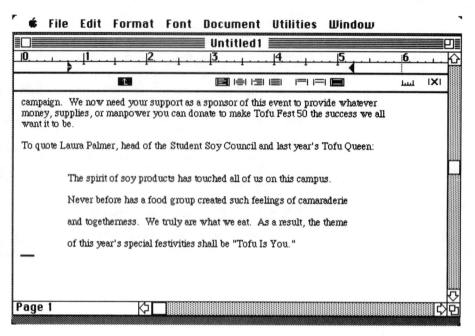

The entire paragraph appears double-spaced. The middle box is for 1 1/2-spacing.

You'll probably agree that the original single-spacing looks best.

Restore single-spacing by clicking on the single-spacing icon.

Alignment

The four **alignment icons** to the left of the spacing icons allow you to vary the alignment of your paragraph. The preset ruler provides left alignment. To change the alignment, simply click the appropriate icon. For center alignment, use the center-alignment icon.

Click the center-alignment icon.

Each line is now centered between the margins.

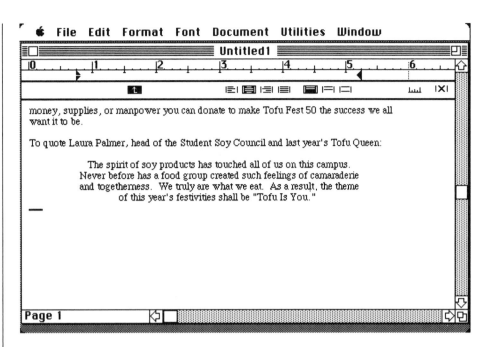

Similarly, for right alignment, use the right-alignment icon.

Click the right-alignment icon.

All lines are now flush up against the right margin. While this might not seem immediately useful, you're sure to come up with an appropriate occasion for right alignment.

With full justification, each line is aligned at both margins. Word does this by inserting small spaces between words to make each line the same length.

Click the full-justification icon.

Note that typed lines that are ended by pressing Return (like the last line of a paragraph) are not aligned. Full justification works only with lines that are word-wrapped.

You'll probably want to stick with left alignment for your letter.

Click the left-alignment icon to restore left alignment.

You're back to where you started.

Hiding Rulers

Sometimes the ruler makes it difficult to see how the document actually looks. In these cases, it can be helpful to hide the ruler.

Choose Hide Ruler from the Format menu.

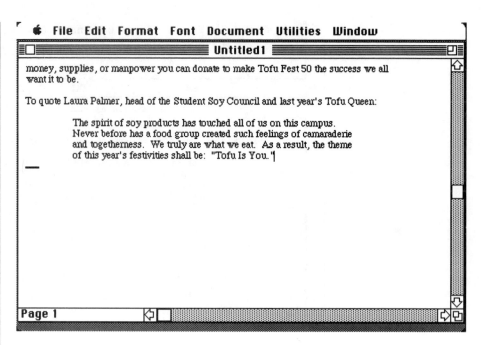

money, supplies, or manpower you can donate to make Tofu Fest 50 the success we all want it to be.

To quote Laura Palmer, head of the Student Soy Council and last year's Tofu Queen:

The spirit of soy products has touched all of us on this campus. Never before has a food group created such feelings of camaraderie and togetherness. We truly are what we eat. As a result, the theme of this year's festivities shall be: "Tofu Is You."

You can now see the document without the ruler getting in the way. But what if you need to change the format?

Choose Show Ruler from the Format menu.

The ruler reappears.

Changing Text Style

In addition to indenting it, you wanted to set the quote off from the rest of the text by changing the style of its text. Word allows you to change your plain text in a variety of ways, including italic, bold, underlined, shadowed, or outlined. It also allows you to combine these styles. To choose a style, or combination of styles, select the text and then choose the appropriate command(s) from the Format menu.

In this case, you want the typestyle of the quote to be in italic.

Select the quote paragraph.

Remember, to select the paragraph, you can drag across the text or use the shift-click method.

Choose Italic from the Format menu.

The paragraph appears in italics.

Saving Your Work

It's a good idea to get into the habit of taking the time to save your work every 10 or 15 minutes. When you save a document, you place a copy of it onto your disk for safekeeping.

Every once in a great while, something unexpected may happen to cause your Macintosh to lose power. Because your Macintosh's memory can't work without power, you might lose work that you were doing at the time. If you save frequently, you'll always have a recent backup copy.

Choose Save from the File menu.

The first time you save your document, a **dialog box** appears, prompting you to give your document a name.

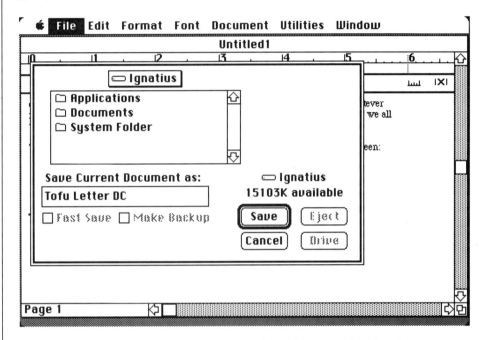

Type "Tofu Letter" followed by your initials as the name for this document. Then, click Save.

In a few moments, the dialog box disappears and your document is now saved on the disk. Now that your document is safe, feel free to take a small break.

Cut, Copy, and Paste

Macintosh's **Cut, Copy,** and **Paste** commands are powerful features that act on words, sentences, paragraphs, and whole documents. These commands let you move blocks of text and graphics within a document or between documents without retyping.

Moving Text

In this case, you've decided to rearrange the paragraphs in your document. You'd like the quote paragraph to come between the first and second paragraphs. You'll use Cut and Paste to move the quote paragraph above the second paragraph. The first step is to select the paragraph that you want to move.

If necessary, scroll to the last paragraph (beginning with "To quote").

You'll use the shift-click method to select the block of text.

Position the I-bar before the words "To quote" and click.

Move the I-bar to the end of the quote (after "Tofu is You."), hold down the Shift key, and click the mouse.

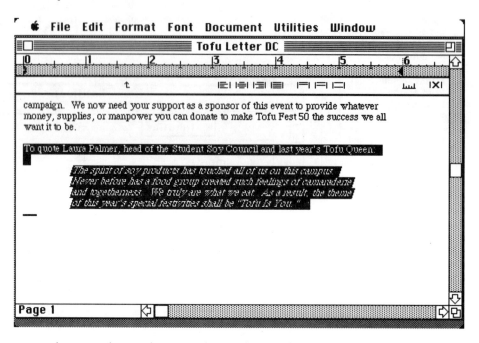

Notice that everything in between the two clicks of the mouse is selected, including the ruler. You're now ready to use Cut.

Choose Cut from the Edit menu.

The selected area disappears. Choosing Cut removes the selected area and places it in a temporary holding area called the **Clipboard.**

Now you'll use the Paste command to transfer the selection from the Clipboard to its new location in the document.

If necessary, scroll up until you reach the end of the first paragraph (the paragraph ends with "university living."), and click to set the insertion point after the final period that ends the paragraph.

Press Return twice to skip a line.

The vertical insertion bar should be flashing on the line below the first paragraph.

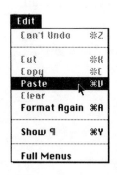

Choose Paste from the Edit menu.

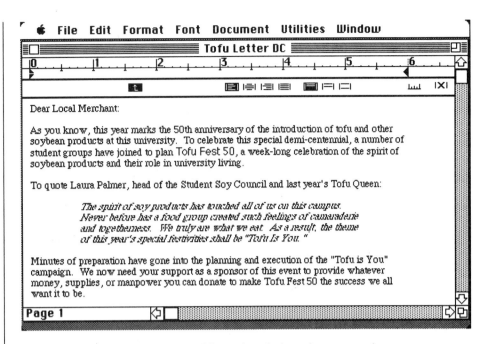

A copy of the paragraph is pasted from the Clipboard into your document.

You can also remove an area by selecting it and pressing the Delete key. However, when you use the Delete key to remove a selection, the selection is *not* placed on the Clipboard, and you won't be able to use the Paste command to reposition it.

Using the Clipboard

A copy of the paragraph remains on the Clipboard even after you've pasted it. If you were to choose Paste again, you could insert another copy of the paragraph. This can be useful if you wish to make a number of copies of the same paragraph.

It's important to remember that the Clipboard holds only one selection at a time. When you choose Cut or Copy from the Edit menu, your selection is placed on the Clipboard and remains there until you use Cut or Copy again.

Finishing Up

You're almost done. You just need to change a few things before you're ready to turn in your document.

First, you need to change the font of "Tofu Fest 50" in the last paragraph so that it is consistent with the first paragraph.

Select the words "Tofu Fest 50" in the last paragraph.

You may have to scroll to see the last paragraph.

Choose Helvetica from the Font menu.

You need to end your document with a little more typing.

Position the insertion point at the end of your document.

Press Return twice and then type "Thanks in advance for your generous contributions."

Now you'll type your closing and leave a space for your signature.

Press Return three times to skip two lines, type "Sincerely," and then press Return four times.

You've left a place to sign your name once it's printed, but now you need to type it. To make it stand out you'd like to have your name be bold.

Changing Styles as You Type

There are two ways to change the style of text. The first way is to select the text that you want to format, and then choose the appropriate commands from the Font menu. You've already done this earlier in the module. The second way is to select the style that you want before you type. You'll do this now to make the text that you type next appear in bold.

Choose Bold from the Format menu.

Type your name, then press Return.

The next line of text should be plain, so you need to cancel the bold.

Choose Plain Text from the Format menu.

Now type "Tofu Fest 50 Coordinator".

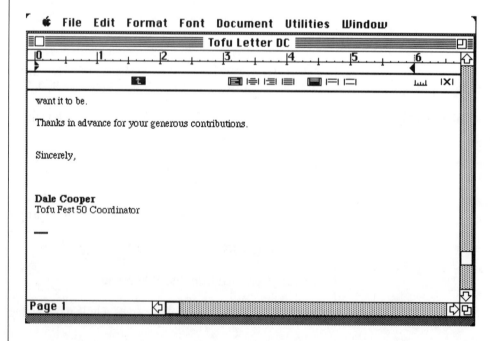

Using Tabs

Like all good letters, this one should have a date at the top of it. You'll add that now.

Scroll to the top of your document and click to set the insertion point before the first word of your letter.

Press Return ten times since there should be some blank lines before the date.

Click on the line above the first line of your letter.

First you'll set a tab at the 4-inch mark on the ruler. You can set tabs by clicking at the appropriate place on the ruler.

Set a tab at the 4-inch mark on the ruler by clicking in the appropriate spot in the middle section of the ruler.

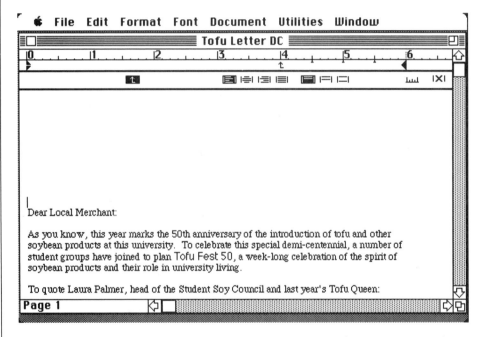

To set tabs correctly, you must click in the middle portion of the ruler, just under the numbers. If you click on the upper portion of the ruler, nothing will happen. If you click on the bottom portion, you might accidently change the alignment or the spacing. Don't get discouraged.

Now you'll tab over to the appropriate spot and type in the date.

Press the Tab key to move the insertion point over to the 4-inch mark.

Type today's date and press Return twice.

There's one more change you want to make. You've decided to give Tofu Fest 50 a more international flair, so you've decided to call it "Tofu Festa 50." You could make the correction by replacing every instance of "Tofu Fest 50" with "Tofu Festa 50." If this were a long document, that could involve a lot of work; in addition, you could easily overlook an occurrence of "Tofu Fest 50." Fortunately, there's a better way. You can use Word's Change... utility to change blocks of text easily. You'll use the Change... utility to change "Fest" to "Festa" everywhere in your document.

Choose Change... from the Utilities menu.

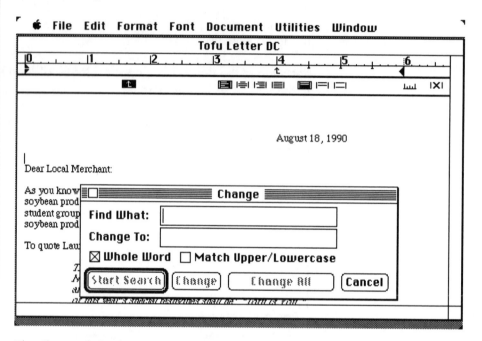

The Change dialog box appears. There are two boxes, one for you to type the text you want to change, and the other for you to type the text you want to replace it with.

Type "Fest" in the Find What box and "Festa" in the Change To box.

If you started changing text now, Word would replace all instances of "Fest " with "Festa." This would cause problems in words that have the letters "fest" in them, such as "infested" and "festival." You can solve this by having word search only for whole words. You'll tell Word to search only for whole words next.

Make sure that the box labeled Whole Word is checked.

The box should be checked (it should have an "x" in it). If it's not, click it again.

Now you're ready to begin changing text. You can either click Change All to have Word search the entire document and make the appropriate changes, or you can click Start Search to have Word search for each instance individually. You'll have

Word search for each instance individually, so you can make sure that you want to make the change before committing to it.

Click Start Search.

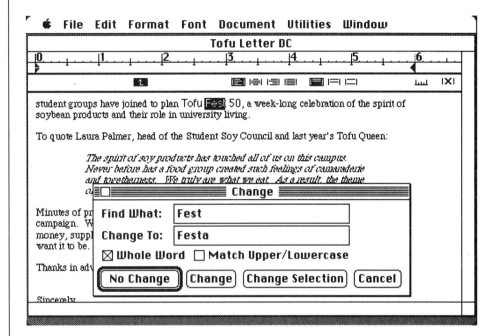

Word finds the first instance of "Fest" and highlights it. You can leave this selection unchanged by clicking No Change. Alternatively, you can click Change to have Word make the change and search for the next occurrence of "Fest." Or you can click Change Selection to have Word change this occurrence of "Fest" and wait to search for the next. You'll click Change to change this occurrence of "Fest" and have Word search for the next.

Click Change.

Word changes the text, finds the next occurrence of "Fest", and highlights it. You'll click Change to have Word search for another occurrence of "Fest".

Click Change to accept the change and search for the next occurrence of "Fest".

Word searches for the next occurrence of Fest.

Click Change to accept the change and search for the next occurrence of "Fest".

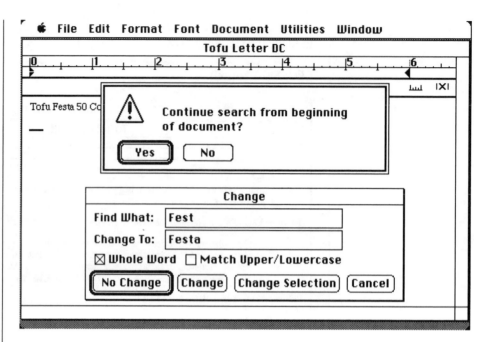

Word changes this occurrence of "Fest" to "Festa", and searches for the next occurrence. A dialog box then appears asking if you want to continue searching from the beginning of the document.

This means that Word has searched to the end of the document and not found any more occurrences of "Fest". Because you started searching in the middle of the document, Word gives you the option of starting over at the beginning to ensure that you haven't missed any changes. You'll click Yes to have Word check the rest of the document.

Click Yes.

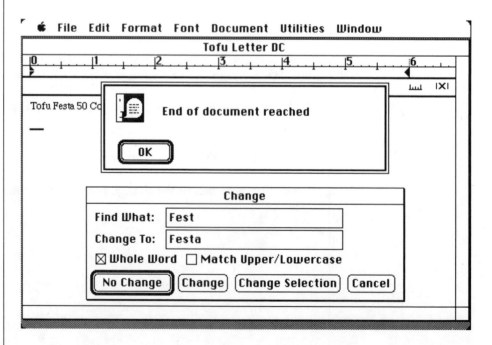

A final dialog box appears, telling you that Word searched the entire document from the beginning and found no more instances of "Fest".

Click OK. Then, close the Change... dialog box by clicking in its close box.

Saving and Printing

Your letter is now finished and ready to be printed and sent out to the local merchants. But first, you should save your completed document.

Choose Save from the File menu.

Since you saved and named your document earlier, Word will not prompt you for a name again. If you should want to save your document under a different name, choose Save As... from the File menu and Word will prompt you for another name.

Now that you've saved your work, you'll want to make a printed copy.

Make sure your printer is chosen correctly, turned on, and ready to print.

Choose Print... from the File menu.

If you'd like multiple copies, type the number of copies you'll need.

Click OK to confirm your print settings.

In a few seconds, your document will begin to print.

Quitting

Choose Quit from the File menu.

If you've made any changes to your document, you'll be asked if you'd like to save them. Click OK.

You're back at the Macintosh desktop. Nice work. If you are in a public Macintosh lab, remember to copy your finished document to your personal data diskette. Then, drag the document that is on the hard disk to the trash.

Review

In this module, you've learned:

- How to create a Word document by typing text
- How to select text by dragging across the words, double-clicking to select single words, and shift-clicking to select large blocks of text
- How to replace text by selecting it and typing
- How to change the font or style of the text using commands from the Font and Format menus
- How to format a document and change ruler settings for margins, indentations, line spacing, and text alignment
- How to save your document on disk
- How to move or copy parts of your document using the Cut, Copy, and Paste commands
- How to change blocks of text with the Change utilitiy.
- How to print your document

What to Turn In

Turn in the printed copy of your letter.

Intermediate
Microsoft Word

The Task

You have written the first draft of a research paper for a class and you would like to revise it in this module. You'll use the basic editing techniques that you used in the Introduction to Microsoft Word module, and you'll also learn some more advanced features, such as footnotes, page numbering, footers, and so on. You'll also learn how to divide a longer document into sections that can be formatted differently.

You'll use these techniques to fix any typos you made while typing the first draft; to create a title page, so that the paper has a more professional appearance; to include footnotes, for which you did not have the proper citation when you typed your first draft; and finally, to include your name and the page number at the bottom of each page.

When you are finished, you will print the revised version of your paper, which should look like the one on the next five pages.

The Wonderful World of Tofu

Bill Berner
Anthropology 136
Food and Culture

Introduction

Tofu is a food made from soybeans. Although not very popular in the U.S. (outside of California, anyway), it is very popular in the Far East. In Japan, for example, there are seven varieties of tofu that are widely used, and tofu is often an important protein source in the Japanese diet.

Nutritional Information

Tofu is high in protein, and can be used as a cheap protein source in many diets. Soybeans, tofu's main ingredient, yield more protein per acre than any other crop (Figure 1). In fact, soybeans are almost 35% protein. Furthermore, the protein in soybeans is complete (it contains all eight of the essential amino acids). Soybeans contain no cholesterol and almost no indigestible saturated fats.

Figure 1

Per Acre Protein Yields for Various Foods

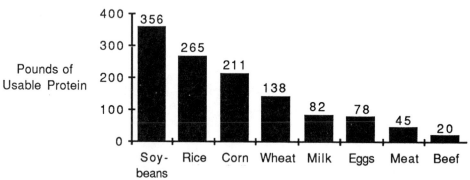

Soybeans are a very good protein source, as measured by both the quantity and quality of protein that result from soybean production.

The quantity of protein found in a food is usually measured in terms of the percentage of the weight of a food that is protein. Figure 2 lists several foods and their percent protein by weight.

Figure 2

Food	% Protein
Dried frozen tofu	53.2
Fish	22.3
Chicken	21.0
Beef	20.0
Tofu	8.1

When evaluating the value of a food as a protein source, it is important to consider not only the *quantity* of protein in that food, but also the *quality* of the protein provided. Net Protein Utilization (NPU) is the measure usually used to compare the quality of protein found in different foods. Net Protein Utilization depends on a food's digestibility and the degree to which the eight essential amino acids making up the protein match the pattern required by the body. The table below lists the Net Protein Utilization of several different foods.

Figure 3

Food	NPU (%)
Fish	80
Beef and hamburger	67
Tofu	65
Chicken	65

The protein found in tofu is a good complement for that found in many grain products. Tofu contains an abundance of lysine, an essential amino acid that many grain products lack. As a result, tofu can be used as a protein booster by combining it with grain products, thus yielding a meal with a higher amount of usable protein than could be obtained by eating either of the foods separately.

Finally, tofu is an ideal diet food. Tofu contains only 9 calories per gram of protein, and only 12 calories per gram of usable protein. Tofu is also rich in minerals, with an abundance of calcium and iron.

The History and Culture of Tofu

A long and colorful history makes tofu as interesting historically and culturally as it is nutritionally. Tofu was known as early as 100 B.C. in parts of China. It became an indelible part of Chinese culture around 520 A.D. when Bhodidarma founded a great Zen school and engaged tofu in "Dharma combat" to prod tofu's understanding of the Buddha's way. He hailed its honest, straightforward nature and its "lovely white robes." Legends of Bhodidarma were passed on verbally; the earliest document to mention tofu was the *seiiroku*, written during the Sung Dynasty (960-1127).

Tofu was brought to Japan in the 8th century by numerous Buddhist monks. Although it appeared in Japan in the 8th century, tofu did not become a fixed part of Japanese culture until the Kamakura period. At that time, tofu blended well with the ruling Samarais' frugal life style.

As the use of tofu spread throughout Japan, the people developed their own methods of production, and Japanese tofu diverged somewhat from its Chinese counterpart in texture and flavor. When the Chinese Zen Master Ingen went to Japan in 1661, he was so taken aback with the form of Japanese tofu that he wrote this famous Japanese proverb:

Mame de
Shikaku de
Yawanaka de

This proverb has a double meaning:

Made of soybeans,		Practicing diligence,
Square, cleanly cut,	*or*	Being proper and honest,
And soft.		And having a kind heart.[1]

Indeed, this is only one of many Japanese proverbs centering around tofu. For instance, when a Japanese person wants to tell someone to "get lost" he may say, "Go bump your head against a corner of a cake of tofu and drop dead." Or when speaking of something as being hopeless, he might say, "It's as futile as trying to clamp two pieces of tofu together."[2]

In the United States, tofu is generally purchased at the supermarket, and only rarely bought from a specialty tofu shop or prepared at home. This is a shame, however, because the traditional tofu maker adds color and variety to the Japanese community. As Shurtleff says in *The Book of Tofu* , "[The tofu maker is] precise and graceful, joined in an effortless rhythm that, at times, [flows] like a dance." Tofu making is an art, and tofu makers are very careful to keep secret methods from slipping into a competitor's hands. In fact, traditional tofu masters have a saying that there are two things that they will not show another person: how to make babies and how to make tofu.[3]

Tofu reaches into one's life in a way that no other food can. Its historical and cultural value combine with outstanding nutrition to bring pleasure and protein to all those whose table it graces.

---

[1]William Shurtleff and Akiko Aoyago, *The Book of Tofu* (Knabawa-ken, Japan: Autumn Press, 1975), p. 95.

[2]Shurtleff and Aoyago, p. 95.

[3]Shurtleff and Aoyago, p. 96.

Bibliography

Abehsera, Michel. *Zen Macrobiotic Cooking*. Edinburgh & London: Albyn Press, 1969.

Cusumano, Camille. *Tofu, Tempeh, and Other Soy Delights*. Emmaus, Pennsylvania: Rodale Press, 1984.

Goulart, Francis Sheriden. *BUM STEERS: How and Why To Make Your Own Delicious High Protein Mock Meats, Fake Fish, and Dairyless Desserts and Avoid Useless Calories, Cholesterol, Sodium Nitrite, Salmonella, Trichinosis, & High Prices*. Old Greenwich: The Chatham Press, 1975.

O'Brien, Jane. *The Magic of Tofu*. New York: Thorsons Publishers Inc., 1983.

Shurtleff, William, and Akiko Aoyago. *The Book of Tofu*. Knabawa-ken, Japan: Autumn Press, 1975.

Getting Started

This module assumes that you are familiar with the basics of using the Macintosh, how to work with a hard disk and/or diskettes, how to choose menu commands, and so on. If these concepts are not familiar to you, please review the Approaching Macintosh module.

Turn on the Macintosh. If you are not using a hard disk, insert the system diskette in the internal diskette drive.

Soon, you'll see the Macintosh desktop.

Next, you'll open Microsoft Word.

Tofu Paper

Copy the "Tofu Paper" document from the Approaching Macintosh diskette onto your hard disk, or, if you are not using a hard disk, onto your system diskette.

If you are using a hard disk, open the "Tofu Paper" document by finding it and double-clicking on its icon.

If you do not have a hard disk, insert the Word program disk in the other diskette drive. Then, open the "Tofu Paper" document by double-clicking on its icon.

If you get a message saying that the Macintosh was unable to open the document because the application could not be found, make sure that Word is installed on your hard disk, or that the Word program disk is in one of the diskette drives.

Using Full Menus

In the introductory module, you used short menus to create your simple letter. In this module, you'll use some of Word's more advanced features, so you'll want Word to display full menus. You'll make sure that Word is displaying full menus now.

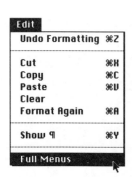

Choose Full Menus from the Edit menu.

Remember that when Word is already displaying Full Menus, the Full Menus command changes to Short menus (so you can switch back and forth). If you see the Short Menus command in the Edit menu, you don't need to do anything.

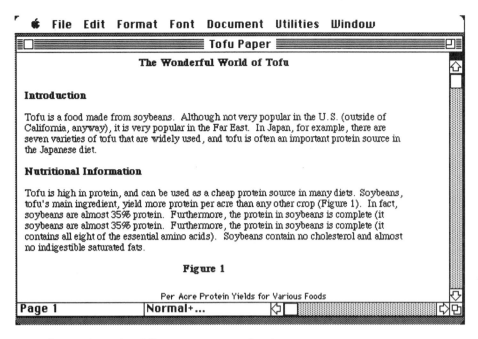

Now that you're using full menus, you can begin.

Advanced Text Selection

Look at the third and fourth lines in the second paragraph (those beginning with "soybeans are"). The first thing you want to do is remove the extra copy of this line. If you remember what you've learned in the Introduction to Microsoft Word module (and you should), then you'll know right away how to do this first step.

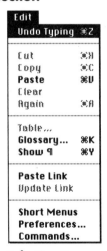

Select the third line in the second paragraph by dragging across it. Then, press the Delete key to remove it from the document.

Remember that the Delete key deletes any selection.

Dragging across text is the simplest way of selecting it. There are, however, other conventions in Word for selecting blocks of text easily. You'll bring that line back now so you can learn more about advanced text selection.

Choose Undo Typing from the Edit menu. Then, click anywhere in the document to deselect the line you just removed.

The Selection Bar

Word uses a **selection bar** to provide other ways of selecting large blocks of text. The selection bar is an invisible area located at the far left edge of your document.

Move the pointer into the selection bar just to the left of the text on the screen.

The pointer shifts right when you are in the selection bar. Because the selection bar is invisible, you may have some trouble locating it. Be persistent, moving the pointer slowly to the left edge of the screen until it changes shape, into an arrow pointing right (See figure below).

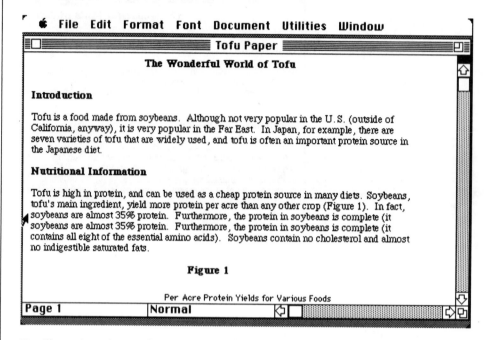

You'll use the selection bar to select the duplicate line.

While the pointer is in the selection bar, position it in front of the first line starting with "soybeans are" in the second paragraph, and press the mouse button.

The entire line is selected and should be highlighted. When the pointer is in the selection bar, clicking in front of a line selects that line. If the line is not selected, try again, making sure that the pointer shifts right before you click.

There are other ways to select large blocks of text in Word. For example, to select:

- **A word:** Double-click anywhere on the word.
- **A sentence:** Hold down the Command key and click anywhere inside the sentence.
- **A paragraph:** Double-click in the selection bar to the left of the paragraph
- **The whole document:** Hold down the Command key and click in the selection bar.

Before continuing, try these advanced selection techniques out and make sure that you are comfortable with using them. They'll save you time later. When you are finished, select the first line starting with "soybeans are" in the second paragraph.

Now you'll delete the line you've selected.

Press Delete.

Delete removes the selected text from the document.

Read the portion of the paper currently shown in the window.

The scroll bar lets you move a long document up or down in the window so you can see different parts of it.

Reading as you go, scroll until you can see the paragraph starting with "The quantity of protein…".

If you are using a large-screen monitor, you may not have to scroll at all.

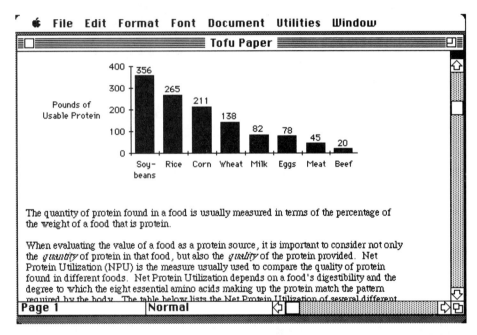

Read over the paragraph starting with "The quantity of protein…"

You want to insert a table showing the percent protein composition of different foods. You will put the table at the end of this paragraph, but first you will label it "Figure 2".

Position the insertion point at the end of the paragraph starting with "The quantity of…" by clicking after the word "protein".

Type in the following sentence (without pressing Return):

Figure 2 lists several foods and their percent protein by weight.

Press Return, and type "Figure 2". Then, move the pointer into the selection bar, and click in front of the line you just typed.

The words "Figure 2" are now selected, and should be highlighted.

You would like "Figure 2" to appear in bold face.

Choose Bold from the Format menu.

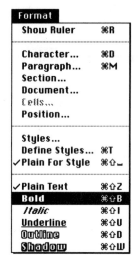

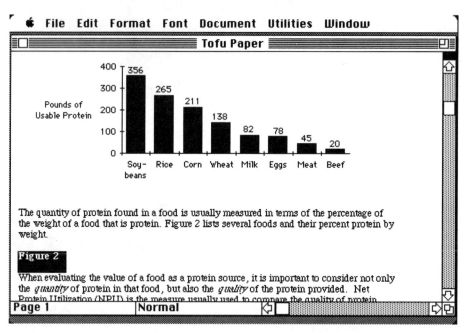

Using Rulers

With Word, whenever you press Return, you create a new paragraph. Therefore, the line containing "Figure 2" is a paragraph, and can be formatted by clicking on the appropriate icons on the ruler. You'll do this in a moment, but first you'll have to tell Word to display the ruler.

Choose Show Ruler from the Format menu.

The ruler should look familiar to you from the Introduction to Microsoft Word module. But it's not the same. Because Word is displaying full menus, there are more icons on the ruler now. The Full Menus ruler is shown below.

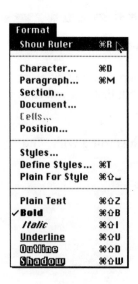

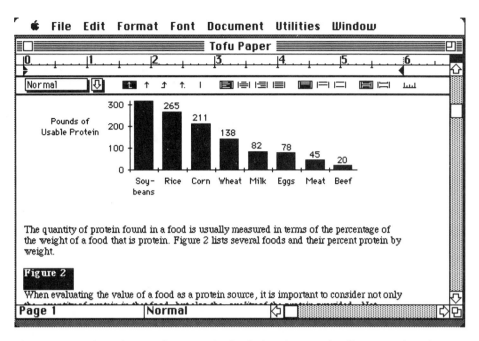

The icons on the ruler are the same for both the Short and Full Menu rulers, but now there are four tab stop icons and one vertical line icon.

You'll use the ruler to format the current paragraph. First, you'll change "Figure 2" to center alignment.

The Center-Alignment Icon

Be sure that the insertion point is somewhere within the text "Figure 2". Then, click on the center-alignment icon on the ruler.

"Figure 2" jumps to the center of the screen.

Remember that before you type in the table, it is necessary to deselect "Figure 2" and place the insertion point at the end of that line.

Use the mouse to position the I-bar to the right of "Figure 2", and click.

The insertion point should now be after the "2" in "Figure 2". Now you'll insert a blank line before typing in your table.

Press Return.

The Left-Alignment Icon

Because Word copies the paragraph format from "Figure 2", the insertion point appears in the center of the screen. However, you would rather use left alignment for the text of your table. You'll change back to left alignment now.

 Click on the left-alignment icon on the ruler.

The insertion point moves back to the left margin.

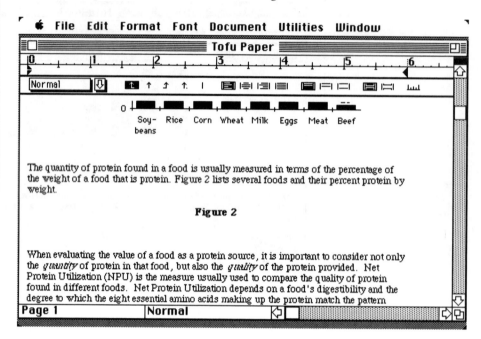

In a moment, you'll type in the data for your table, but first you'll move the left indent marker in so the table is set off from the rest of the paper.

☞ **Drag the left indent marker to the 1-inch point on the ruler.**

Remember that when you drag the left indent marker, the first line indent marker moves with it. Also remember that the left indent marker is the lower of the two markers. If you accidently drag the first line indent marker, don't get discouraged. Just drag it back and try again.

Using Tabs

You are now ready to type in the information for the table. But first you must set a tab stop. You learned how to set tab stops in the introductory module by clicking on the Short Menus ruler. With Full Menus, you set tabs the same way, but now there are four different tab stop icons to choose from.

The use of the four tab stop icons is illustrated on the next page.

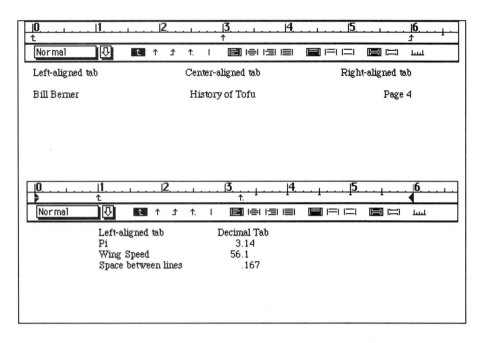

Your table will have two columns. The first will contain text labels, and the second will contain numbers. Because the second column will contain only numbers, you'll use a **center-aligned tab stop** for the second column heading, so the numbers will line up nicely beneath it.

Inserting Center-Aligned Tab Stops

You insert a single tab by clicking the appropriate icon and then clicking at the appropriate place on the ruler. You'll set a center-aligned tab at the 4-inch mark now.

↑ **Set a center-aligned tab at the 4-inch mark by first clicking on the center-aligned tab icon and then moving the pointer into the area just below "4" on the ruler and clicking.**

A tab marker appears at the place you clicked, indicating that the tab is set.

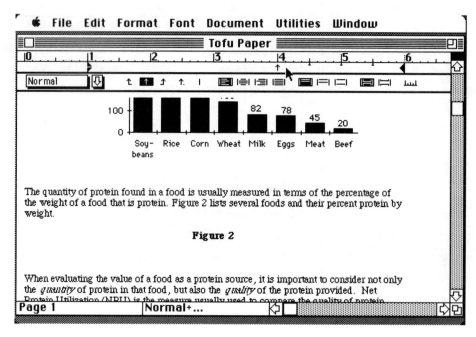

Note that you must click on the center portion of the ruler, below the numbers.

If you insert the tab in the wrong spot, you can use the mouse to reposition it by dragging it left or right to the appropriate position. You can also remove a tab by dragging it off the bottom of the ruler.

You are ready to type column headings for your table.

Type "Food". Then, press Tab. Finally, type "% Protein". Then, press Return.

The formatting for your paper is set so Word automatically inserts a blank line spacing between paragraphs, that is, each time you press Return. For the main text of the paper, this is fine, because you want a blank line between paragraphs. But you would not like a blank line spacing between the lines of the table; therefore, you will use the Paragraph... command from the Format menu to change this.

Press Delete to delete the blank line you just inserted, then choose Paragraph... from the Format menu.

Formatting Paragraphs

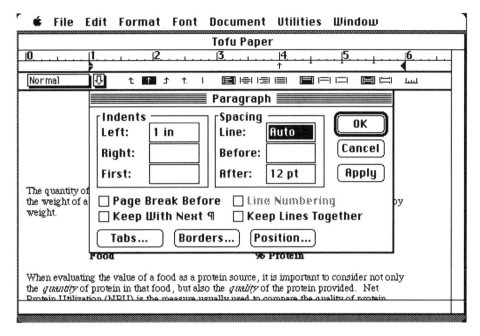

A dialog box appears. Here you can specify a paragraph's left and right indentation, as well as the indentation of its first line (from the left edge of the paragraph).

Line Spacing

You can also specify line spacing. **Auto** is the preset value; it means that Word adjusts spacing between lines automatically. Use **Spacing Before** and **Spacing After** to insert extra space before or after the paragraph.

Notice that the entry in the Spacing After box is "12 pt". This means that Word will insert a blank space 12 points tall after the paragraph. (If you are using a 12-point text size, this is equivalent to 1 line.) You'll change this value to 0 now.

Select the text in the Spacing After box by dragging across it. Then, type "0 pt". When you are done, click OK.

Now when you press Return, you won't get a blank line between paragraphs.

Press Return to move to the next line.

You are now ready to type in data for the table. The headings for the table are in bold type, but you don't want the data for your table to be bold. When you insert text, Word formats the new text exactly like the text immediately preceding the insertion point, so you'll need to specify plain text formatting before typing the rest of the table.

Choose Plain Text from the Format menu.

Using Decimal-AlignedTab Stops

Before typing in the numbers for your table, you'll change the center-aligned tab stop to a **decimal-aligned tab stop,** a tab stop that forces the decimal points of numbers to line up.

To make the change, you'll remove the center-aligned tab , and then replace it with a decimal-aligned tab at the same location.

You'll remove the center-aligned tab now by dragging it off the bottom of the ruler.

Click on the center-aligned tab stop that you set at the 4-inch mark on the ruler. Then, drag it off the bottom of the ruler and release the mouse button.

The tab icon disappears from the ruler. Now, you'll set a decimal-aligned tab in the same spot.

↑.

Set a decimal-aligned tab stop at the 4-inch mark on the ruler by first clicking the decimal-aligned tab stop icon and then clicking below the 4-inch mark on the ruler.

A decimal-aligned tab appears at the appropriate spot on the ruler.

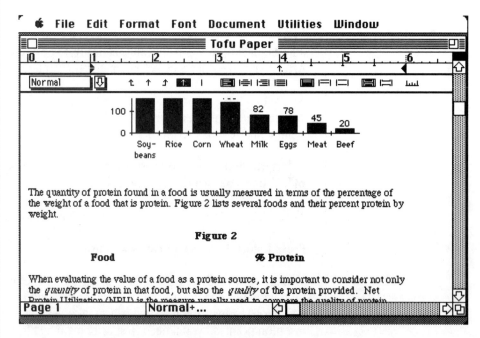

Now, you're ready to enter the data for your table.

Enter the following text for the body of the table, being sure to press Tab after each text label, and Return at the end of each line:

Dried frozen tofu	53.2
Fish	22.3
Chicken	21.0
Beef	20.0
Tofu	8.1

Your table should now look like this:

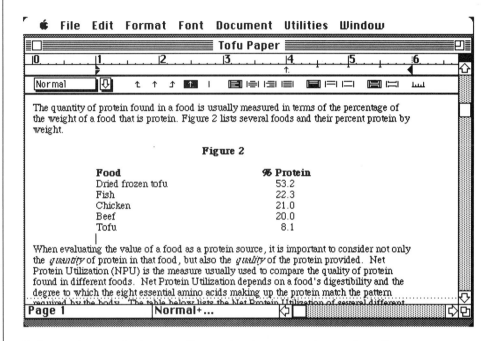

Saving Often

Before going any further, you'll save the changes you've made so far.

Choose Save from the File menu.

It's a good idea to save your documents often. This way you won't lose very much work if the power goes off unexpectedly (or your pet rabbit chews through the power cord).

Adding Another Table

You are now ready to type in the third figure for your paper. (The chart at the beginning and the table you inserted were the first two.) This will be a table very similar to the last one, but the steps are listed in case you have forgotten. First, you'll set the insertion point in the appropriate spot.

Set the insertion point at the end of the paragraph beginning with "When evaluating..." by positioning the I-bar after the word "foods." and clicking.

You may have to scroll to see the entire paragraph. Notice the dotted line between the fifth and sixth lines of this paragraph. Although you haven't seen that before, it's nothing to be concerned about. That's just the way that Word marks the beginning of a new page.

Now you're ready to insert your table.

Press Return.

Word inserts a blank line, and you are ready to type the table heading.

Choose Bold from the Format menu, and then type "Figure 3".

Next, align it correctly.

Click on the center-alignment icon on the ruler. Then, press Return.

You're ready to type in the table, but first you must format it correctly.

Click on the left-alignment icon, then drag the left margin marker to the 1-inch mark on the ruler.

Next, you'll set a center-aligned tab.

Set a center-aligned tab at the 4-inch mark by first clicking on the center-aligned tab icon and then moving the pointer to the position just below "4" on the ruler and clicking.

Finally, you'll enter your table headings.

Type "Food", press Tab, and finally type "NPU (%)".

You'll change formats so that there is no blank line between paragraphs.

Choose Paragraph... from the Format menu.

A dialog box appears.

Change the value for Spacing After to 0. When you are finished, click OK.

Now, you'll type in the NPU data.

Press Return, then choose Plain Text from the Format menu. Finally, replace the center-aligned tab with a decimal-aligned tab.

Remember that to do this you need to complete the following steps:

- Drag the center-aligned tab off the bottom of the ruler.
- Click on the decimal-aligned tab icon.
- Click just below the "4" on the ruler.

Now, you're ready to type in the data for your table.

Type in the following text for the body of the table. (Don't forget to press Tab after each text label, and Return at the end of each line.)

Fish   80
Beef and hamburger   67
Tofu   65
Chicken   65

Your table should now look like this:

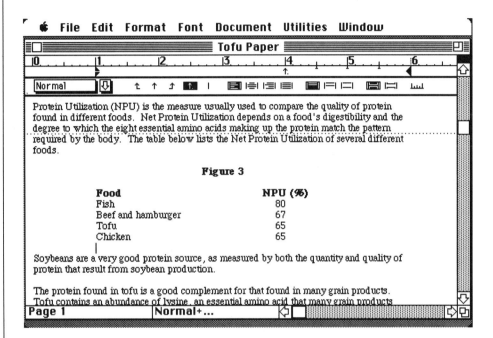

Before going on, remember to save the changes that you've made so far.

Choose Save from the File menu.

The paper would read better if the next paragraph came before the two tables that you just inserted. Word's selection bar and the Cut, Copy, and Paste commands of the Macintosh make moving paragraphs easy.

To move a paragraph, just select it, move it to the Clipboard with the Cut command, set the insertion point to the new location, and use the Paste command to reposition the paragraph. You'll move the paragraph now.

Use the mouse to move the pointer into the selection bar anywhere to the left of the paragraph starting with "Soybeans are a very good...". Then, double-click.

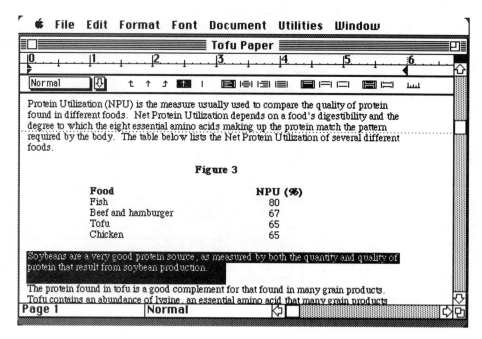

The paragraph is selected and should be highlighted. When the pointer is positioned in the selection bar, double-clicking selects the entire paragraph. If you have trouble selecting the paragraph, make sure that the pointer is in the selection bar (the arrow points right) before you double-click.

Now, you'll move the paragraph to the Clipboard with the Cut command.

Choose Cut from the Edit menu.

The paragraph is removed from the document and placed on the Clipboard.

Next, you'll move to the new position.

Click in the gray bar above the scroll box until the chart scrolls into view.

Before you can paste the paragraph, you need to set the insertion point.

Position the I-bar directly before the "T" at the beginning of the paragraph starting with "The quantity of protein..." and click to set the insertion point.

Now, you'll paste the paragraph back in.

Choose Paste from the Edit menu.

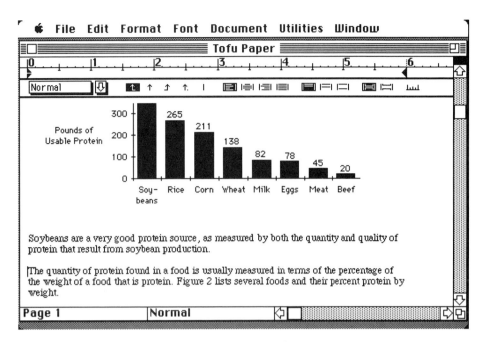

The paragraph moves into position just below the chart.

You've moved backward a few screenfuls, so you'll have to catch up.

Reading as you go, scroll through the document until you come to the boldface header for the next section. The title of the next section is "The History and Culture of Tofu".

Read the first several paragraphs of this section, stopping after the paragraph beginning with "Indeed, this is only one…".

Using Footnotes

It's obviously great prose, but you'll want to include a footnote to cite the source that you used for this information.

Use the mouse to position the I-bar at the end of the paragraph (after the word "together."), and click.

Choose Footnote… from the Document menu.

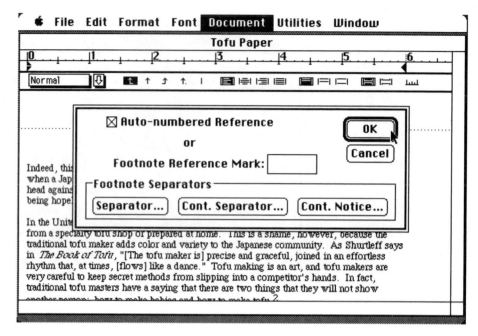

A dialog box appears, asking if you would like an **Auto-numbered Reference** or a **Footnote Reference Mark.** There are also some buttons for specifying footnote separators.

If you choose Auto-numbered Reference, Word will number your footnotes for you. If you add or delete footnotes anywhere in your document, Auto-numbering will also renumber them correctly. Alternatively, you can specify a Footnote Reference Mark (the Footnote Reference Mark appears in your document text to indicate the corresponding footnote text). A Footnote Reference Mark can be a letter, a number, or a phrase up to 10 characters long. For this paper, you want an Auto-numbered Reference.

Click OK.

Word places a "2" in your document, divides the screen in two, and also places a "2" in the lower window. The top window contains your document. The bottom window is the footnote window, the place where you insert your footnote text. A "2" has been inserted because it is this document's second footnote (you may have seen the first on the previous screen). The reference for this footnote is the same as that for the last footnote, so you only have to type the author's name, and the page number.

Type "Shurtleff and Aoyago, p. 95.".

To follow standard footnote style, you need to indent the first line of the reference. You'll use the first line indent marker to indent it now.

Indent the footnote reference 1/2 inch by moving the first line indent marker to the 1/2-inch mark on the ruler.

In case you've forgotten, there are two markers at the left edge of the ruler. The marker on top is the first line indent marker.

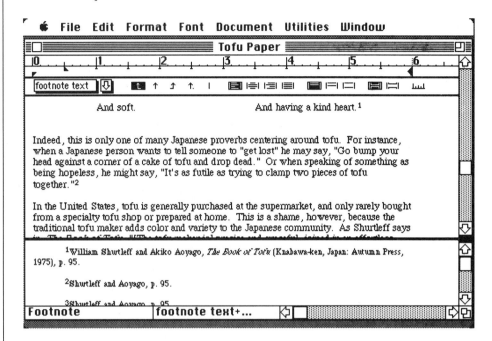

Look at the black line that divides the main text of your document from the footnote window.

The Split Bar

The small black rectangle in the scroll bar at the right of your screen is called the **split bar.** You can close the footnote window by dragging the split bar off the screen.

You'll close the footnote window now.

 Position the pointer over the split bar. It will change shape to two bars with vertical arrows. Close the footnote window by clicking and dragging the split bar to the bottom of the window.

The footnote window disappears. Note that if you drag too far, the footnote window will not go away. Be sure to drag only as far as the resize box. If you dragged too far the first time, try again.

Read the rest of the text on the screen, then scroll to see the next screen.

Using a Footer

A **header** or **footer** is a block of text that appears on every page of the section (more on sections later). A header appears at the top of the page; a footer appears at the bottom. Next, you'll create a footer so that your name and the page number appear at the bottom of each page.

Choose Open Footer... from the Document menu.

A window opens for you to insert your footer. At the top of the window, there are icons for adding the page number, the date, and the time to your footer (you'll use one of these to enter the page number in a moment). There is also a grayed-out button that says "Same as Previous". In a document with several sections, you could use this button to set footnotes equal between them. Your document has only one section, so the button is grayed-out.

First, you'll include your name at the left edge of the footer.

Type your name.

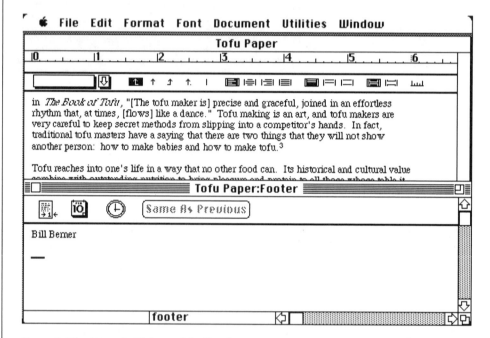

Type ": The Wonderful World of Tofu".

Adding the Page Number

You would like the page number to appear flush right against the right margin. You can do this easily because there is a preset right-aligned tab stop at the right edge of the page. There is also a preset center-aligned tab stop, so you'll have to press tab twice to move to the right margin.

Press Tab twice, then type "page" and a space.

Be sure to type a space after the word "page" so there will be a space between the word "page" and the page number. Now you'll have Word insert the page number.

Click on the page icon to add the page number to your footer (the page icon is the left-most of the three icons at the top of the footer window).

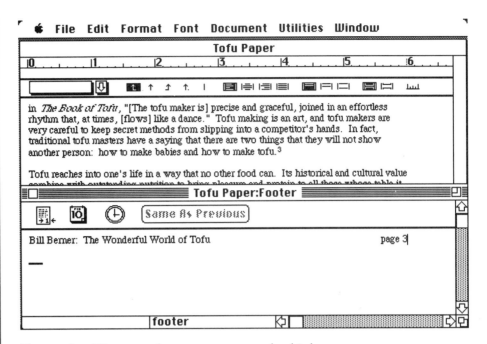

The number "3" appears because you are on the third page.

Using Sections

A document can be divided into different **sections** that you can format differently.

Different sections can have unique headers or footers, as well as different styles of page numbering. In a longer manuscript (such as a thesis or a book), there may be many sections with similar headers and footers, although the text of the headers or footers will not be the same for all sections. For example, the footers in *Approaching Macintosh* use the chapter's title, so each chapter is a separate section. There may also be sections (such as a preface or an appendix) in which you want to use a different style of numbering entirely (perhaps Roman numerals rather than Arabic ones).

You'll create a title page, but first you must close the footer window and scroll to the beginning of the document.

Click in the close box of the footer window.

The footer window disappears from the screen.

Scroll to the beginning of the document. Then, click after the word "Tofu" in the title.

Inserting a Page Break

To create a title page, you need to insert a **page break** to force Word to start a new page, leaving the title of your paper on its own page. In Word, you insert a page break by holding down the Shift key and pressing Enter.

Hold down the Shift key and press Enter.

A dotted line signifies a page break. Although you can't see the entire page, you can be confident that the first page will end right after the title of your paper.

Remember that the footer you created appears at the bottom of every page in this section of the document. If you printed now, the footer would appear at the bottom of your title page. You don't want this, so you need to adjust the formatting of the section. You can change the format of a section with the Section... command.

Choose Section... from the Format menu.

A dialog box appears.

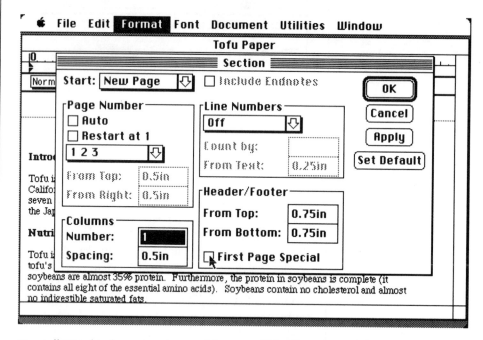

You tell Word to leave headers and footers off the first page of the section by clicking the box labeled "First Page Special". You'll do that now.

Click in the box next to the text "First Page Special". Then, click OK.

Now, you'll add the course number and title to the title page.

Click after the word "Tofu" in the title, press Return, and type your name.

Press Return, and type in the following two lines to complete the title page:

    Anthropology 136
    Food and Culture

To make the title stand out from the rest of the text on the page, you can insert some extra line spacing after the paragraph containing the title.

Click anywhere inside the line "The Wonderful World of Tofu", and Choose Paragraph... from the Format menu.

A dialog box appears. You would like 10 blank lines before and after the title.

Set the values of Space Before and Space After to "10 li".

"10 li" stands for 10 lines.

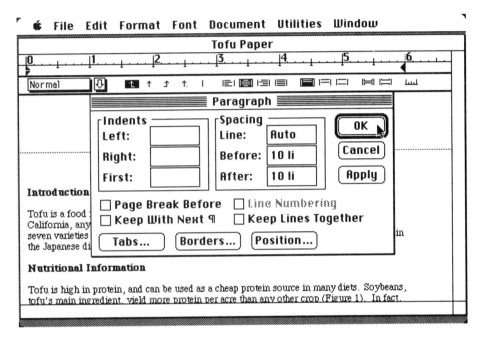

Finishing Up

Spell Checking

When you are done, click OK.

Now that you've finished your revision, you'd like to make sure that you haven't spelled any words incorrectly, and then you'd like to get a printout.

Before using Word's spell checker, you'll make sure that there's at least one error for it to find.

Use the mouse to set the insertion point after the "o" in "Wonderful". Press Delete to remove the "o" and then type a "u" to replace it.

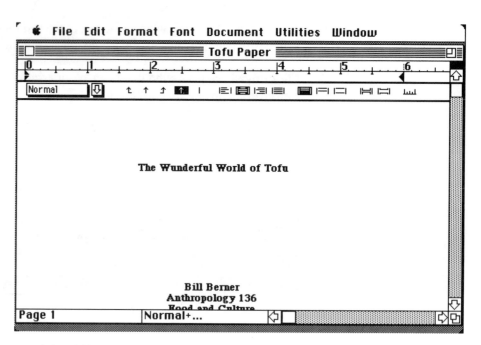

Word should have no trouble finding a misspelling. Now, you'll open the spell checking utility.

Choose Spelling... from the Utilities menu.

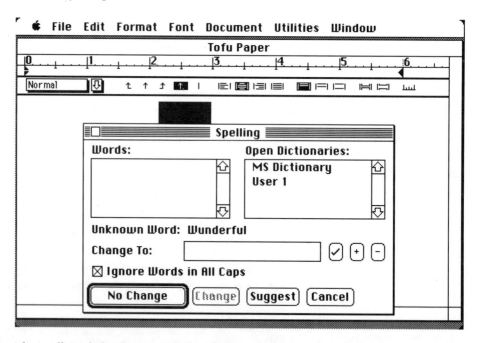

The spelling dialog box appears. At the top of the dialog box, there are two lists. Words contains suggested replacements for the current word. Dictionaries is a list of dictionaries that Word will use to check the spelling of the words in your document. The spelling checker works by comparing the words in your document with all of the words in the dictionaries that are open. If it doesn't find a match, it stops and allows you to enter a replacement in the Change To box.

At the bottom of the dialog box there are four buttons. **No Change** tells Word to accept the current spelling of the word. **Change** replaces the word with the contents of the Change To box. Change is grayed out because you haven't entered a replacement yet. **Suggest** tells Word to enter possible replacements in the Words list. **Cancel** ends spell checking and returns you to the document.

You'll ask Word to suggest alternatives for "Wunderful."

Click Suggest.

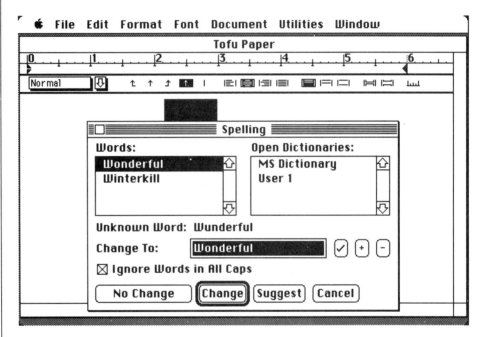

Word suggests both "Wonderful" and "Winterkill." Note that "Wonderful" is selected in the Words list, and Change is no longer grayed out. You'll accept Word's suggestion.

Click Change to replace "Wunderful" with "Wonderful".

Word makes the change, and jumps to the next word that it doesn't understand (probably your name). You could continue to check the document, but for now you'll assume everything else is spelled correctly. (You can do this because we spell-checked the whole thing when we wrote the book.)

Click Cancel.

Now check that Word has fixed the misspelling (you may have to scroll to see the beginning of the document).

Saving and Printing

Your revision is now complete and ready to be printed and turned in. But first, you should save your document.

Choose Save from the File menu.

Now you're ready to print, but first, make sure your printer is chosen correctly, turned on, and ready to print.

Choose Print... from the File menu.

If you'd like multiple copies, type the number of copies you need.

Click OK to confirm your print settings.

In a few seconds, your document will begin to print.

When you have finished printing, you'll return to the desktop.

Quitting

Choose Quit from the File menu.

If you've made any changes to your document, you'll be asked if you'd like to save them. Click OK.

Your Word document closes, and you find yourself back at the desktop. If you are in a public Macintosh lab, you should copy your finished Tofu Paper to your personal data diskette. Then, drag the document that is on the hard disk to the trash.

Review

In this module, you have learned:

- How to use the selection bar to select large blocks of text
- How to set decimal-aligned tabs
- How to use footnotes
- How to define footers and headers to display the same text and the page number, the date, or the time on every page of the document
- What sections are, and how to format them
- How to format paragraphs to include blank lines before or after the paragraph
- How to use the spell checker

What to Turn In

Turn in a copy of your revised Tofu Paper document.

Advanced
Microsoft Word

The Task

Imagine that you're a student looking for a job (not too difficult, is it?). You've prepared a standard resume and cover letter to send to a number of prospective employers. To make the best possible impression, you'd like to tailor each letter to the specific employer and type of position. But you'd rather not have to retype the bulk of the letter again and again for each employer.

Fortunately, using Microsoft Word's **print merge** capability, you can create "customized form letters" for each person on your list.

To do this, you'll modify your original cover letter and resume so that they can be easily customized. The resulting document is called the **main document** and contains the basic form of your letter, along with instructions on how to customize each individual letter.

Next, you'll create a list of the names and addresses of those who you want to receive the document, and the unique elements that will customize each letter. This list is called the **merge document,** because it contains the special information that merges with the main document to create the customized letters.

Finally, you'll **merge print** the customized letter. For each employer listed in your merge document, Word will create a customized letter by customizing the main document letter with the information that you entered in your merge document. The result will be letters that are similar—but personalized. Examples are shown on the next few pages.

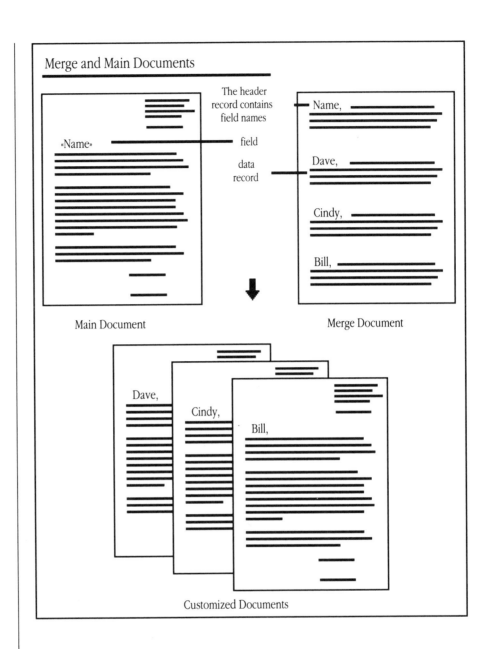

Merge and Main Documents

The header record contains field names

«Name»

field

data record

Name,

Dave,

Cindy,

Bill,

Main Document

Merge Document

Dave,

Cindy,

Bill,

Customized Documents

1006 Broadway Avenue
San Jose, California 95125

January 13, 1991

Mr. Leo Johnson
Director of Personnel
Soya-Nara Soy Foods, Incorporated
31529 Rancho San Carlos Road
Carmel, California 94705

Dear Mr. Johnson:

In June of this year, I will be graduating from Stanford University with a Bachelor's degree in Science and Slavic Languages, and I am interested in obtaining a position with your firm as a soybean processor at your Carmel facility.

Ever since my early childhood, I have been fascinated by the soy foods industry and have recognized Soya-Nara Soy Foods, Incorporated as a leader in that industry. In addition, my coursework in Science has given me a great deal of experience in laboratory settings.

I am sure you will agree that my background in Science and Slavic Languages provides me with the depth and breadth of experience necessary to work as a Soya-Nara Soy Foods, Incorporated soybean processor.

My resume is enclosed and provides additional details about my undergraduate work and extracurricular activities. I would appreciate the opportunity to meet with you to discuss how my education and experience would be consistent with your needs. I will call you in the next few days to answer any questions you might have about my qualifications and hopefully at that time we can set up a time to meet.

Thank you for your consideration.

Sincerely,

Dale Cooper

enclosure

Dale Cooper

1006 Broadway Avenue
San Jose, California 95125
(415) 898-0725

Objective   To obtain a position as a soybean processor with a leading soy-food
              manufacturer.

Education   **Stanford University,** Stanford, California.
9/87-6/91   B.A.S. degree in Science and Slavic Languages, with a
              concentration in alternative food technologies. Extensive course
              work in soy-food research, statistics, and plant biology.
              Honors: Phi Beta Kappa, Tau Delta Pi.

Experience   **President.** Slavic Languages Society. Stanford University,
              Stanford, California.
1/89-Present Organized finances and coordinated group activities. Conceived,
              designed, and managed first-ever Slavic Translate-a-Thon. Tripled
              membership during tenure.

8/88-1/89   **Laboratory Technician.** New Food Laboratory, Stanford
              University, Stanford, California.
              Performed research on alternative food products. Was a member of
              the team to first successfully synthesize dijon mustard from ordinary
              sludge.

6/88-8/88   **Maintenance Manager.** Roche Motel, Lodi, California.
              Responsibilities included maintaining facilities and managing large
              cleaning staff. Developed benzene solution to control pests with
              only minor carcinogenic effects on hotel maintenance personnel.

6/87-9/87   **Production Assistant.** *Arabian Horses Magazine*, Milpitas,
              California.
              Assisted in the production of a leading four-color magazine.

Additional   Tofu King, 1989 Tofu Fest.
Information   Director, 1989 Stanford Chorale Round-Up.
              Enjoy horses, chemistry, and pipe organs.

References   Available upon request.

1006 Broadway Avenue
San Jose, California 95125

January 13, 1991

Ms. Audrey Horne
Director of Personnel
Foreign Sport Magazine
586 Mayfield Avenue
East Palo Alto, California 94303

Dear Ms. Horne:

In June of this year, I will be graduating from Stanford University with a Bachelor's degree in Science and Slavic Languages, and I am interested in obtaining a position with your firm as a translator at your East Palo Alto facility.

Ever since my early childhood, I have been fascinated by the sports magazine industry and have recognized Foreign Sport Magazine as a leader in that industry. My three years as head of the Stanford Slavic Languages Society has given me experience in managing interpersonal relationships.

I am sure you will agree that my background in Science and Slavic Languages provides me with the depth and breadth of experience necessary to work as a Foreign Sport Magazine translator.

My resume is enclosed and provides additional details about my undergraduate work and extracurricular activities. I would appreciate the opportunity to meet with you to discuss how my education and experience would be consistent with your needs. I will call you in the next few days to answer any questions you might have about my qualifications and hopefully at that time we can set up a time to meet.

Thank you for your consideration.

Sincerely,

Dale Cooper

enclosure

Dale Cooper

1006 Broadway Avenue
San Jose, California 95125
(415) 898-0725

Objective
To obtain a position translating Yugoslavian sports medicine journals for a leading sports magazine.

Education
9/87-6/91
Stanford University, Stanford, California.
B.A.S. degree in Science and Slavic Languages, with a concentration in alternative food technologies. Extensive course work in soy-food research, statistics, and plant biology.
Honors: Phi Beta Kappa, Tau Delta Pi.

Experience

1/89-Present
President. Slavic Languages Society. Stanford University, Stanford, California.
Organized finances and coordinated group activities. Conceived, designed, and managed first-ever Slavic Translate-a-Thon. Tripled membership during tenure.

8/88-1/89
Laboratory Technician. New Food Laboratory, Stanford University, Stanford, California.
Performed research on alternative food products. Was a member of the team to first successfully synthesize dijon mustard from ordinary sludge.

6/88-8/88
Maintenance Manager. Roche Motel, Lodi, California.
Responsibilities included maintaining facilities and managing large cleaning staff. Developed benzene solution to control pests with only minor carcinogenic effects on hotel maintenance personnel.

6/87-9/87
Production Assistant. *Arabian Horses Magazine*, Milpitas, California.
Assisted in the production of a leading four-color magazine.

Additional Information
Tofu King, 1989 Tofu Fest.
Director, 1989 Stanford Chorale Round-Up.
Enjoy horses, chemistry, and pipe organs.

References
Available upon request.

Getting Started

Cover Letter

Resume

Complete the Introduction to Microsoft Word module and the Intermediate Microsoft Word module.

Many of the concepts explained in the introductory modules will be necessary to complete this one. Make sure that you've completed these modules and understand the basics of Word.

Copy the documents "Cover Letter" and "Resume" from your Approaching Macintosh disk onto your hard disk, or onto your personal data diskette if you are using one to store your personal files. If you're not sure how to do this, consult the Approaching Macintosh module.

You'll begin working with the "Cover Letter" document.

Double-click on the "Cover Letter" document to open it.

Creating the Main Document

Your first step is to convert your standard cover letter into the **main document** used to generate the customized letters. To do this, you'll replace the employer-specific parts of the letter with **merge fields.** Merge fields are placeholders that mark the position where Word will insert the special information for each customized letter.

For example, since the name and address for each letter are obviously different, you create merge fields to tell Word to look for a different employer name, street address, city, state, and ZIP code for each letter and to insert them in the appropriate positions when the letter is printed.

Creating Merge Fields

To create a merge field, you first think of a name for it. Then you type the name, enclosing it in special characters, "«" and "»", which tell Word that the enclosed text is a field. Note that these are **not** doubled less than and greater than signs, but special characters that you type in a special way:

- To get the "«", hold down the **Option** key and press the backslash (\) key.
- To get the "»", hold down the **Shift** and **Option** keys and press the backslash (\) key.

Make sure that you understand how to type these characters before continuing.

When you "merge print" copies of the main document, Word stops at each merge field and looks in the merge document to find the information that should be inserted at that position.

Merge Instructions

Aside from the merge fields, you can also place **instructions** in your main document to tell Word what you want to do.

Instructions are information you provide Word to control the printing of your customized documents. You type instructions inside the special characters "«" and "»" so that Word knows they're instructions and won't print them.

Using the DATA Instruction

The **DATA** instruction must be the first instruction in the main document (it doesn't have to be the first word in your document, but it must come before any other instructions or fields). The DATA instruction tells Word the name of the merge document that contains the customized information that will be used in this document.

When you create your merge document later in this module, you'll call it "Cover Letter Data."

Use the mouse to move the I-bar to the beginning of the first line of the document, and click to set the insertion point.

Note that if you move the pointer too far to the left (inside the selection bar), you'll select the entire line rather than set the insertion point. If this happens, move the pointer slightly to the right, and click again to set the insertion point.

Type «DATA Cover Letter Data».

Remember:

- To get the "«", hold down the **Option** key and press the backslash (\) key.
- To get the "»", hold down the **Shift** and **Option** keys and press the backslash (\) key.

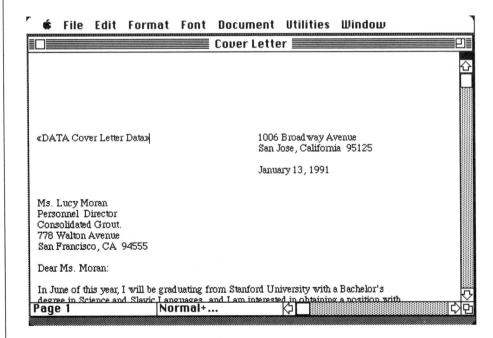

ADVANCED MICROSOFT WORD

You have now told Word that you'll be merging parts of the document "Cover Letter Data" with this document. Note that it's not necessary to type the instructions in capital letters, but it does make them easier to recognize.

The first thing you'll do is delete the employer name and address in this letter, and define appropriate merge fields to replace them.

Select the entire name and address by dragging through it. See the screen, below, if this is unclear.

The entire area should be highlighted. Be sure not to select the blank line after the address, or it will be more difficult for you to do what comes next.

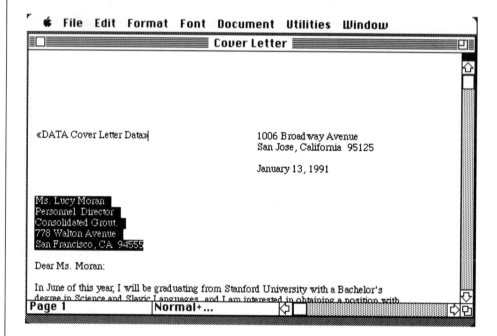

Press Delete to delete the selection.

You can now create merge fields for the employer's name and address. The merge fields will act as placeholders for the unique information that you want to include in each letter. The example below shows how you will replace the current name and address with merge fields that can be customized for each letter.

Ms. Lucy Moran
Personnel Director 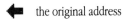 the original address
Consolidated Grout
778 Walton Avenue   fields created from
San Francisco, CA 94555   the original address

«Contact Title» «Contact First» «Contact Last»
«Contact Position»
«Company Name»
«Company Street»
«Company City», «Company State» «Company ZIP»

First, you'll create fields for the name of the contact person who will receive your letter.

Type "«Contact Title» «Contact First» «Contact Last»".

By replacing "Ms. Lucy Moran" with the fields Contact Title, Contact First, and Contact Last, you tell Word to find the title, first name, and last name of the addressee for each letter in the "Cover Letter Data" document. This way, you can just as easily write to a "Mr. Leo Johnson" as a "Ms. Audrey Horne".

Now you'll replace the contact's position and the company name and address with appropriate fields.

Press Return. Then, type the following four lines:

    «Contact Position»
    «Company Name»
    «Company Street»
    «Company City», «Company State» «Company ZIP»

Your document should now look like this:

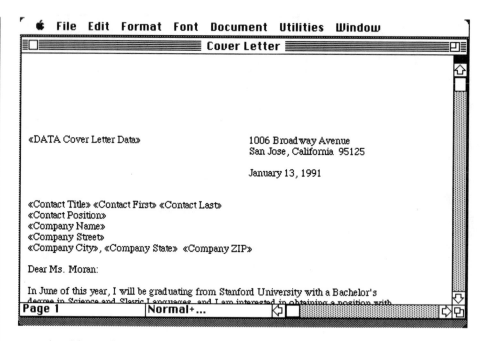

You should now begin to see the form that the main document will take. Before continuing, try to think of what other merge fields you will need to define before your letter will be complete.

Using the SET Instruction

Each time you print a batch of customized letters, you'd like to have Word ask you for the current date and use that date in every letter printed. The **SET** instruction allows you to set the content of any field, in this case the date field, equal for all documents printed at that time. You can also use the SET instruction to have Word ask you, when you are print merging, for the value you'd like to use.

To use the SET instruction, you first define the field that you would like to set. Then, you insert the SET instruction itself «SET Date=? What is the Date?», which has three parts:

- First, you type "SET" to tell Word that you'll be setting the value of a field equal for all documents printed.
- Second, you type the name of the field that you'd like to set.
- Finally, you type an equal sign (=) followed by either a value for Word to assign, or a question for Word to ask you before printing.

If you know the value that you would like to assign to a field when you are creating the main document, then use that value. If, on the other hand, you are uncertain of the value that you'd like assigned to the field, you can have Word ask you for it when you do the actual printing.

To use a value, you simply type it in after the "=" sign. But if you want to have Word present you with a question, or **prompt,** then first type a question mark (?) and then the prompt that you would like. For example:

> ? What is the date?

The first question mark tells Word that what follows is a prompt, and "What is the date?" is the prompt Word will show before printing.

You'll create a field for the date now, and then use the SET instruction to have Word ask you for the date before printing.

Select the date by dragging across it. Be sure not to include the blank line after the date in the selection. Then, type "«Date»" to replace it.

The Date field is now created. Next, you'll type the SET command.

Now use the mouse to position the I-bar at the beginning of the line with the «Date» field in it, and click to set the insertion point.

Type "«SET Date=? What is the Date?»".

This tells Word to ask "What is the Date?" each time that you print a set of cover letters and resumes.

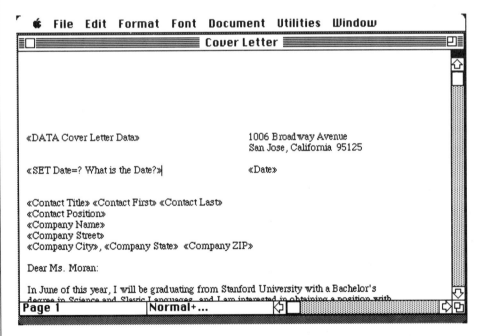

Note that the SET instruction can be placed anywhere on the page, because it will not be printed. The Date field, however, must be placed where you want it to be printed—in this case, underneath the return address.

Next, you'll change the greeting.

Select "Ms. Moran" from the greeting, then type "«Contact Title» «Contact Last»".

If you accidently deleted the colon (:), type another.

Read over the first paragraph.

You may have to scroll to see all of it.

In this letter, you are applying to be a technician, but this may be different depending on the company you're contacting. You should create a field to store the title of the position you're applying for.

Select "technician", then type "«Position»".

Now you can apply for any job you'd like and your letter will always be accurate.

You'll also replace "San Francisco" with the field «Company City».

Select "San Francisco" and type "«Company City»" to replace it.

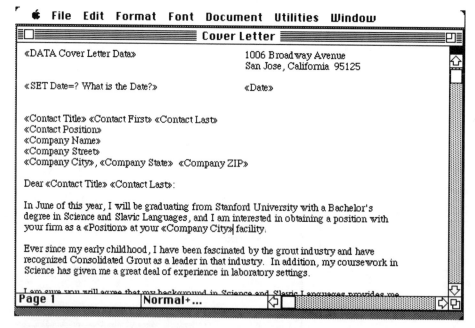

Read over the next paragraph.

Can you see what text needs to be changed in this paragraph? If you apply to companies that make different products, you'll want to define a field to replace "grout" in the first sentence. You'll do that now.

Select "grout" and type "«Product»" to replace it.

Certainly "Consolidated Grout" in this letter must be replaced by the field "Company Name".

Select "Consolidated Grout", then type "«Company Name»" to replace it.

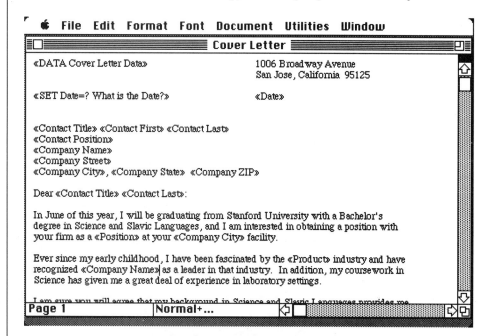

Read the sentence starting with " In addition, my coursework in…".

This sentence won't work with some of the letters you'll be sending. For some employers, you would like to stress your science background. For others, you would rather emphasize your familiarity with Slavic languages. You can use the **IF…ELSE…ENDIF** instruction to have Word insert one block of text if the job is technical, and a different block of text if it is not.

The IF…ELSE…ENDIF instruction begins with a condition. In this case, the condition is "Is the job technical?" So the first portion of this conditional statement (the "IF" part) reads as follows:

«IF Job Type = "technical"»

After the "IF" part, you insert the text that you would like to include if the condition is true. Next, you type the ELSE instruction:

«ELSE»

And then the text that Word should insert if the condition in the "IF" part is false. In this case, you would type the text that you want Word to insert when you are applying for a job that is nontechnical.

Finally, you type the «ENDIF» instruction to mark the end of the instruction.

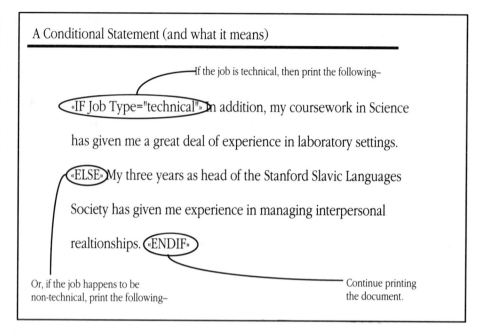

You'll enter the IF...ELSE...ENDIF instruction now.

Use the mouse to set the insertion point between the first and second sentences in this paragraph (between the words "industry." and "In"), and type the following instruction:

«IF Job Type="Technical"»

Next, set the insertion point at the end of the paragraph (after the word "settings.") and type:

«ELSE»My three years as head of the Stanford Slavic Languages Society has given me experience in managing interpersonal relationships.«ENDIF»

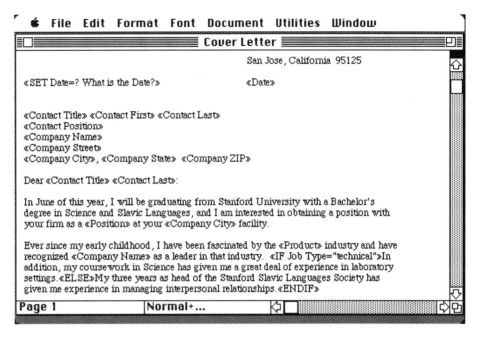

Note that for every IF instruction, there need not be an ELSE, but there must be an ENDIF instruction. This allows you to have one block of text inserted if a certain condition is true, and nothing if it is false.

Use the Scroll Bar to see the next paragraph.

There are two more blocks of text that must be replaced with appropriate fields.

Select "Consolidated Grout" and type "«Company Name»", then select "technician" and type "«Position»".

The INCLUDE Instruction

The **INCLUDE** instruction is used to have the contents of another Word document merged with the main document when you are print merging. The INCLUDE instruction needs one piece of information. The name of the document to be merged. You'll use the INCLUDE instruction now to include a copy of your resume with each cover letter.

The contents of the document specified in the INCLUDE instruction are inserted at the exact spot where the INCLUDE instruction appears. If you type the INCLUDE statement right at the end of your cover letter, your resume will start on the same page as the letter, and you'll probably remain unemployed. Instead, you can insert a page break before typing the INCLUDE statement, so your resume begins on a new page after the cover letter.

Click to set the insertion point after the word "enclosure" (at the very end of the document).

In Word, you insert a page break by holding down the Shift key and pressing the Enter key. You'll do this now.

Hold down the Shift key, and press Enter to insert a page break.

A page break is represented on the screen by a dotted line.

Now you'll be sure that the resume will print on its own page.

Click to set the insertion point below the dotted line, and type "«INCLUDE Resume»".

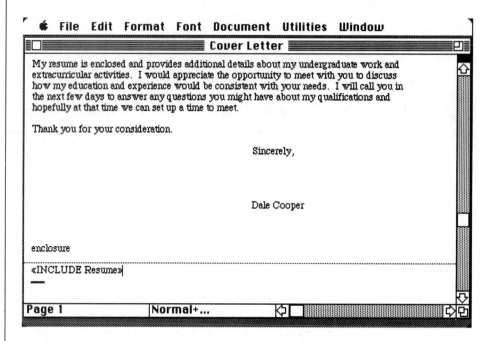

The INCLUDE instruction always has the form «INCLUDE Name». It inserts the text of the document "Name" at the point of the INCLUDE instruction. In this case, the document named "Resume" will be printed at the same time as your cover letters, but on a separate page, of course.

Editing Multiple Documents

There is still one more change that you want to make. You need to replace the job objective in your resume with a field, so that you can write a specific objective for each company you apply to.

Because Word allows you to have multiple windows open at a time, you can work with your Resume document in one window without closing your letter in the other.

But first, you'll save the changes you've made.

Choose Save from the File menu.

Choose Open from the File menu.

A dialog box appears with a list of documents from which to choose.

Open the "Resume" document by clicking on it and then clicking Open.

Note that if there are many documents on your disk, you may have to scroll to see the Resume document.

A window containing your resume appears on the screen.

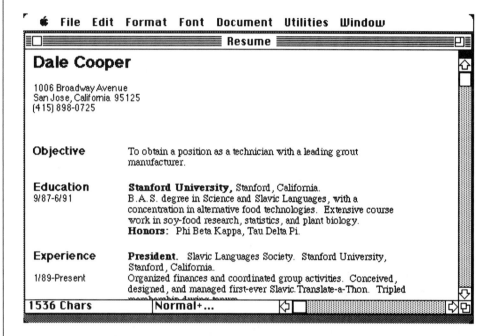

You'll use one of Word's short cuts to select the job objective now.

Hold down the Command key and click anywhere inside the sentence containing the job objective.

Holding down the Command key and clicking inside a sentence selects that sentence. You can now easily replace the text with a field definition.

Type "«Objective»".

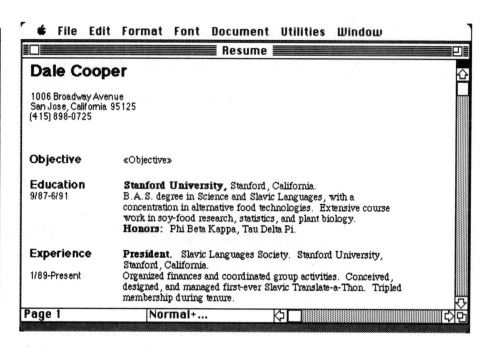

That's it! You can now close the Resume document, saving the changes you have made.

Choose Save from the File menu.

Choose Close from the File menu.

The Merge Document

You now have your form letter written, but you still need to tell Word how many letters to print out. You must also specify values for each of the fields (Company Name, Company Street, and so on) in each of the letters to be printed. You store this information in the merge document.

Now you'll open a new document for the employer-specific merge data.

Choose New from the File menu.

Creating a Merge Document

A new document opens on the screen. This will be your merge document.

You're ready to type in your merge document.

You've made the main document as general as possible by inserting fields in place of each piece of text that will change from one copy of the cover letter to another. In the merge document, you provide Word with the information it needs to customize the main document for each of the recipients.

A merge document is made up of **data records.** Data records hold the fields of text that will be merged into the main document. Each separate data record holds the text for a different version of the main document. In your case, you will have one data record for each employer to whom you wish to mail a copy of the letter and resume.

The first record in a merge document is a special one called the **header record.** This record lists the **field names** to be used in the merge document. For instance, in your document, you would like the header record to contain the following fields: Contact Title, Contact First, Contact Last, Contact Position, Company Name, Company Street, Company City, Company State, Company ZIP, Position, Product, Job Type, and Objective.

When you type in the header record, be sure not to press Return until you're finished. A Return in the merge document signifies the end of a data record, so "early" Returns will end the header record prematurely.

If you would like a Return that does *not* end a data record (for aesthetic purposes, perhaps), you can hold down the Shift key while pressing Return, and the data record can be continued beyond Return.

Type in the following line. Don't press Return until the very end.

Contact Title, Contact First, Contact Last, Contact Position, Company Name, Company Street, Company City, Company State, Company ZIP, Position, Product, Job Type, Objective

Press Return to mark the end of the header record.

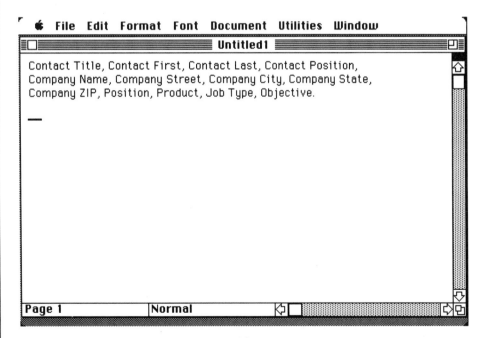

Now you're ready to enter the data records for each of the employers who you want to receive your letter. You create a data record the same way you create a header record, only you use the appropriate information for each employer.

Type in the following data record (remember not to use Return):

Mr., Leo, Johnson, Director of Personnel, "Soya-Nara Soy Foods, Incorporated", 31529 Rancho San Carlos Road, Carmel, California, 94705, soybean processor, soy foods, Technical, To obtain a position as a soybean processor with a leading soy-food manufacturer.

Press Return to complete the data record.

Note that the value for Company Name has quotations around it. When you are typing in the merge records, you use commas to separate fields. If you want to include a comma in the text for a field, you must enclose the entire field in quotation marks.

You'll enter one more sample now.

Type in the following line (again, don't press Return until the very end):

Ms., Audrey, Horne, Director of Personnel, Foreign Sport Magazine, 586 Mayfield Avenue, East Palo Alto, California, 94303, translator, sports magazine, Nontechnical, To obtain a position translating Yugoslavian sports medicine journals for a leading sports magazine.

Press Return to enter this record.

Remember that you must end each record with a Return.

Your document should now look like this:

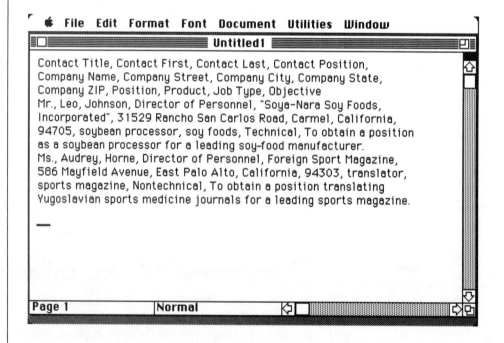

Finishing Up

That's it for the merge document. You could type a long list of prospective employers, but for now, use these two as a sample.

Saving the Merge Document

Choose Save from the File menu.

You are presented with a dialog box asking you to name the document. Remember that inside the main document, you specified (in the DATA instruction), that you were going to use the file "Cover Letter Data" when you did your print merging; therefore, you must assign that name to your merge document.

Type "Cover Letter Data", then click Save.

The merge document is saved onto your disk.

Merge Printing

It's time to do some printing. But first, you need to bring your Cover Letter document to the front. You do this by selecting it in the Window menu.

Choose Cover Letter from the Window menu.

Your main document comes to the front. Once your main document is active, you can print out your form letters.

Choose Print Merge... from the File menu.

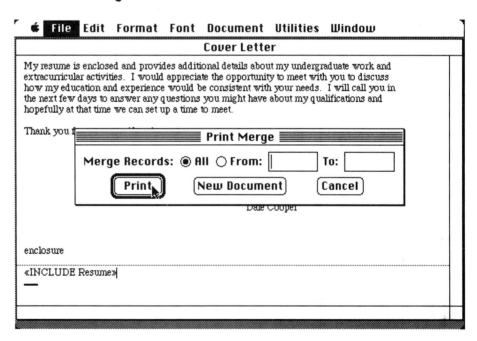

In a few seconds, you are presented with a dialog box asking you if you'd like to print all of the letters or just a subset. You want to print them all.

Click Print.

In a few seconds, you are presented with a dialog box asking you what the date is.

Remember that we used the **SET** instruction to tell Word to prompt us for the date, and insert it in each letter that it prints.

Type in the date, for example:

January 13, 1991

When you are finished, click OK.

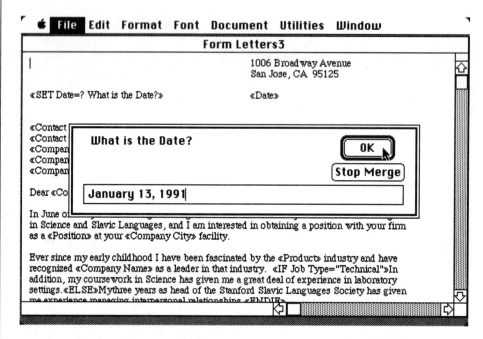

Next, you'll be presented with the Print dialog box.

Choose options as you would to print any other document.

When you are finished, click OK to start printing.

Soon, your two form letters are sitting in front of you.

Choose Quit from the File menu.

Quitting

If you have inadvertently made any changes to either of your files since the last time that both of them were saved, Word will ask you if you would like to save the changes before quitting.

Review

If all has gone well, you've learned to do the following:

- Create a main document for print merging, defining necessary merge fields and instructions
- Work with multiple documents
- Use conditional instructions (IF-ELSE-ENDIF)
- Use the INCLUDE instruction to combine documents for print merging
- Create a merge document for print merging

What to Turn In

Turn in your two completed form letters and your two completed resumes.

Serving the Soy Community
for Over Two Years

Special Issue: Tofu Fest 50

This year marks the 50th anniversary of the introduction of soybean products to this university. To celebrate, a number of student groups have joined to plan Tofu Fest 50, a week-long celebration of the spirit of soybean products and their role in university living.

This special edition of The *Tofu Times* will cover the exhibits and events that will make Tofu Fest 50 one of the truly great gatherings of the year.

Tofu Queen Pageant

The 50th annual Tofu Queen Pageant is expected to draw nearly twenty competitors from the university and neighboring communities. The audience is expected to be larger than last year's record crowd of 4,000 attendees.

The festivities will begin with an address by the president of the senior class, Rupert Broadbones III, who will speak on the topic "Tofu and the Quality of Life." Rupert has been very active in the "Tofu—It's Not Just for Californians Anymore" campaign.

The meat of the pageant (no pun intended) comes right after Rupert's speech. This year's pageant will be divided into two parts. There will be an evening gown competition and a swimsuit competition. The soybean costume competition was dropped after several contestants complained that last year's competition favored contestants who could afford Peruvian designer costumes.

The new Tofu Queen will, of course, be crowned by the reigning 1984 queen, Laura Palmer.

Tofu Wrestling

Certainly you've all tried to work wonders with tofu, but at Tofu Fest 50, you'll get a chance to work wonders *in* tofu. That's because this year's festivities will include a tofu wrestling tournament. Men and women of all ages will compete for the top prize—a month's supply of soy milk!

Tofu Dunking Pool

For those of you who are better suited to noncontact sports, there will once again be a tofu dunking pool where you can test your throwing ability. Members of the Soy Products Association and faculty from the School of Agriculture will take turns sitting in the booth. This should be great fun for all ages.

Tofu Exhibitions

Virtually all local manufacturers and retailers of soy foods will have a booth in the exhibition hall. There will certainly be many sources of drinks and snacks. In fact, booth space has been reserved for over twenty soy-milk bars, with products ranging from "Tofu Mongo Punch" to "Tofu Sesame Seed Cheese Dip". However, not every booth will contain snack foods, and those who want to purchase a full meal will certainly be able to find one. (Experienced tofu gourmets recommend both the soybean burrito at *Senor Soya* and the tofu pot pies from *Soys-R-Us*.) Certainly, no one will go home hungry.

Although most of the booths will contain food items, there will be a section of the exhibit hall reserved for nonfood soy items. This ambitious project, known as "Tofu Out of the Kitchen: A Struggle for Freedom" was masterminded by Bubona Plage, president of the Computer Science Undergraduate Association. Plage was the first to suggest that imitation frozen squid (a nonmeat product made almost entirely of soy derivatives) be added to the food service menu.

Description

The *Tofu Times* is a multi-column document created using Microsoft Word. To create a multi-column document with Word, you use the Section command from the Format menu to change the number of columns to two or more.

With a multi-columned document, only one column will appear on the screen. To see the document exactly as it will look when printed, you can use the Page View command from the Document menu.

Bean Quiz

Biology 387
Bean Quiz

Name: _____   Date: _____

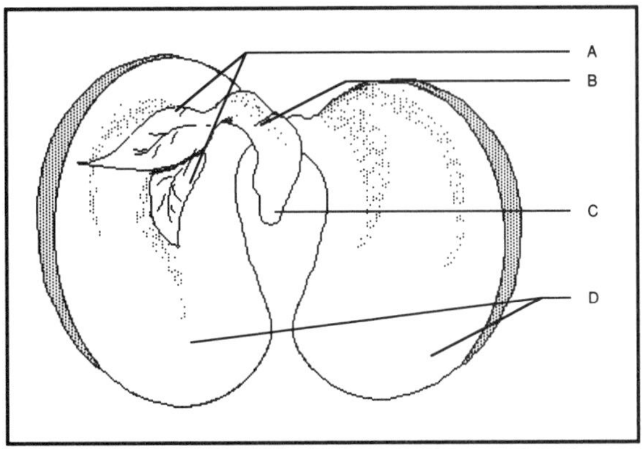

The diagram above shows the major parts of a young bean plant. Fill in the name of each part and give a brief description of its function.

A: Name: _____   Description: _____

_____   _____

B: Name: _____   Description: _____

_____   _____

C: Name: _____   Description: _____

_____   _____

D: Name: _____   Description: _____

_____   _____

Description

This quiz was created using Microsoft Word. The solid lines were created by specifying a leader for the tab stops.

A leader is a pattern that is repeated from the last piece of text to the tab stop. To specify a leader, you click the Tabs button in the format paragraph dialog box.

When you define tabs in Word, you can select a leader, if you choose to use one. Then, when you press Tab, the space between the insertion point and the next tab stop is filled with the leader.

The graphic used in this quiz was created using two applications, MacPaint and MacDraw.

Exercises

1. Based on your experience with word processing software, describe how you think writing a paper using a word processor differs from using a typewriter. Which would you rather use? Why?

2. What is a What You See Is What You Get (WYSIWYG) word processor? Why is WYSIWYG important?

3. Why is the ability to integrate information from other applications important? Give examples of when you might use this ability.

4. How do you select an arbitrary block of text in Word? Give the short cuts for selecting each of the following:

- A word.
- A line.
- A sentence.
- A paragraph.
- An entire document.

5. Think of a good use for Word's Print Merge capability. Create your own merge and main documents, and print the resulting customized documents.

6. Modify the "Resume" document from the Advanced Microsoft Word module so that it contains information about you.

7. Modify the Footer from the "Tofu Paper" document so that it is in 10-point type and so that the name of the class appears centered in the footer.

8. What is a section (in terms of a Word document)? In the Intermediate Microsoft Word module, you formatted the first section so your title page would not have a footer on it. Modify the Tofu Paper document so that the bibliography is in a separate section. Then format the bibliography to use lower case roman numerals (i, ii, iii, and so on) instead of Arabic numerals (1, 2, 3, and so on).

Hint: In Word, you create a section divider by holding down the Command key and pressing Return.

9. Design a table to hold information about a portfolio of stocks. Your table should contain 4 columns: one for the name of the company, and one each for the number of shares, the price at which the stock was bought, and the current price of the stock. Be sure to use decimal tabs for any column that contains numbers.

10. In your cover letter, you used the «Company Name» field in both the employer's address and in the sentence, "Early in my coursework at Stanford, I began thinking seriously about eventual employment with «Company Name»". This sentence will sound a little awkward, however, if the value for Company Name is "Apple Computer, Inc." It would be better if you used "Apple" in the body of the letter. Change the Cover Letter and Cover Letter Data documents now to include a new field, «Informal Company Name», and use this field in place of «Company Name» in the body of the cover letter.

11. Use Word to write a short autobiography.

HOWDY DO!

4 Spreadsheets

A9

MBA Analysis

	A	B	C	D	E	F
1	MBA Net Present Value Calculation					
2		Year 1	Year 2	Year 3	Year 4	Year 5
3						
4	**Increased Earnings**	($35,000)	($35,000)	$10,000	$15,000	$20,000
5						
6	Costs					
7	Tuition	($15,000)	($15,000)	$0	$0	$0
8	Books	($1,000)	($1,000)	$0	$0	$0
9						
10						
11						
12						
13						
14						
15						
16						
17						
18						
19						

About Spreadsheets

A spreadsheet is a group of items (numbers or text) arranged in horizontal rows and vertical columns to emphasize relationships among them. One common application of a spreadsheet is an accountant's ledger books, where the columnar tables are used to keep track of the flow of money. Your checkbook register is a more familiar example of a spreadsheet. Each column of the register contains one piece of information for every transaction, and each row contains all of the information for one transaction.

For people who use traditional spreadsheets to record a large number of complex numbers and relationships, a problem arises when the information in the spreadsheet needs to be changed. Imagine that you use the tabular format of a spreadsheet to calculate your payments on a car loan that you're thinking of taking out. You'd probably want to include numbers like the interest rate, the number of payments, the principal, and so on.

If a single number changed, you'd have to recalculate all of the numbers affected by the change. A tedious and unpleasant task if you have a large spreadsheet, or one that changes often.

Enter spreadsheet applications software for your personal computer. An electronic spreadsheet: With it, the computer can do your calculations for you—even complex calculations—fast and with a high level of accuracy. You enter the numbers into the spreadsheet grid, enter formulas elsewhere in the grid, and the computer does the computation. A formula is a relationship between one or more numbers in the spreadsheet. For example, the formula

Profit = Income – Expenses

expresses the relationship between the number for profit and the numbers for income and expenses.

Using the numbers and formulas you enter, a spreadsheet can quickly calculate the result. So quickly, in fact, that you can change the numbers in the spreadsheet and watch as the computer recalculates and updates the other related numbers automatically.

The ability to update formulas instantly is especially useful for what are often called "What If?" analyses. With "What If?" analyses, you use formulas to create numerical models that express the relationships between different quantities. "What if my sales are lower in March? How much lower would my profit be?" "What if I purchased a cheaper car for my business? How much lower would my expenses be?" This kind of numerical modeling is used often in the engineering and financial worlds to predict the behavior of various systems, whether they be mechanical systems such as the structure of an airplane, or economic systems such as the relationship between defense spending and inflation.

About Microsoft Excel

Microsoft Excel is an electronic spreadsheet program for the Macintosh. Excel features include:

Automatic Recalculation. Excel will automatically recalculate the formulas in your spreadsheet whenever you change some of the information in it.

Functions. Excel allows you to use several predefined functions to create complex formulas. These functions include NPV (Net Present Value), AVERAGE, SUM, and others.

Linking. Excel can dynamically link two or more spreadsheets so that changes made to one are automatically reflected in the other.

Multiple Formatting Options. Excel allows you to use different formats for numbers and text. Formatting options for numbers include Dollar, Percent, Decimal, and Scientific. For text, Excel allows you to choose different fonts, type sizes, and typestyles (**bold,** *italic,* underline, and so on).

Introduction to Microsoft Excel

The Task

As a budding entrepreneur, you decide to form a small business to deliver sushi to the student body. This idea seems like a winner, but to be sure, you want to calculate some of your expenses in order to estimate your expected profit.

One of your largest expenses will be purchasing and operating an automobile for picking up supplies and delivering sushi to various student residences.

You realize that once you include car payments, insurance, and gasoline, your calculations can become quite complex. Therefore, you have decided to use Microsoft Excel to help you estimate your car expenses.

You'll learn the basic spreadsheet techniques in Excel and use them to design a spreadsheet that calculates the monthly cost of owning and operating an automobile. For each element contributing to the total cost (such as car payments, insurance, and gasoline), you'll list the relevant prices and quantities and calculate a subtotal. Then you'll calculate a grand total based on this information. Throughout the module, you'll use "What If?" analysis to answer questions like, "What if I decide not to buy the rusty old Buick?"

You'll use the results from this spreadsheet in the Advanced Excel module, where you'll calculate the total revenues and expenses of your business.

When you're finished, your spreadsheet will look like the one shown on the following page.

Item	Amount
Car Payments	
Price of Car	$5,000
Down Payment	$1,250
Principal	$3,750
Number of Payments	60
Interest Rate	1%
Subtotal	$83
Insurance	
Liability	$50
Collision	$0
Comprehensive	$1
Subtotal	$51
Gasoline	
MPG	25
Price/gallon	$1.22
Miles/month	500
Subtotal	$24
Grand Total	$159

Getting Started

This module assumes that you are familiar with the basics of using the Macintosh, how to work with a hard disk and/or diskettes, how to choose menu commands, and so on. If these concepts are not familiar to you, please review the Approaching Macintosh module.

First, you'll start from the Macintosh desktop.

Turn on the Macintosh. If you are not using a hard disk, insert the system diskette in the internal diskette drive.

Soon, you'll see the Macintosh desktop.

Next, you'll open Excel.

Microsoft Excel

If you are using a hard disk, find the Excel icon and double-click on it to open Excel.

If you do not have a hard disk, insert the Excel program disk, wait for the disk icon to appear, and double-click on the Excel icon to open the application.

A new worksheet appears on the screen.

Using Full Menus

Before you get started, you'll set the spreadsheet to ensure that the instructions in the module make sense.

Like Microsoft Word, Excel has two sets of menus: Full Menus and Short Menus. Because you'll use some of the Full Menus commands in this module, the first thing you'll do is set Excel to display full menus.

If necessary, choose Full Menus from the Options menu.

If Excel is already displaying full menus, the Full Menus command won't appear in the Options menu; instead, the Short Menus option will be there. If you see Short Menus, you don't need to do anything.

The **reference area** contains the **current cell address.**

The **row heading** is the identifier for the row. Click here to select the entire row.

The **current cell** has a black border around it. Anything you type will appear in the current cell.

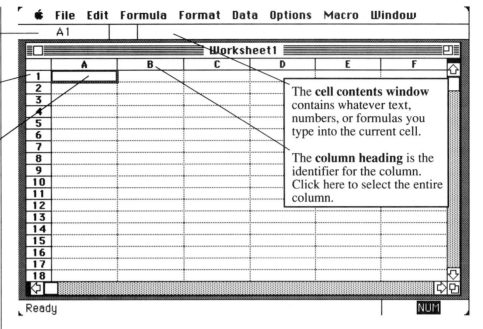

The **cell contents window** contains whatever text, numbers, or formulas you type into the current cell.

The **column heading** is the identifier for the column. Click here to select the entire column.

The Excel Worksheet

An Excel spreadsheet is made up of many small boxes called **cells.** In an Excel spreadsheet, cells are used to store pieces of information. A single cell can contain a text label, a number, or a **formula** (a relationship between other cells).

Each cell is referred to by a row and column identifier.

Rows run horizontally across the worksheet. Each row is identified by a number appearing in the **row heading** to the left of it.

Columns run vertically down the worksheet. Each column is identified by a letter appearing in the **column heading** at the top of it.

The Formula Bar

Notice the two boxes above your worksheet. One contains the text "A1" and the other is blank. These two boxes make up the **formula bar.** The box on the left is the **reference area.** It contains the **current cell address,** which tells you the row and column of the current cell. When you start a new worksheet, the current cell is always A1. As you move around the worksheet, however, the current cell address constantly changes to let you know where you are.

To the right of the current cell address is the **cell contents window.** This window holds the actual information in the current cell. If the current cell contains a label or a number, you'll see it here. If the current cell contains a formula, you'll see the formula here and the computed result of the formula in the worksheet.

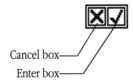

Cancel box
Enter box

There are two other items of interest in the formula bar—the **cancel box** and the **enter box**—but you can't see them now. The reason you can't see them is because you haven't done anything, so there isn't anything to cancel or enter. As soon as you type something in the current cell, the cancel and enter boxes appear in the formula bar.

Now you'll enter some text into the worksheet so that you can see how the cancel icon works.

Type your name.

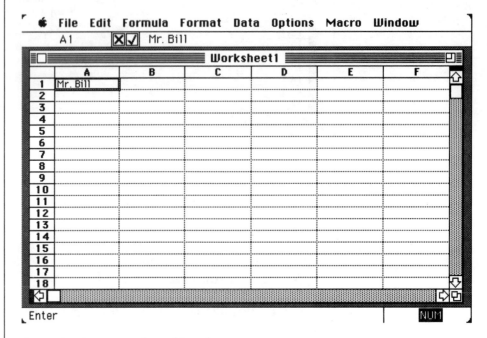

As you begin to type, three things happen:

- First, the text that you enter appears in the current cell.
- Second, the same text also appears in the cell contents window of the formula bar.
- Third, two small boxes appear between the current cell address and the cell contents window in the formula bar.

The box on the left, with the "X" in it, is the cancel box. By clicking on the cancel box, you cancel changes you have made to the current cell. In this case, clicking on the cancel icon will erase the text that you've typed.

Click the cancel icon.

Your name disappears from both the formula bar and the current cell. The box on the right, with the check mark in it, is the enter box. By clicking on the enter box, you tell Excel to accept the changes that you make to the current cell.

Many of the remaining items on the screen (the menu bar, title bar, scroll bars, zoom box, and size box) should be familiar to you by now. If they are not, consult the Approaching Macintosh module.

One other thing that you haven't seen before is the box at the bottom of the screen with the word "Ready" in it. This is the status box. The status box gives you hints to help prevent you from getting lost. For example, right now, it displays "Ready" because it's waiting for you to begin work.

Typing Labels

You start creating your worksheet by typing labels in cells. Before you do this, however, you'll set the standard font for the document so it will look good on both an Apple ImageWriter and a LaserWriter printer.

Choose Standard Font... from the Options menu.

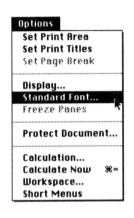

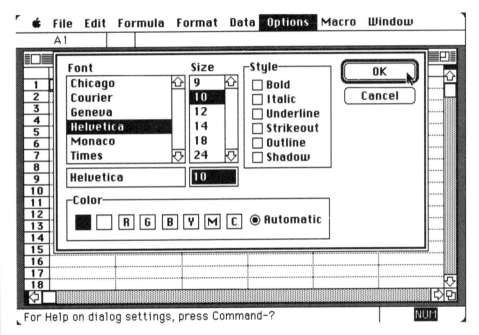

A dialog box appears. Here you can specify the font you want to use for your spreadsheet. You'll use Helvetica because that font looks good when printed on both ImageWriter and LaserWriter printers.

Click on Helvetica to change the font. Then, click OK.

Now you're ready to begin work.

The first labels you'll enter will be column headings for your spreadsheet. There will be two columns: one will contain labels describing the expenses, and the other will contain the corresponding values. You'll enter the two column heading labels first.

To select a cell, position the pointer on the cell and press the mouse button. You'll select cell A1, the cell at the intersection of the first row and first column, now.

If A1 is not already the current cell, move the pointer into cell A1 and click.

This cell, now the current selection, has a black border.

Typing Text in the Current Cell

All text, numbers, and formulas that you type will be inserted into the current cell. The characters will also appear in the cell contents window.

Type "Item".

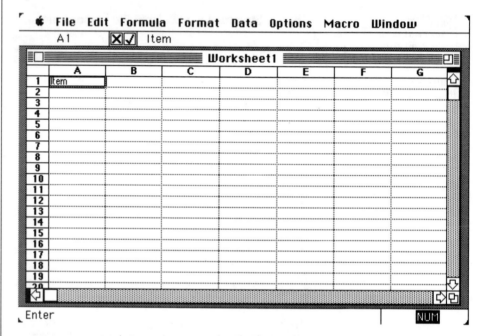

If you make a mistake while typing this label, use the Delete key to correct the error. Alternatively, you can use the mouse to move the cursor within the cell contents window and correct the error using the Cut or Clear... commands from the Edit menu. If all else fails, click the cancel box and try entering the label again.

The Enter Key

Press Enter to accept this label.

When you are entering labels, numbers, or formulas, pressing the Enter key causes Excel to accept the entry but does not change the current cell location. Before a label or number is entered, you can't change its formatting.

Moving through Your Spreadsheet

Next, you'll insert a label in cell B1, the cell directly to the right of the current cell. You could use the mouse to select this cell, but there is an easier way. You can use the arrow keys to move through your spreadsheet:

- The **down arrow** moves the current cell **down** to the next row.
- The **up arrow** moves the current cell **up** to the previous row.
- The **right arrow** moves the current cell **right** to the adjacent column.
- The **left arrow** moves the current cell **left** to the adjacent column.

Alternatively, you can use the Return, Tab, and Shift keys to move through the spreadsheet. Note that Shift-Return means to hold down the Shift key while pressing Return. Shift-Tab means to hold down the Shift key while pressing Tab.

- **Return** moves the current cell **down** to the next row.
- **Shift-Return** moves the current cell **up** to the previous row.
- **Tab** moves the current cell **right** to the adjacent column.
- **Shift-Tab** moves the current cell **left** to the adjacent column.

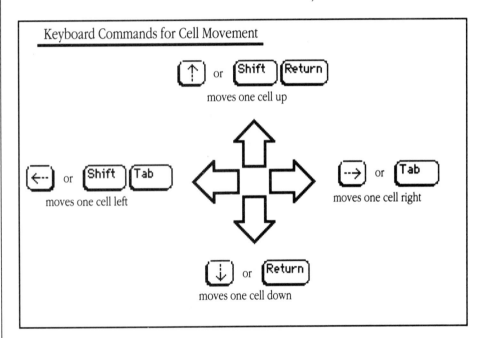

You'll use the Tab or right arrow key to move the current cell to the next column now.

Press the right arrow key to move the current cell to the right.

B1 becomes the current cell.

If you use keys to move beyond the area of the spreadsheet that is visible on the screen, Excel will automatically scroll the spreadsheet for you so that the current cell remains on the screen. To move more quickly through your spreadsheet, use the scroll bars along the right and bottom sides of the window.

Practice moving around the spreadsheet. When you are done, move back to cell B1.

Type "Amount" to enter a label for the second column.

Next, you'll enter a label for "Car Payments", the first expense that you'll calculate. But first you'll have to change the position of the current cell.

From B1, use the arrow keys to move down one row, and then to move one cell left to cell A2. Then type "Car Payments".

The next cell that you want to enter a label in is A3.

Press the down arrow key to make A3 the current cell.

Your spreadsheet will be divided into four parts—Car Payments, Insurance, Gasoline, and Grand Total. Under the labels for each of these items, you'll list the expenses that determine the cost of that item. For example, to calculate your monthly car payment you need to know the price of the car, the down payment, the number of payments, and the interest rate.

Type "Price of Car".

You'll enter the value 8000 for the price of the car in the cell to the right of the label you typed.

From cell A3, press the right arrow key to move to cell B3.

Cell B3, just to the right of "Price of Car", is now the current cell.

Type "8000", then press Enter to accept the label.

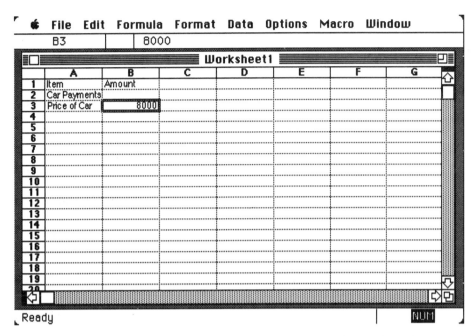

Notice that Excel "pushes" numbers against the right edge of the cell, and text against the left edge.

You're ready to type in the rest of the information needed to calculate your car payments.

From cell B3, move down to the next row, and then one column to the left to cell A4.

The current cell should now be A4, directly below the cell containing "Price of Car". Now, you'll enter a text label for the down payment.

Type "Down Payment". Then, press the right arrow to move one cell to the right to B4.

Using Formulas

You're ready to enter the down payment value for your car now. You have talked to a banker, and you know that you will have to provide a down payment of 25% to get a car loan. That is, the down payment can be calculated by the formula:

Down Payment = 25% x Price of Car

In our example, the down payment is 2000 (25% of 8000).

Noticing this, you could simply enter 2000 in cell B4, but then you would have to recalculate the value and reenter it each time that the price of the car changed. Because you will be considering many different cars, this would be a lot of work. By using a **formula,** however, you can tell Excel to perform calculations on values contained in the cells and to display the results of these calculations automatically.

You'll enter a formula for down payment now.

The Equal Sign

In Excel, you must start all formulas with an equal sign, so that Excel knows they are formulas and not just text or numbers.

Make sure that cell B4 is the current cell. Select it if it's not. Then, type an equal sign, "=".

Cell References

To calculate the down payment, you need to multiply the price of the car by 25%. You'll type a formula to **reference** the cell that contains the price of the car.

The easiest way to reference a cell in a formula is to simply type the cell's row and column address. You'll enter the formula for the down payment as the price of the car (B3) multiplied by 25%. This formula tells Excel to take the number in cell B3, multiply it by 25%, and store the result in B4.

Type "B3*25%", then press Enter.

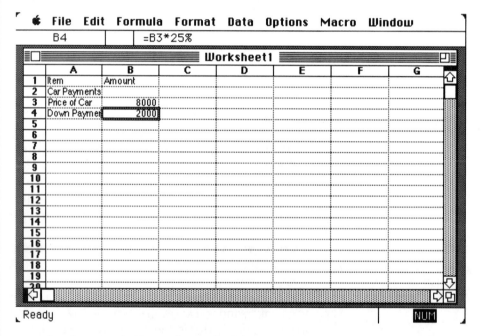

Note that the asterisk (*) signifies multiplication. In computer applications, the asterisk (*) and the slash (/) are often used to signify multiplication and division, respectively. Notice that when you press Enter, the formula is still displayed in the formula bar, but that the result (2000) is now displayed in the worksheet.

The formula is now complete.

Next, you'll enter a text label and a formula to compute the principal of your loan.

Move from cell B4 to cell A5. Then, type "Principal".

Move one cell to the right to cell B5.

Now, you'll enter the principal for your car loan, that is, the amount of money that you will have to borrow. The principal can be calculated from the price of the car and the down payment by using this formula:

Principal = Price of Car − Down Payment

In our example, the principal is 6000 (8000 − 2000).

Noticing this, you could simply enter "6000" in cell B5, but then you would have to recalculate the value and reenter it each time either the price of the car or the down payment changed. Because you will be considering many different cars, this would be a lot of work. You'll use a formula instead.

Type "= B3− B4", then press Enter.

By now you should be getting good at entering formulas.

There are two more values you will need to compute the amount of your car payments: the number of payments that you will make and the interest rate. You'll enter these values now.

Move from cell B5 to cell A6.

A6 should be highlighted.

Type "Number of Payments". Then, press Enter to accept the label.

Changing Column Widths

Notice that a small part of the label extends into cell B6. There is nothing in that cell, so that's okay. If, however, cell B6 had contained some text or numbers, then only the part of the label that could fit in cell A6 would show up. The rest would still be there, but it would be hidden. When you enter a value for the down payment in B6, the part of the label that extends into B6 will be hidden, and the spreadsheet will look very cramped.

Fortunately, Excel allows you to change the width of a column so that you can fit more or less text in it. You can change the width of the column containing the current cell by dragging the appropriate column heading divider to the left or right.

Use the mouse to position the pointer between the column headings for column A and column B.

The pointer should change shape to show a double arrow as you position the pointer between the two column headings.

When the pointer changes shape, you can change the width of the column by dragging to the right or left.

Press the mouse button and drag to the right until column A is approximately twice its original width.

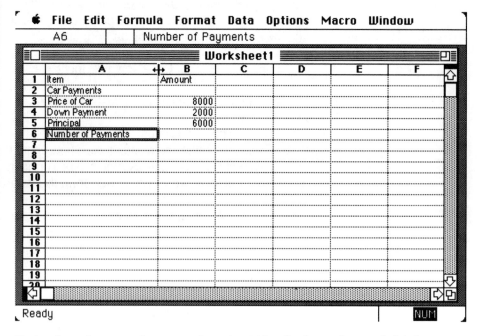

Notice that when you change a column's width, all other columns shift left or right to accommodate the change.

Now, enter a value for the number of payments. Your car loan will be paid off in 60 monthly payments.

Press the right arrow key to move one cell to the right to cell B6. Then, type "60".

Finally, you'll enter the interest rate.

Move from cell B6 to cell A7.

A7 should be highlighted.

Type "Interest Rate", and then move one cell to the right.

To calculate the amount of your car payments, you will need the interest rate per month, not per year. For simplicity, we are going to assume a 12% per year rate, so the monthly rate will be 1% or .01.

Type ".01", then press Enter.

You now have enough information to calculate your monthly car payments. But first, you'll need to type in a label.

$(C + E + P) - O$

Move to cell A8.

Type "Subtotal", then press the right arrow key to move to B8.

Using Functions

You are now ready to enter a formula to compute the amount of your car payments. Your first thought might be to enter the formula like this:

Payment = Principal / Number of Payments

This would not be quite right because it doesn't take into account the monthly interest on the loan balance. The actual formula is very complicated. When you look at it, don't be alarmed; you'll use a short cut to get the answer.

$$\text{Car Payment} = \cfrac{\text{Principal}}{\cfrac{1}{\text{Interest Rate}} - \cfrac{1}{\text{Interest Rate} \times (1 + \text{Interest Rate})^{\text{Number of Payments}}}}$$

This is a very complicated formula. Fortunately, Excel provides a large number of **functions** to make complex calculations (like this one) easier. You use a function by typing in its name and a list of **arguments.** An argument is a piece of information that is required to compute the final result. In the formula above, the arguments are Principal, Interest Rate, and Number of Payments.

You'll use the PMT( ) (Payment) function to calculate the amount of your car payments now.

You use a function either by typing its name directly into the formula bar, or else by having it inserted automatically using the Paste Function command from the Formula menu. Once you've inserted the name of the function, you insert the arguments, enclosed in parentheses, after the name.

You'll insert the PMT( ) function now.

Choose Paste Function... from the Formula menu.

You are presented with a list of functions that Excel recognizes.

Notice the check box marked "Paste Arguments". By clicking on this check box, you can have Excel provide "hints" for the arguments that the function requires. You won't need to use the hints this time.

Using the scroll bar, scroll down until the function PMT( ) is in view.

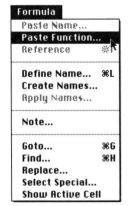

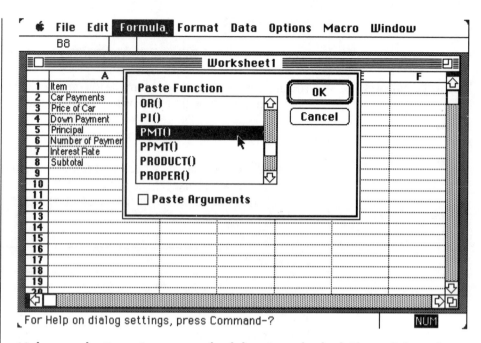

Make sure the Paste Arguments check box is unchecked. Then, click on the PMT( ) function, so that PMT( ) is highlighted. Then, click OK.

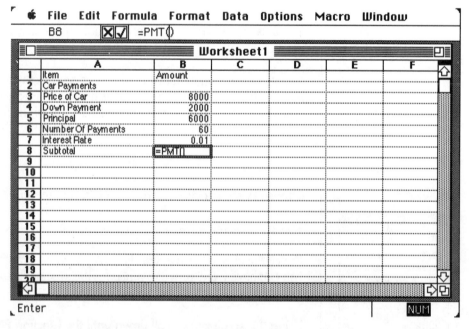

The beginning of the PMT( ) function appears in the formula bar with the insertion point between the two parentheses.

You include the arguments of the function in parentheses. You'll enter the arguments to the function as references to the cells that contain them. When you entered the formulas for Down Payment and Principal, you used absolute references. That is, you looked up the address for each of the cells you referenced, and then typed it in. This can be a long and tedious process. Fortunately, there is a better way.

Entering Arguments to Functions

When you define a formula, you can have Excel automatically add cell references for you by simply clicking in the cell that you would like to reference. You'll enter the arguments to the PMT( ) function this way.

You have three arguments to enter: Interest Rate, Number of Payments, and Principal. Note that you must enter the arguments in the proper order so Excel doesn't get confused.

With the insertion point still between the two parentheses, click on cell B7.

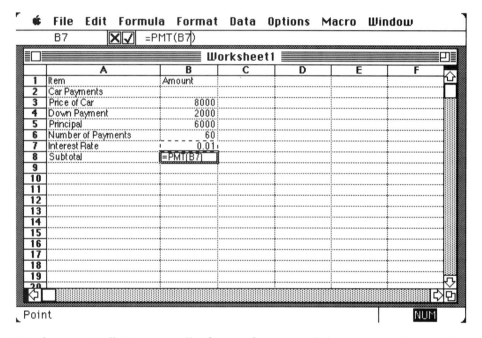

Excel automatically inserts a cell reference for you, and places a marquis around the cell B7.

You'll enter the second argument now, but first you'll type a comma to separate it from the first argument.

Type ",", then click on cell B6.

Your formula is almost complete, but you still need to add one more argument for the principal of the loan.

Type ",", then click on cell B5.

Your formula is now complete.

Press Enter to accept the formula.

| | File | Edit | Formula | Format | Data | Options | Macro | Window |

B8 | =PMT(B7,B6,B5)

Worksheet1

	A	B	C	D	E	F
1	Item	Amount				
2	Car Payments					
3	Price of Car	8000				
4	Down Payment	2000				
5	Principal	6000				
6	Number of Payments	60				
7	Interest Rate	0.01				
8	Subtotal	-133.46669				
9						
10						
11						
12						
13						
14						
15						
16						
17						
18						
19						

Ready | NUM

The formula remains in the formula bar, but the result, -133.46669 appears in the cell B8. The PMT( ) function gives a negative number because the auto payment is subtracted from your savings—it is a cash outflow. Because you're going to use this number to add to other costs later in this module, you'd rather have it appear as a positive number. You can do this by inserting a minus sign (–) before the PMT( ) function in the cell contents window.

Set the insertion point by moving the I-bar between the equal sign (=) and the PMT( ) function in the cell contents window and pressing the mouse button.

The blinking cursor shows the location of the insertion point.

Type a minus sign, "–", and then press Enter to accept the change.

| | B8 | | =-PMT(B7,B6,B5) | |

Worksheet1

	A	B	C	D	E	F
1	Item	Amount				
2	Car Payments					
3	Price of Car	8000				
4	Down Payment	2000				
5	Principal	6000				
6	Number of Payments	60				
7	Interest Rate	0.01				
8	Subtotal	133.466686				
9						
10						
11						
12						
13						
14						
15						
16						
17						
18						
19						
20						

Ready   NUM

The result of the formula changes to 133.466686.

Using "What If?" Analysis

You've finished calculating your car payments, but you may be wondering why you used a spreadsheet in the first place; you probably could have done all of this figuring on a pocket calculator in two minutes. Spreadsheets are invaluable, however, when you want to do "What If?" analysis. "What If?" analysis involves three steps:

- First, you ask a "What If?" question about your spreadsheet. For example, "What if the price of the car I'm buying were $10,000 instead of $8,000?"
- Second, you alter the appropriate cell or cells in your spreadsheet. In this case, to change the price of the car to $10,000, you would change the value of B3 to 10000.
- Third, you observe how different values in the spreadsheet change. In this case, you would probably be most interested in the final amount of your car payments.

Next, you'll do a small-scale "What If?" analysis on the portion of the spreadsheet that you've completed so far by changing the price of the car you'll be buying to 10000 from 8000.

Click on cell B3 to select it. Then, type "10000". Finally, press Enter to accept the change.

B3	10000

Worksheet1

	A	B	C	D	E	F
1	Item	Amount				
2	Car Payments					
3	Price of Car	10000				
4	Down Payment	2500				
5	Principal	7500				
6	Number of Payments	60				
7	Interest Rate	0.01				
8	Subtotal	166.833358				
9						
10						
11						
12						
13						
14						
15						
16						
17						
18						
19						

Ready   NUM

Several things happen. First, the value in B3 is changed to 10000, which is probably not surprising to you.

Second, the down payment of your loan, given in cell B4, changed from 2000 to 2500. Remember that the down payment is given by the formula:

Down Payment = 25% x Price of Car

From this formula, you can see that if the price of the car has increased by 2000 (from 8000 to 10000), then the down payment must increase by 25% of 2000, or 500. The new down payment is now 2500.

Third, the principal of your loan, given in cell B5, has changed from 6000 to 7500. Remember that the principal of the loan is given by the formula:

Principal = Price of Car – Down Payment

From this formula, you can see that if the price of the car is increased by 2000, and the price of the down payment is only increased by 500 , then the principal must increase by the difference, 1500. When one cell in the spreadsheet changes, Excel recalculates all of the formulas in the spreadsheet to reflect the change; this is why it's important to use formulas to express relationships between cells.

The final change occurred in cell B8, your monthly car payments. The amount of each car payment has gone from 133.4666686 to 166.833358. Because you used cell references as arguments to the PMT( ) function, the new result is calculated automatically when the value of one of the arguments changes.

This completes your introduction to "What If?" analysis, but you'll use it again once you've completed more of your spreadsheet.

Saving Your Work

Before you calculate your insurance and gasoline costs, you should save the work that you've done so far.

Choose Save from the File menu.

You are presented with the Save dialog box. You'll type in the name for your document.

Type "Car Costs", as the document name, then choose the disk and folder where you would like the document to be placed. Finally, click Save.

The work you've done so far is now saved to disk.

Using Regions

A **region** is a group of cells that lie next to each other in the spreadsheet. You can simplify the process of entering information by selecting the region of cells where the information will reside *before* entering it. When you select the region first, Excel knows in advance which cells to use. As a result, both formatting and moving through the cells of the region is faster than working with each cell individually. You'll see how this works in a minute.

Selecting Regions

First, you'll select the region of cells you'll be using for this section.

Click on cell A9 and drag down and to the right until the pointer is on top of cell B12. Then, release the mouse button.

	É	**File**	**Edit**	**Formula**	**Format**	**Data**	**Options**	**Macro**	**Window**

A9

Car Costs

	A	B	C	D	E	F
1	Item	Amount				
2	Car Payments					
3	Price of Car	10000				
4	Down Payment	2500				
5	Principal	7500				
6	Number of Payments	60				
7	Interest Rate	0.01				
8	Subtotal	166.833358				
9						
10						
11						
12						
13						
14						
15						
16						
17						
18						
19						
20						

Ready

NUM

Eight cells should be highlighted, indicating that they are selected and the current cell should be A9. Note that when you select a region, the current cell is white. To move from cell to cell within a region, you use the Enter key.

Next, you'll type the label for the section in the first cell of the region, and use the Enter key to move to the next cell.

Type "Insurance", then press the Enter key twice.

Moving through Regions

Notice that each time you pressed the Enter key, Excel accepted your entry and moved to the next cell in the selection. Excel moves through a region in the same way that you would move through a page of a book you were reading—from left to right and top to bottom.

When you reach the last cell in the selection, pressing the Enter key again moves the current cell back to the first cell of the selection. In this way, you can go back to make corrections, if necessary. You'll use the Enter key now to practice moving completely through the selection and back to the beginning.

Press Enter until the current cell moves throughout the entire selected region and back to cell A10. You should have to press Enter once for each cell in the region, eight times in all.

You're now ready to enter the information you'll need to calculate the amount of your insurance premiums. You'll be buying three kinds of insurance—liability, collision, and comprehensive. First you'll enter a label for liability insurance.

Type "Liability" in cell A10. When you are finished, press Enter.

The current cell should now be B10. Note that you can also use the Return, Tab, Shift-Return, and Shift-Tab keys to move through the region. If, however, you pressed one of the arrow keys by mistake, then the region will be deselected. Reselect it and start over, being sure to press Enter after you type the first label.

You'll enter the estimate that you have for liability insurance. You know that it will cost you $150 for six months, so you'll use a formula to enter a monthly estimate of $150 divided by 6.

Type "=150/6", then press Enter.

Notice that Excel jumps right to the next cell.

Now you'll enter information for collision insurance. It's $100 for six months.

Type "Collision". When you are finished, press Enter and type "=100/6".

Your final estimate is for comprehensive insurance. It's $50 for six months.

Press Enter to move to cell A12.

Type "Comprehensive", press Enter, and finally, type "= 50/6". When you are finished, press Enter to accept this formula.

All cells in the region should be completely filled, and the current cell should be A9.

	File	Edit	Formula	Format	Data	Options	Macro	Window

A9		Insurance

Car Costs

	A	B	C	D	E	F
1	Item	Amount				
2	Car Payments					
3	Price of Car	10000				
4	Down Payment	2500				
5	Principal	7500				
6	Number of Payments	60				
7	Interest Rate	0.01				
8	Subtotal	166.833358				
9	Insurance					
10	Liability	25				
11	Collision	16.6666667				
12	Comprehensive	8.33333333				
13						
14						
15						
16						
17						
18						
19						

Ready   NUM

If you've made any errors, use the Enter key to move through the region and correct the mistake.

Next, you'll calculate a subtotal for insurance.

Select cell A13 by clicking on it. Then, type "Subtotal". Finally, press the right arrow key to move to cell B13.

Next, you'll define a formula to calculate the total cost of your insurance premiums.

Using the SUM( ) Function

You might enter the formula using cell references and addition signs:

= B10 + B11 + B12

But it is easier to add cell values using the Excel function SUM( ). You'll use SUM( ) now to calculate the insurance subtotal.

Choose Paste Function... from the Formula menu.

The Paste Function dialog box appears.

Use the scroll box to scroll through the list until you find the function named "SUM( )". Click on it, and then click OK.

The beginning of a function, =SUM( ), appears in the formula bar with the cursor between the two parentheses. Excel automatically adds the equal sign for you.

Referencing a Range

You can specify an argument to a function as a **range** of cells when the argument is made up of a group of cells that lie next to each other on the spreadsheet. You specify a range of cells by typing a reference to the first cell, then typing a colon (:), and finally a reference to the last cell in the range.

This diagram shows several cell ranges, and the text you would type to include them as an argument to a function:

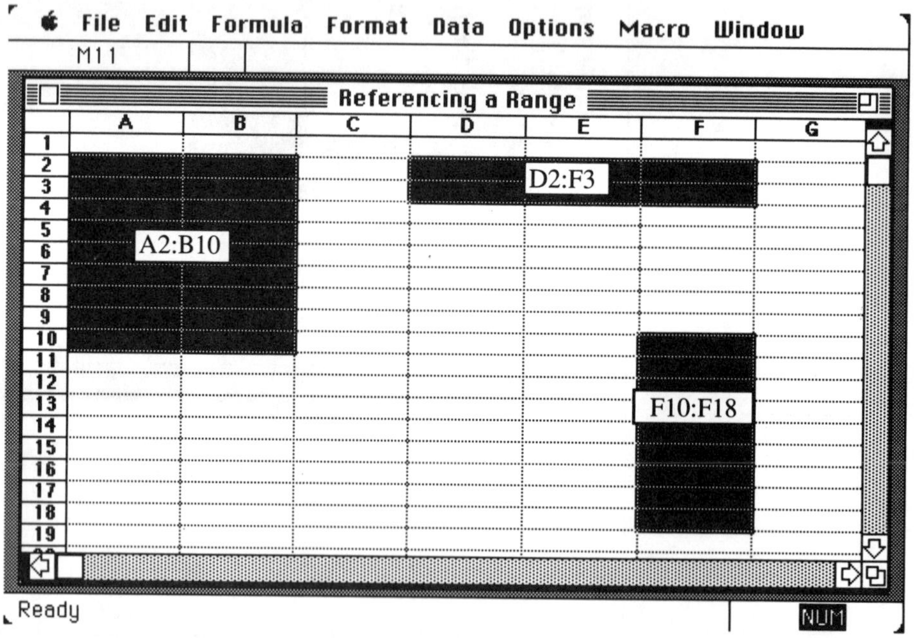

Selecting a Range

Instead of typing in the cell references that define a range, you can enter a range as an argument by clicking on the first cell in the region (the one at the top left), and dragging through the region.

In this case, you want to sum cells B10, B11, and B12. You'll enter a reference to the region they define as an argument to the SUM( ) function now.

Position the mouse pointer on cell B10. Press and hold the mouse button and drag down to cell B12. Then, release the mouse button.

As you drag, "B10:B12" appears in the formula bar to reflect the range that you've selected with the mouse. If you make a mistake, don't worry. Just press the Delete key to erase what you've typed, then try again.

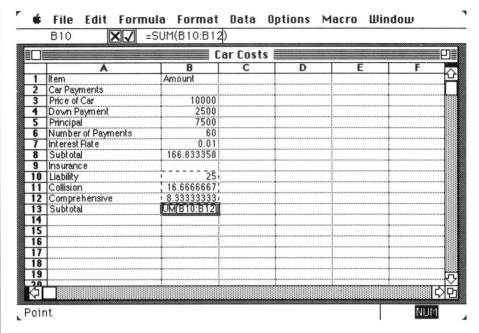

Your formula is now complete.

Press Enter.

Excel accepts the formula. The result 50 should appear in the current cell.

You have one more subtotal to calculate, and then you'll be able to calculate the total cost of operating the car.

You'll be calculating the amount of money that you expect to spend on gasoline each month. There are three things you'll need to include: the number of miles per gallon (MPG) you expect your car to get, the price per gallon you think you'll have to pay, and the number of miles you think you'll be driving each month. The total gasoline cost (per month) will be given by the formula:

$$\text{Total Gasoline Cost} = \frac{\text{Miles/Month}}{\text{MPG}} \times \text{Price/Gallon}$$

You can enter all of the information at once by first selecting a region, and then typing the information. You'll need a region five rows tall and two columns wide, which you'll select now.

Click on cell A14 and drag down to the right to cell B18. Then release the mouse button.

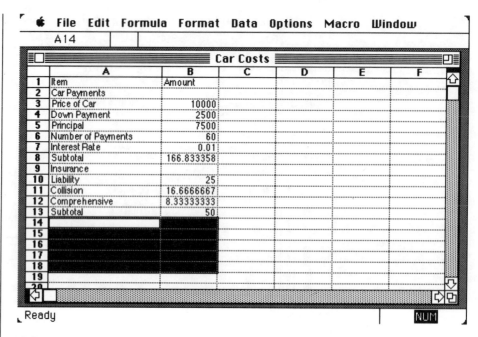

If the region you've selected doesn't look exactly like the one shown here, try again.

Now you'll enter the information that you have for your monthly gasoline expenses.

Fill in the selected cells with the text shown below. Be sure to use Enter to move from one cell to the next. You can simply press Enter twice after the first cell to leave the second one blank. Click in the appropriate cells to create the cell references in the subtotal cell.

Gasoline	
MPG	25
Price/gallon	1.22
Miles/month	500
Subtotal	= B17 / B15 * B16

A14   Gasoline

```
╔══════════════════ Car Costs ══════════════════╗
         A              B        C     D     E     F
 1  Item            Amount
 2  Car Payments
 3  Price of Car         10000
 4  Down Payment          2500
 5  Principal             7500
 6  Number of Payments      60
 7  Interest Rate         0.01
 8  Subtotal         166.833358
 9  Insurance
10  Liability               25
11  Collision        16.6666667
12  Comprehensive    8.33333333
13  Subtotal                50
14  Gasoline
15  MPG                     25
16  Price/gallon          1.22
17  Miles/month            500
18  Subtotal              24.4
19
20
```

Ready   NUM

Using Names

You've now entered all of the information that you'll need to calculate your monthly car payments. Now, you'll obtain a grand total using this formula:

$$\text{Monthly Grand Total} = \text{Car Payment} + \text{Insurance} + \text{Gasoline}$$

Defining Names for Cells

So far, you've been entering formulas with cell references. A more intuitive way to reference cells is by using **names.** You can give a name to a single cell or a group of cells and then reference them in formulas using the name. For example, the formula that calculates the amount of your car payments is in cell B8. If you would rather refer to B8 by name, you could call it something meaningful like Car_Payment. Excel's rules for naming cells are:

- Names must start with a letter, but can consist of letters, numbers, periods (.), and underscores (_).
- Names *cannot* include spaces.
- Names cannot be cell references (for example, B8).
- Names can be up to 255 characters long.

You'll define names for each of the subtotals in your document.

Click on cell B8, then choose Define Name... from the Formula menu.

The Define Name dialog box appears and prompts you for a name that will refer to the cell. The window with the scroll arrows shows previously defined names. Since you have not defined any names yet, none appear.

Below the window, there is a box in which you enter the name you will give to the cells that are selected.

Formula

Paste Name...
Paste Function...
Reference   ⌘T

Define Name... ⌘L
Create Names...
Apply Names...

Note...

Goto...   ⌘G
Find...   ⌘H
Replace...
Select Special...
Show Active Cell

If the cell adjacent to the selected cell (or the first cell in the selected range) contains a label, Excel will suggest that label as the cell name. In this case, "Subtotal" is the label for the selected cell, so Excel suggests the name "Subtotal". You might click OK to accept Excel's suggestion, but in this case, you want a more descriptive name.

You'll name the cell "Car_Payment".

Type "Car_Payment", then click OK.

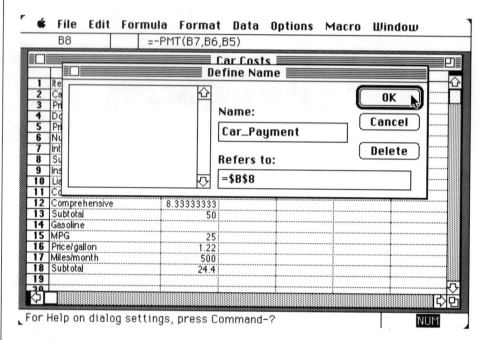

Note that you must put an underscore between the two words because Excel doesn't allow blank spaces in names.

Before entering a formula for the total cost, you'll define names for Insurance and Gasoline.

Use the procedure outlined above to define the name "Insurance" for cell B13 and "Gasoline" for cell B18.

Remember that to define each name, you must:

- Select the cell.
- Choose Define Name from the Formula menu.
- Type in the name, and click "OK".

Using Names in Formulas

Finally, you'll define a formula to calculate the total monthly cost of operating your car, but first you'll have to enter a label.

Select cell A20 and type "Grand Total".

Press the right arrow key to move one cell to the right.

The current cell should be B20.

Enter the following formula:

= Car_Payment + Insurance + Gasoline

Note that instead of cryptic cell references in your formula, you used the names that you had defined. This makes it much easier to check your formulas for errors.

Press Enter to accept the formula.

```
 File   Edit   Formula   Format   Data   Options   Macro   Window
      B20              =Car_Payment+Insurance+Gasoline
```

	A	B	C	D	E	F
2	Car Payments					
3	Price of Car	10000				
4	Down Payment	2500				
5	Principal	7500				
6	Number of Payments	60				
7	Interest Rate	0.01				
8	Subtotal	166.833358				
9	Insurance					
10	Liability	25				
11	Collision	16.6666667				
12	Comprehensive	8.33333333				
13	Subtotal	50				
14	Gasoline					
15	MPG	25				
16	Price/gallon	1.22				
17	Miles/month	500				
18	Subtotal	24.4				
19						
20	Grand Total	241.233358				

Ready   NUM

"241.233358" appears in cell B20 if you've done everything correctly.

If an error message appears, make sure that you have not made any typing errors while entering the formula. If there is still a problem, redefine each of the names, and then reenter the formula, being sure that the names you defined are exactly the same as the names you use in the formula.

Your spreadsheet is complete, so you can experiment with the power of "What If?" analysis. You'll do that in a moment, but first, you'll format some of the cells in your spreadsheet to make them more attractive and more functional.

Formatting Spreadsheets

You'd like the two column labels—"Item" and "Amount"— to stand out. You'll do this by formatting them so that they're centered in their cells and in bold type.

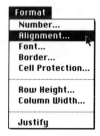

Click on cell A1 to select it. Then, choose Alignment... from the Format menu.

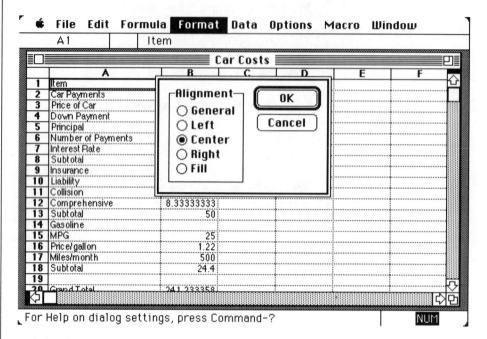

A dialog box appears with a list of alignment options. General is the default. When General is chosen, Excel pushes text against the left edge of the cell and numbers against the right edge. Fill is used to repeat the text as many times as necessary to completely fill the cell.

You'll use center alignment for your column heading.

Select Center for alignment. Then, click OK.

Next, you'll format your column heading so that it is in bold type.

Choose Font... from the Format menu.

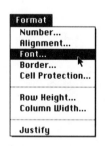

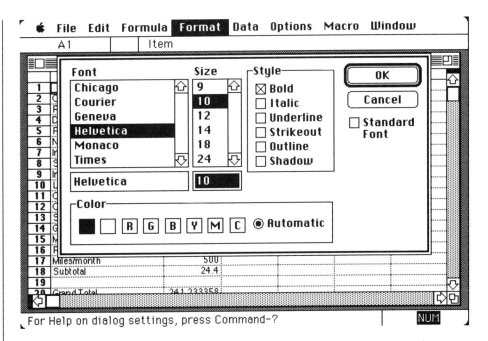

You are presented with a dialog box that allows you to format the text in the current selection. You can choose different fonts, styles, sizes, and color (if you're fortunate enough to have a color monitor).

You'll choose bold for your text label.

Choose "Bold" for style by clicking on the check box next to it. Then, click OK.

Your label is now properly formatted. Next you'll format the label for your second column the same way.

Follow the procedure outlined above to format cell B1 the same way that you've formatted cell A1.

Next, you'll format your Subtotal and Grand Total labels so they are also in bold.

Format each of the Subtotal labels (cells A8, A13 , and A18) and the Grand Total label (A20) so that they are pushed against the right edge of the cell and so that they are in bold type.

Remember that to do this, you'll need to:

- Click on the appropriate cell to select it.
- Choose Alignment… from the Format menu.
- Select Right for alignment. Then, click OK.
- Choose Font… from the Format menu.
- Select Bold for style. Then, click OK.

Finally, you'll format your section headings—"Car Payments," "Insurance," and "Gasoline"—so that they are italicized.

Follow the procedure outlined above to format the three section headings, cell A2, A9, and A14, so that they are italicized.

When you are finished, your spreadsheet should look like the one shown here:

File	**Edit**	**Formula**	**Format**	**Data**	**Options**	**Macro**	**Window**

C20

Car Costs

	A	B	C	D	E	F
1	Item	Amount				
2	*Car Payments*					
3	Price of Car	10000				
4	Down Payment	2500				
5	Principal	7500				
6	Number of Payments	60				
7	Interest Rate	0.01				
8	Subtotal	166.833358				
9	*Insurance*					
10	Liability	25				
11	Collision	16.6666667				
12	Comprehensive	8.33333333				
13	Subtotal	50				
14	*Gasoline*					
15	MPG	25				
16	Price/gallon	1.22				
17	Miles/month	500				
18	Subtotal	24.4				
19						
20	Grand Total	241.233358				

Ready

NUM

Formatting Numbers

Now, you'd like to format the numbers on your spreadsheet so they are easier to read. Specifically, you'll format all the dollar amounts with commas and dollar signs, so that the price of the car appears as $10,000 instead of 10000.

First, you'll format the cell that holds the price of the car.

Select cell B3. Then, choose Number… from the Format menu.

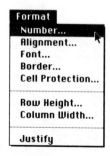

Format
Number…
Alignment…
Font…
Border…
Cell Protection…

Row Height…
Column Width…

Justify

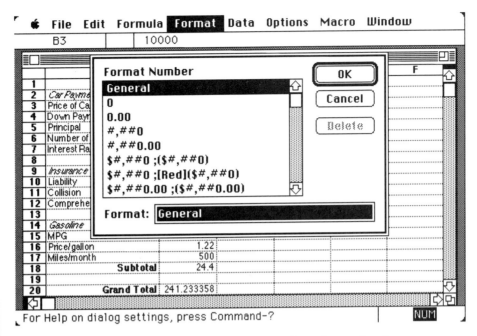

You are presented with a dialog box that lists all of Excel's number formats. At first, the dialog box probably looks intimidating. Don't worry—once you read the explanation for the different formatting options, it should be much clearer.

The default option is **General**. With general formatting, Excel displays numbers without dollar signs or commas, and displays as many digits as possible after the decimal point. In your spreadsheet, all numbers are currently displayed in the general format.

The second option, **0**, is used to display numbers without commas and with *no* numbers after the decimal point. With this format chosen, Excel would display the number 36144.6338 as 36145.

The **0.00** format displays numbers with no commas, but with two numbers after the decimal point. 36144.6338 appears as 36144.63 with this format chosen.

The **#,##0** format tells Excel to display numbers with commas and without any numbers after the decimal point. With this format chosen, Excel would display the number 36144.6338 as 36,145.

Can you imagine how numbers with the **#,##0.00** format are displayed? They are shown with commas but with only two numbers after the decimal point. With this format chosen, Excel would display the number 36144.6338 as 36,144.63.

The next three formatting options are for dollar amounts. They are similar to the other options, but they display numbers with a dollar sign before them. Negative numbers are displayed in parentheses with these formats. With the **$#,##0;($#,##0)** format chosen, Excel would display the number 36144.6338 as

$36,145. Excel would display the number -36144.6338 as ($36,145). There is an option to display negative numbers in red on color screens.

You will need to scroll to see the next set of options.

Scroll to see the next screenful of formatting options by clicking in the gray area of the scroll bar.

Here you see options for percents, scientific notation, and dates.

An example of each of the formatting options is shown below.

"Regular" Number		Date	
General	36144.6338	m/d/yy	12/3/62
0	36145	d-mmm-yy	3-Dec-62
0.00	36144.63	d-mmm	3-Dec
#,##0	36,145	mmm-yy	Dec-62
#,##0.00	36,144.63		
$#,##0($#,##0)	$36,145	**Time**	
$#,##0.00($#,##0.00)	$36,144.63	h:mm AM/PM	8:14 AM
		h:mm:ss AM/PM	8:14:26 AM
Percent		h:mm	8:14
General	0.69	h:mm:ss	8:14:26
0%	69%	m/d/yy h:mm	12/3/62 8:14
0.00%	69.00%		
Scientific Notation			
General	36144.6338		
0.00E+00	3.61E+04		

You'll choose the $#,##0;($#,##0) format for the price of the car.

Choose the $#,##0;($#,##0) format by clicking on it and then clicking OK.

B3		10000				

Car Costs

	A	B	C	D	E	F
1	Item	Amount				
2	*Car Payments*					
3	Price of Car	$10,000				
4	Down Payment	2500				
5	Principal	7500				
6	Number Of Payments	60				
7	Interest Rate	0.01				
8	Subtotal	166.833358				
9	*Insurance*					
10	Liability	25				
11	Collision	16.6666667				
12	Comprehensive	8.33333333				
13	Subtotal	50				
14	*Gasoline*					
15	MPG	25				
16	Price/gallon	1.22				
17	Miles/month	500				
18	Subtotal	24.4				
19						
20	Grand Total	241.233358				

Ready　　　　　　　　　　　　　　　　　　　　　NUM

10000 now appears as $10,000, which certainly looks better. Note that the formatting does not change even if the value in the cell is changed.

Formatting Groups of Cells

When you have many cells to format, it's easier to format groups of cells together. You can do this by first selecting the group of cells you want formatted, and then choosing the format you want.

You'll format the numbers for Down Payment and Principal now.

Select cells B4 and B5 by clicking on B4 and dragging down. Then, choose Number... from the Format menu.

The Format Number dialog box appears.

Choose the $#,##0;($#,##0) format by clicking on it. Then, click OK.

Both numbers are now formatted correctly. The next number, the Number of Payments, doesn't need to change at all. However, you'd like the Interest Rate to appear as "1%" instead of "0.01".

You'll format the interest rate now.

Click on cell B7 to select it. Then, Choose Number... from the Format menu. Finally, scroll to see the 0% format and click on it to select it. When you are finished, click OK.

Discontiguous Selection

That certainly looks better. Now you should be able to apply the dollar format to the other numbers in your spreadsheet. You could format each of these cells individually, but that involves a lot of steps. You can't drag across the cells to select them, because they are not all contiguous. Fortunately, there is a way to select discontiguous groups of cells. To select two discontiguous regions, you simply select the first region, and then hold down the Command key while selecting additional regions. You'll use this short cut now to format all remaining dollar amounts at once.

Click on cell B8, then hold down the Command key and click on cell B10.

| | File | Edit | Formula | Format | Data | Options | Macro | Window |

| B10 | =150/6 |

Car Costs

	A	B	C	D	E	F
1	Item	Amount				
2	*Car Payments*					
3	Price of Car	$10,000				
4	Down Payment	$2,500				
5	Principal	$7,500				
6	Number of Payments	60				
7	Interest Rate	1%				
8	Subtotal	166.833358				
9	*Insurance*					
10	Liability	25				
11	Collision	16.6666667				
12	Comprehensive	8.33333333				
13	Subtotal	50				
14	*Gasoline*					
15	MPG	25				
16	Price/gallon	1.22				
17	Miles/month	500				
18	Subtotal	24.4				
19						
20	Grand Total	241.233358				

Ready   NUM

The selection is extended to include B10. Next, you'll extend the selection to include all remaining dollar amounts.

While continuously holding down the Command key, drag across cells B11, B12, and B13. Then, click on cell B18. Finally, click on cell B20.

When you are finished, you're selection should look like this:

B20   =Car_Payment+Insurance+Gasoline

Car Costs

	A	B	C	D	E	F
1	**Item**	**Amount**				
2	*Car Payments*					
3	Price of Car	$10,000				
4	Down Payment	$2,500				
5	Principal	$7,500				
6	Number of Payments	60				
7	Interest Rate	1%				
8	**Subtotal**	166.833358				
9	*Insurance*					
10	Liability	25				
11	Collision	16.6666667				
12	Comprehensive	8.33333333				
13	**Subtotal**	50				
14	*Gasoline*					
15	MPG	25				
16	Price/gallon	1.22				
17	Miles/month	500				
18	**Subtotal**	24.4				
19						
20	**Grand Total**	241.233358				

Ready   NUM

Now you're ready to apply the $#,##0;($#,##0) format to all of these numbers at once.

Apply the $#,##0;($#,##0) number format to the current selection.

Remember, to format numbers using the $#,##0;($#,##0) format, you need to do the following:

- Choose Number... from the Format menu.
- Select the correct format in the Format Number dialog box—in this case, $#,##0;($#,##0).
- Click OK.

The numbers you used to calculate the cost of gasoline for your car are Miles per Gallon, Price per Gallon, and Miles per Month. The Miles per Gallon and Miles per Month numbers don't need to be reformatted, but you'll want to use a dollar format for Price per Gallon.

If you choose the same format that you used for other dollar amounts in the spreadsheet, the 1.22 would appear as $1. With this number, the cents are just as important as the dollars, so you want Excel to display two places after the decimal point. The $#,##0.00;($#,##0.00) format does just that.

You'll format price per gallon now.

Select cell B16 by clicking on it. Then, choose Number... from the Format menu. Select the $#,##0.00;($#,##0.00) format by clicking on it, and then click OK.

When you are finished, your spreadsheet should look like the one shown here.

	File	Edit	Formula	Format	Data	Options	Macro	Window

C20

Car Costs

	A	B	C	D	E	F
1	Item	Amount				
2	*Car Payments*					
3	Price of Car	$10,000				
4	Down Payment	$2,500				
5	Principal	$7,500				
6	Number of Payments	60				
7	Interest Rate	1%				
8	Subtotal	$167				
9	*Insurance*					
10	Liability	$25				
11	Collision	$17				
12	Comprehensive	$8				
13	Subtotal	$50				
14	*Gasoline*					
15	MPG	25				
16	Price/gallon	$1.22				
17	Miles/month	500				
18	Subtotal	$24				
19						
20	Grand Total	$241				

Ready
NUM

"What If?" Analysis Revisited

Now that your spreadsheet is complete, you can experiment with the full power of "What If?" analysis. The spreadsheet that you've created calculates the monthly cost of owning and operating a car, so your "What If?" analysis should be centered around the question: "What if I buy this car rather than that one?" You'll complete this cost analysis now for the following two cars:

	Porsche 944 (red)	Old Buick (rust)
Price of Car	$33,000 (new)	$5000 (used)
Liability	$300/6 months	$300/6 months
Collision	$250/6 months	$0/6 months
Comprehensive	$100/6 months	$6/6 months
MPG	15 (maybe)	25

You'll calculate the monthly car operating costs for both of these cars.

Enter the information given in the previous table for the Porsche 944. When you are done, your spreadsheet should look like this:

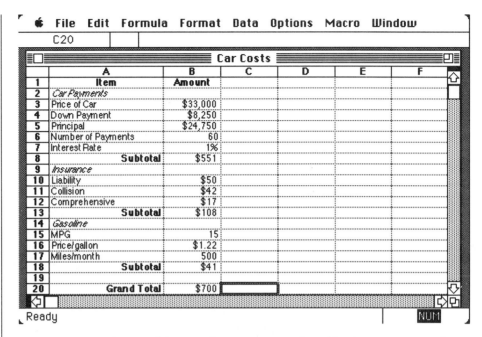

As you can see, the monthly cost of owning a Porsche 944 is $700. Now, you'll calculate the monthly cost of owning an old rusty Buick.

Enter the information for the old Buick given in the table on the previous page. When you are done, your spreadsheet should look like this:

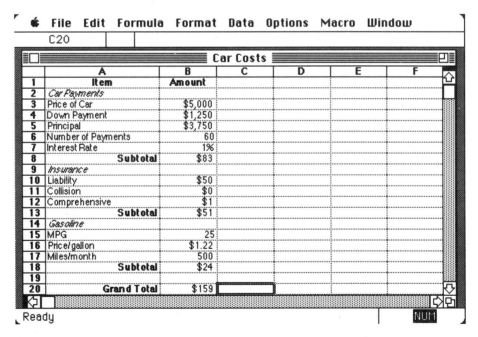

The cost of owning an old rusty Buick is only $159. Perhaps now you can truly appreciate the power of "What If?" analysis. You could have made these same calculations on paper, but you probably wouldn't have; it would have taken too long. "What If?" analysis takes much of the number crunching out of decision making, allowing managers to consider more options, and hopefully make better decisions.

Finishing Up

Before closing, you will want to print your worksheet.

When you print an Excel spreadsheet, you tell Excel how to format the page using the Page Setup command.

The Page Setup Command

Choose Page Setup... from the File menu.

Here you can choose to print your spreadsheet with or without row and column numbers and gridlines. You can print it with a header or footer—or both—on each page, if you like. The default header is "&f", which means that Excel will print the file name at the top of every page you print out. The default footer is "Page &p", which means that Excel will print "Page" and then the page number at the bottom of every page. You can also control the margins.

Uncheck the box for "Print Row and Column Headings" so that the printer won't print row or column numbers. Then, set the left margin to 2.75 inches and the top margin to 2 inches. If you are using a laser printer, make sure that Font Substitution is checked. Finally, click OK.

Printing

Finally, you'll print your spreadsheet. But first, make sure that the printer is connected, turned on, and selected correctly in the Chooser.

Choose Print... from the File menu.

You are presented with the Print dialog box.

Click OK when you're ready to print your spreadsheet.

You're about ready to quit Excel, but first you'll get one more printout. This time, you'll have Excel print the formulas in each of the cells. With this printout, it will be easier for someone to check your work for accuracy.

You'll set Excel to display formulas now.

Choose Display... from the Options menu.

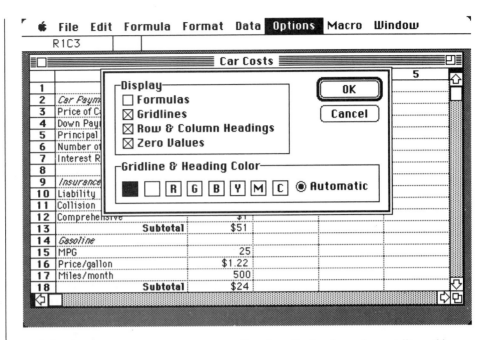

A dialog box appears. Here you can set Excel to display formulas, gridlines (the lines that define cell boundaries), row and column headings, zero values, and a color.

Set Excel to display formulas by clicking in the box labeled formulas. Then, click OK.

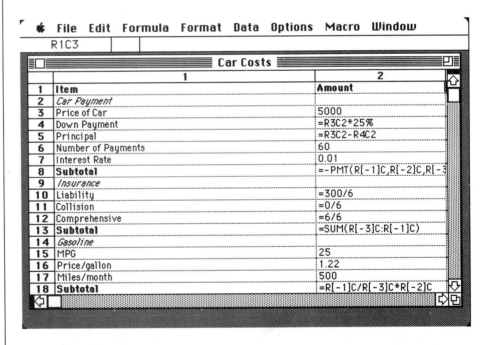

INTRODUCTION TO MICROSOFT EXCEL

Excel enlarges each column so the entire formula can be seen when printed. Before you print, you'll change the margins so the entire spreadsheet will fit on one page.

Choose Page Setup… from the File menu. Set the left margin to .75 inch and the top margin to 1 inch. Then, click OK.

Now you're ready to print your formulas.

Choose Print… from the File menu. When you are presented with the dialog box, click OK to print your formulas.

In a few moments, you'll have another spreadsheet with your formulas printed on it. Because you'll use the "Car Costs" spreadsheet in the advanced module, you'll set Excel to display values again before you quit.

Choose Display… from the Options menu. When the dialog box appears, uncheck the box labeled "Formulas". Then, click OK.

Excel displays values once again. Note that Excel restores the original column widths. You're finished now, but you'll want to save your worksheet before quitting.

Choose Save from the File menu.

Your document is now saved on disk.

Quitting

Now, you're ready to return to the desktop.

Choose Quit from the File menu.

Review

You've completed the introductory Microsoft Excel exercise for the Macintosh. If all has gone well, you've learned:

- How to type text labels in cells
- How to type numbers in cells
- How to enter formulas
- How to define names
- How to use names in formulas
- How to format cells
- How to print the worksheet and formulas

What to Turn In

Turn in a copy of both of your printed spreadsheets. Be sure to save this document; you'll need it to complete the Advanced Excel module.

Advanced
Microsoft Excel

The Task

As stated in the Introduction to Microsoft Excel module, you are thinking of starting a business to sell sushi in the student union. You have already done some preliminary cost analysis. Specifically, you have calculated the expected cost of owning and operating an automobile used to pick up supplies and deliver sushi to retail outlets around campus. You will now prepare a spreadsheet that will use that information, plus other projected costs and expected income, to calculate the amount of profit that the business will produce if all of your projections are accurate.

Because the job will be complicated, you've decided to use Excel to create a spreadsheet to store and manipulate data.

There will be several parts to this exercise. First, you'll create a list of business expenses.

Next, you'll dynamically link the document you created in the introductory module into the spreadsheet that you'll create in this one. Specifically, you'll insert your final result from the "Car Costs" document into a list of business expenses.

Finally, you'll use the Fill Right command to copy the formulas you've defined to expand your one-month profit projection into a three-month profit projection.

When you're finished, your spreadsheet should look like the one shown on the next page.

	A	B	C	D	E
1		Sushi Dreams Profit Worksheet			
2					
3		January	February	March	Total
4	Number of Samplers	200	300	300	800
5					
6	Expenses				
7	Rent	$600	$600	$600	$1,800
8	Car	$109	$109	$109	$326
9	Raw Materials	$600	$900	$900	$2,400
10	Wage Cost	$400	$400	$400	$1,200
11	Total Expenses	$1,709	$2,009	$2,009	$5,726
12					
13	Income				
14	Sushi Samplers	$1,600	$2,400	$2,400	$6,400
15	Total Income	$1,600	$2,400	$2,400	$6,400
16					
17	Profit	($109)	$391	$391	$674

Getting Started

Make sure that you have completed the Introduction to Microsoft Excel module.

Many of the concepts explained in the introductory module will be needed to complete this one. You will also link the spreadsheet you create in this module with the one that you created in the introductory module.

And, while completing this advanced module, don't be shy about having another look at the introductory module to remind yourself about entering text and numbers, defining names, using formulas and functions, and other topics that it covered.

First, you'll start from the Macintosh desktop.

Turn on the Macintosh. If you are not using a hard disk, insert the system diskette in the internal diskette drive.

Soon, you'll see the Macintosh Desktop.

Next, you'll open Excel.

Microsoft Excel

If you are using a hard disk, find the Excel icon and double-click on it to open Excel.

If you do not have a hard disk, insert the Excel program disk, wait for the disk icon to appear, and double-click on the Excel icon to open the application.

Excel creates a new, untitled document for you.

You will use Full Menus in this advanced module.

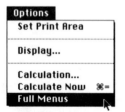

If necessary, choose Full Menus from the Options menu.

Remember that if Excel is already displaying full menus, the Full Menus command will not appear in the Options menu. Instead, the Short Menus command will appear, and you don't need to do anything.

Formatting the Worksheet

The spreadsheet that you will create in this module will be similar to the one that you created in the introductory module. Specifically, you will have labels along the left side of the worksheet, with the corresponding values to the right of them. Before entering text labels, you'll change the standard font to Helvetica.

Choose Standard Font... from the Options menu. When the dialog box appears, click Helvetica to select it. Finally, click OK.

From the introductory module, you know that the labels generally take up more room than the preset column width. Therefore, before entering any text or numbers in the spreadsheet, you'll increase the width of the first column.

Increase the width of the first column to approximately double its original size.

Remember that to change the width of a column, you must:

- Use the mouse to position the pointer between the column heading for the column you want to change and the column next to it.
- When the pointer changes shape to show a double arrow, click and drag to the right or left to change the width of the column.

Entering Text Labels

You are now ready to enter a title for your worksheet.

Select cell B1 and type "Sushi Dreams Profit Worksheet". Then, press Enter to accept the label.

&	**File**	**Edit**	**Formula**	**Format**	**Data**	**Options**	**Macro**	**Window**

| B1 | Sushi Dreams Profit Worksheet |

Worksheet1

	A	B	C	D	E	F
1		Sushi Dreams	Profit Worksheet			
2						
3						
4						
5						
6						
7						
8						
9						
10						
11						
12						
13						
14						
15						
16						
17						
18						
19						

Ready   NUM

Remember that extra text will flow from one cell into the cell to the right as long as that cell is empty.

In the introductory module, you entered each row in order—first the label, then the number or formula. However, now that you're familiar with Excel's basic editing techniques, it'll be easier for you to first enter all of the labels, then the numbers, and then do the formatting. This is because some of the tasks that you did for each cell in the introductory module could be done to many cells at the same time, such as formatting numbers or labels, and defining names.

Your spreadsheet will be divided into two areas: expenses and income.

Because there will be several types of information in the first column, you must be careful about how you format different cells. You'll use three kinds of alignment:

- The two headings for expenses and income will be centered.
- The three totals (total expenses, total income, and profit) will be aligned right.
- The rest of the cells will be aligned left.

Now, you'll fill the first column with labels for your spreadsheet.

Enter the labels in the first column of your worksheet until it looks like the one shown here. Use the Alignment... command from the Format menu to align them as described above and displayed below.

Remember, to align the text in a cell, you

- Select the cell by clicking on it.
- Choose Alignment... from the Format menu.
- Select the alignment you want.
- Click OK.

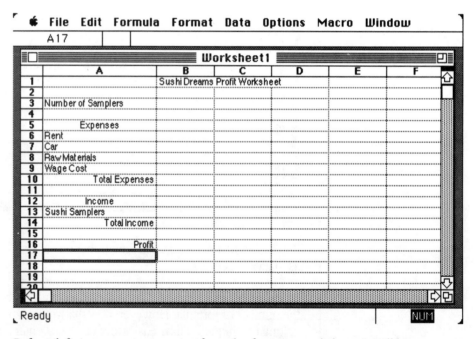

Relative versus Absolute References

Before defining names or creating formulas for your worksheet, it will be important for you to understand the two different types of references that Excel uses: **absolute references** and **relative references**.

An absolute reference in a formula is identified by dollar signs before the row and column identifiers. For example, an absolute reference to cell B3 is written as B3. An absolute reference is a reference that always refers to the same cell, even if the formula that it is in that cell gets copied or moved to another cell. For example, if you use the reference B3 to create a formula in cell B5, and then copy the formula to cell C5, the reference will still be to cell B3.

Relative references are different. When you use relative references to create a formula, you are referring to a cell that is in a certain position relative to the current cell. For example, if you use the relative reference B7 to create a formula in cell B10, you are not only creating a reference to B7, but you are telling Excel to reference the cell that is "three rows up and in the same column." If you copy the formula to another cell, say C10, then the reference will no longer be to B7, because B7 is no longer the cell that is "three rows up and in the same column." Instead, the reference will be to cell C7, the cell that is three rows up and in the same column as C10.

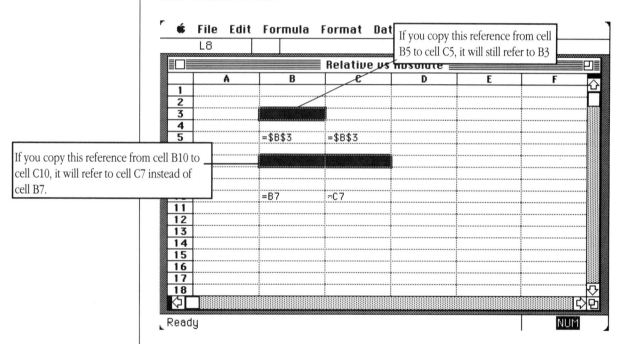

Relative and absolute references work exactly the same way as long as you don't move your formulas to different parts of the worksheet. Even if you insert cells in the middle of your spreadsheet (you'll see how to do this later in the module), Excel will automatically adjust all references (both relative and absolute) for you so that you don't have to retype them to account for the new cells.

Be sure that you understand the difference between relative references and absolute references before going on.

Naming Rows

Because this spreadsheet is going to be a complicated one, you'll use names for cell references wherever possible so that the formulas you define are easily understood. Instead of naming single cells, however, you'll name entire rows for this worksheet. This is because after you create a profit projection for one month, you'll use a copying short cut to extend the analysis for three months. But to do this, you'll want the names you define to refer to entire rows, rather than single cells. That way, when you say:

Rent + Car

in a formula, Excel will understand that you mean the value in the "rent row" for this month plus the value in the "car row" for this month.

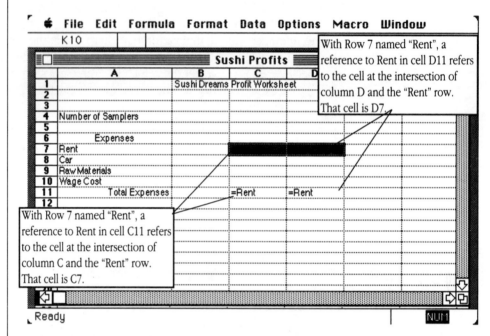

When you define a name to a group of cells and then use that name in a formula, the reference will be a relative one to the cell that is at the intersection of the named region and the row or column that the current cell is in. This is an important concept, but is not easily grasped; be sure that you understand how references to named cells work before you go on.

You'll name row 3 "Number_of_Samplers" now, but you must select a region before you can name it.

Click on row 3 in the row heading.

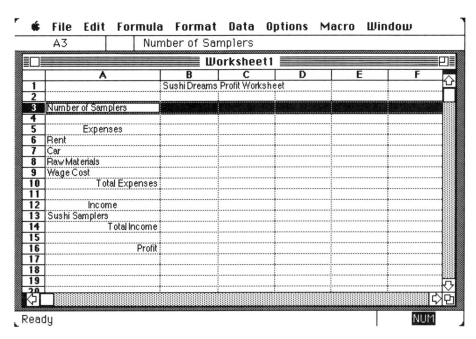

The entire row is selected, and should be highlighted.

Choose Define Name... from the Formula menu.

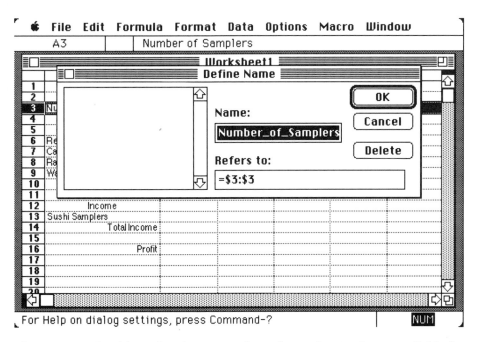

This time you should see the phrase "Number_of_Samplers" in the Name field of the dialog box. Excel put the name there because it found that label in the first column of row 3. "Number_of_Samplers" is a good name for the row because it describes the row's contents.

Click OK.

Define names for the following rows:

Give this row	This name
row 6	Rent
row 7	Car
row 8	Raw_Materials
row 9	Wage_Cost
row 10	Total_Expenses
row 13	Sushi_Samplers
row 14	Total_Income
row 16	Profit

Remember that to define a name for a row, you must:

- Select the row by clicking in its row header.
- Choose Define Name... from the Formula menu.
- When the dialog box appears, either type in a name, or click OK to accept the name that Excel suggests (in this worksheet, you'll always accept Excel's suggestion).

Entering Numbers and Formulas

You're ready to enter numbers and formulas into your worksheet.

The first row in your worksheet, the one labeled "Number of Samplers", will contain your estimate of the number of "Sushi Samplers" that you'll be able to sell in one month (each plate of sushi that you sell will actually contain three kinds of sushi, so it's called a "Sushi Sampler") .

From the surveys you've taken to estimate demand, you project that you'll be able to sell 200 Sushi Samplers the first month. You'll enter "200" for the number of samplers now.

Select cell B3 by clicking on it. Then, type "200".

Next, you'll enter the amount that you'll have to pay for rent. This will be $600.

Select cell B6 by clicking on it. Then, type "600". Finally, press Enter to accept this number.

Eventually, you'll want to use a Dollar format with "Rent", but you'll take care of that later, after you've entered all of your numbers and formulas.

Linking Spreadsheets

The next expense that you'll enter is the cost of operating the car that you'll use to pick up supplies and deliver sushi to various retail outlets around campus. You'll enter a total for that now, but you'll want to use the value you calculated in the introductory module.

You could copy the number from your "Car Costs" spreadsheet, but each time you changed a number in the first spreadsheet (for example, to consider several different cars you are thinking of purchasing), you'd have to remember to update the number in this spreadsheet to reflect the change.

Fortunately, there is a better way. You can **link** the two spreadsheets so that every time the Grand Total cell in the "Car Costs" document changes, the changes will be reflected in this spreadsheet, too.

To link two spreadsheets, you simply enter a formula that uses a cell reference of the spreadsheet you are linking to. Excel remembers where the information came from, and each time you open this spreadsheet, it also reads the linked information from the other.

For example, to link the "Car Costs" document with this one, you'll open the "Car Costs" document. Then, you'll begin a formula in cell B7 of the "Sushi Profits" document by typing an equal sign (=) in it. Next, you'll click on the cell containing the Grand Total in the "Car Costs" document to create a reference to it. Finally, you'll press Enter to enter the formula.

You'll open the "Car Costs" document in a moment, but first you'll save the changes you've made so far.

Choose Save from the File menu.

If Save is disabled, you have probably forgotten to press Enter to accept the number "600". Make sure you press Enter before trying to select Save from the File menu.

Because this is a new document, you are asked to name it.

Type "Sushi Profits".

You'll want to keep this document with the "Car Costs" document, so you'll save "Sushi Profits" on the same disk and in the same folder with "Car Costs".

If necessary, click the drive button or use the pop-up menu to select the folder and disk where you have stored the "Car Costs" document. Then, click Save.

Now, you're ready to open the "Car Costs" document.

Choose Open from the File menu.

You are presented with the Open File dialog box. You want to open "Car Costs". If there are many documents on your disk, you might have to use the scroll arrows to see it.

Select the document named "Car Costs". Then, click Open.

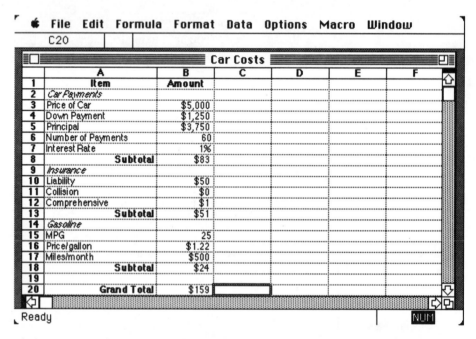

The "Car Costs" document opens on your desktop.

You'll begin your formula on the "Sushi Profits" worksheet, but first you'll have to bring that worksheet to the front. In Excel, when you are working with multiple documents, you can bring a document to the front by selecting it in the Windows menu.

You'll bring "Sushi Profits" to the front now.

Choose "Sushi Profits" from the Window menu.

The "Sushi Profits" document jumps to the front. Next, you'll begin a formula to link the two spreadsheets.

Select cell B7 by clicking on it. Then, type "=".

Now you're ready to link the two spreadsheets. To do this, you'll bring the "Car Costs" worksheet to the front and click in the Grand Total cell.

Choose "Car Costs" from the Window menu.

The "Car Costs" document comes to the front. Now, you'll enter a reference to the cell containing the grand total by clicking on it.

Click on cell B20.

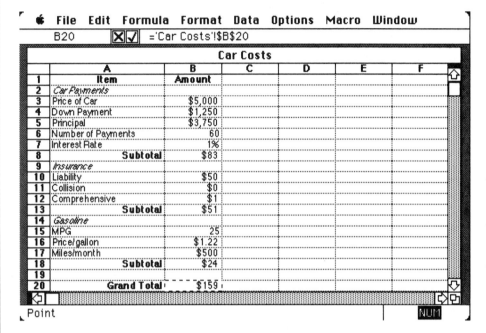

Look in the formula bar. Excel has entered a reference to cell B20, but this reference looks different. It has the text "'Car Costs'!" before it. This tells Excel to look in the "Car Costs" spreadsheet for the value that goes here.

Press Enter to accept the formula.

When you press Enter, Excel brings the original spreadsheet to the front. The cell reference is displayed in the formula bar, and the value from cell B20 in the "Car Costs" document is displayed in the worksheet.

| A1 | ='Car Costs'!B20 |

Sushi Profits

	A	B	C	D	E	F
1		Sushi Dreams Profit Worksheet				
2						
3	Number of Samplers	200				
4						
5	Expenses					
6	Rent	600				
7	Car	158.816679				
8	Raw Materials					
9	Wage Cost					
10	Total Expenses					
11						
12	Income					
13	Sushi Samplers					
14	Total Income					
15						
16	Profit					
17						
18						
19						
20						

Ready   NUM

More Formulas and Numbers

Now, you'll enter numbers for raw materials and wage cost.

You've determined that it will cost you $3.00 in raw materials to produce each sushi sampler; therefore, your monthly raw material cost will be the number of sushi samplers you sell in a month multiplied by three. Next, you'll enter a formula to calculate your monthly raw material cost.

Select cell B8. Then, type "= 3 * ".

Remember that you've already named row 3 as "Number_of_Samplers". By including "Number_of_Samplers" in the formula, you'll add a relative reference to the cell that is at the intersection of row 3 and the column that the current cell is in. In this case, the reference will be to B3.

Choose Paste Name... from the Formula menu and select the name "Number_of_Samplers". When you are done, click OK.

Press Enter to accept this formula.

B8	=3*Number_of_Samplers

Sushi Profits

	A	B	C	D	E	F
1		Sushi Dreams Profit Worksheet				
2						
3	Number of Samplers	200				
4						
5	Expenses					
6	Rent	600				
7	Car	158.816679				
8	Raw Materials	600				
9	Wage Cost					
10	Total Expenses					
11						
12	Income					
13	Sushi Samplers					
14	Total Income					
15						
16	Profit					
17						
18						
19						
20						

Ready   NUM

"600" (3 * 200) appears in cell B8 if you've done everything correctly.

You're ready to enter a formula to calculate your wage cost. Unlike your raw material cost, which depends on the amount of sushi that you sell, your wage cost is a fixed cost; it stays the same every month. In fact, you know that you'll have to hire someone to work 100 hours a month (approximately 25 hours each week), and that you'll pay them $4 an hour.

You could just enter $400 in B9 , because you know that the amount will be fixed. You'll use a formula, however, in case you either have to pay more than $4 an hour to lure people out of the library, or you need to hire more than 25 hours of help per week.

Press the down arrow key to move down one cell to B9. Then, type "= 100 * 4". Finally, press Enter to accept this formula.

You're ready to sum your expenses to obtain a total. You've defined names for the rows containing each of your expenses; therefore, you can use the following formula to calculate their sum:

Total Expenses = Rent + Car + Raw_Materials + Wage_Cost

Press the down arrow key to move down one cell to B10. Then, type "= Rent + Car + Raw_Materials + Wage_Cost".

Note that you can type a name in a formula instead of pasting it in with the Paste Name... command.

Press Enter to accept the formula.

```
 	  File   Edit   Formula   Format   Data   Options   Macro   Window
      B10              =Rent+Car+Raw_Materials+Wage_Cost
```

```
                            Sushi Profits
            A              B          C       D       E       F
 1                 Sushi Dreams Profit Worksheet
 2
 3   Number of Samplers        200
 4
 5          Expenses
 6   Rent                      600
 7   Car              158.816679
 8   Raw Materials             600
 9   Wage Cost                 400
10        Total Expenses  1758.81668
11
12          Income
13   Sushi Samplers
14          Total Income
15
16          Profit
17
18
19
20
```

Ready   NUM

If you've done everything correctly, "1758.81668" appears in cell B10.

If things didn't work out exactly as they should have, don't worry too much. Working with defined names in formulas can be tricky.

If you do get an error message, check to be sure that all of your names have been defined correctly. Also check to make sure that you typed the underscore character in the names for Raw_Materials and Wage_Cost; if you don't type the underscore character, you'll get an error. If all else fails, try redefining names for the rows that you are using, and reentering the formula.

You're ready to enter values for the Income area of your worksheet.

Your only source of income will be from selling sushi samplers. To determine the amount of money you will make from selling sushi, you'll need to know how many samplers you'll sell, and the price you'll receive for each one.

The number of samplers has already been entered (in row 3). Because you've decided to charge $8 for each sushi sampler, your total income will be the number of samplers you sell multiplied by 8. You'll enter a formula to calculate this amount now.

Select cell B13 and type "= 8 * Number_of_Samplers". Press Enter to accept the formula.

"1600" appears in cell B13.

Finally, you'll calculate total income and profit. Because your total income comes from selling sushi samplers, your total income will simply equal sushi income.

Press the down arrow key to move down one row.

The current cell should be B14.

Type "= Sushi_Samplers". Then, press the down arrow twice to enter the formula and move down two rows to cell B16.

You'll make a formula for profit, which is simply total income minus total expenses.

Type "= Total_Income– Total_Expenses". Then, press Enter to accept this formula.

"–158.81668" should appear in cell B16.

```
 File   Edit   Formula   Format   Data   Options   Macro   Window
    B16              =Total_Income-Total_Expenses
```

	A	B	C	D	E	F
1		Sushi Dreams Profit Worksheet				
2						
3	Number of Samplers	200				
4						
5	Expenses					
6	Rent	600				
7	Car	158.816679				
8	Raw Materials	600				
9	Wage Cost	400				
10	Total Expenses	1758.81668				
11						
12	Income					
13	Sushi Samplers	1600				
14	Total Income	1600				
15						
16	Profit	-158.81668				
17						
18						
19						

Ready

Formatting a Group of Cells

Your profit statement is nearly complete. But you'll want to use a dollar format with some of the numbers in your spreadsheet.

It would be faster to format all of the cells at once, but you can't select all of column 2 and then use a dollar format with it because one of the numbers in column 2 (Number_of_Samplers) shouldn't have a dollar format. You'll select the region of cells from rent (row 6) to profit (row 16) now. Then, you'll give all of the cells in the region a dollar format.

Select the region between cell B6 and cell B16.

Remember that to select a region you must:

- Move the pointer on top of the first cell in the region.
- Press and hold the mouse button while dragging through the region to the last cell in the region.
- Release the mouse button.

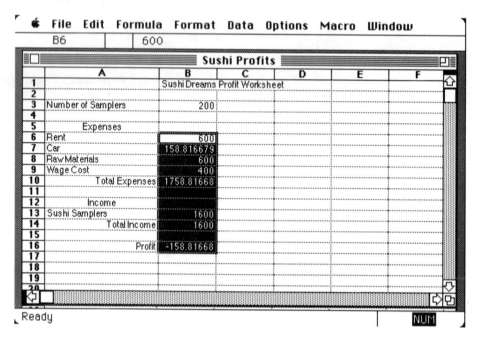

You format numbers with the Number... command from the Format menu.

Choose Number... from the Format menu. Select the $#,##0;($#,##0) format by clicking on it. Then, click OK.

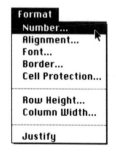

All of the selected cells now have a dollar format. Notice that the result for profit has parentheses around it. That's because your profit was negative. Remember that the $#,##0;($#,##0) format uses parentheses, rather than a minus sign (–), for negative numbers.

You've finished your profit statement for the first month. The results are not good, and it looks like you'll lose money if you go ahead with the business. But there is something important that you've ignored so far. Although you think that you'll only be able to sell 200 samplers the first month, you'll probably be able to sell many more during the second month after more people have heard about your business from friends.

You'll expand your analysis to include figures for the first three months to see how the increase in sales will affect your profits. When you do this, you'll want to include the name of the month at the top of each column.

Inserting a Row

You'll want to insert an extra row to hold the names of the months. Excel allows you to insert a row by selecting the row below where you want the new row and choosing the **Insert...** command. You'll insert a row above row 3 now.

Select row 3 by clicking in its row heading (the number 3 at the left of the screen).

The row is selected and should be highlighted.

Choose Insert... from the Edit menu.

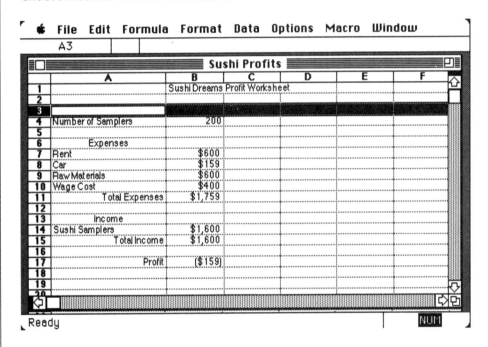

A new row is inserted, and all of the text and numbers below it are shifted down to make room.

Don't worry about any of your references becoming incorrect; Excel will update them for you.

**Entering Column
Headings**

Before entering column headings, you must select the cells where they belong.

Select the region from cell B3 to E3 (by dragging through it).

	File	Edit	Formula	Format	Data	Options	Macro	Window

B3

	A	B	C	D	E	F
1		Sushi Dreams Profit Worksheet				
2						
3						
4	Number of Samplers	200				
5						
6	Expenses					
7	Rent	$600				
8	Car	$159				
9	Raw Materials	$600				
10	Wage Cost	$400				
11	Total Expenses	$1,759				
12						
13	Income					
14	Sushi Samplers	$1,600				
15	Total Income	$1,600				
16						
17	Profit	($159)				
18						
19						
20						

Ready   NUM

Now, you'll enter the column headings.

Type "January", press Enter, type "February", press Enter, type "March", press Enter. You should now be at cell E3. Type "Total" and press Enter to accept this fourth label.

Note that if you use the right arrow key instead of Enter, the four cells will be deselected. Reselect them and start over.

You'll want center alignment for these headings.

With the region still selected, choose Alignment... from the Format menu. When the dialog box appears, select Center for alignment. Then, click OK.

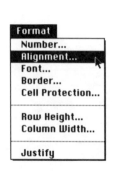

Format
Number...
Alignment...
Font...
Border...
Cell Protection...

Row Height...
Column Width...

Justify

| B3 | | January |

Sushi Profits

	A	B	C	D	E	F
1		Sushi Dreams Profit Worksheet				
2						
3		January	February	March	Total	
4	Number of Samplers	200				
5						
6	Expenses					
7	Rent	$600				
8	Car	$159				
9	Raw Materials	$600				
10	Wage Cost	$400				
11	Total Expenses	$1,759				
12						
13	Income					
14	Sushi Samplers	$1,600				
15	Total Income	$1,600				
16						
17	Profit	($159)				
18						
19						
20						

Ready

NUM

Filling Formulas

You're ready to copy the formulas in column 2, but don't worry, you won't have to type in all of the formulas and numbers again, or even paste them one at a time. Using the **Fill Right** command, you'll be able to copy the formulas and numbers for January into the columns for February and March.

To use Fill Right, you first must select the area that will be filled, as well as the area that you will fill it with.

Move the pointer to cell B4, press the mouse button, and drag down and to the right to cell D17. Then, release the mouse button.

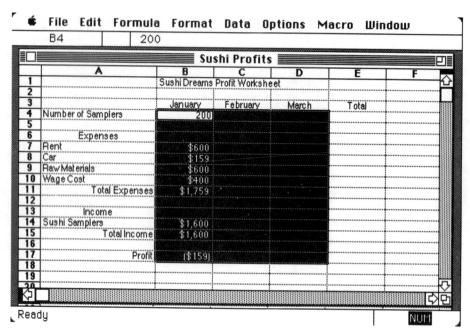

The region is selected and should be highlighted.

Now, you'll fill the columns for February and March with the numbers and formulas for January.

Choose Fill Right from the Edit menu.

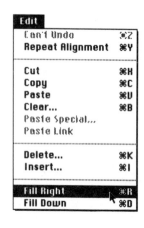

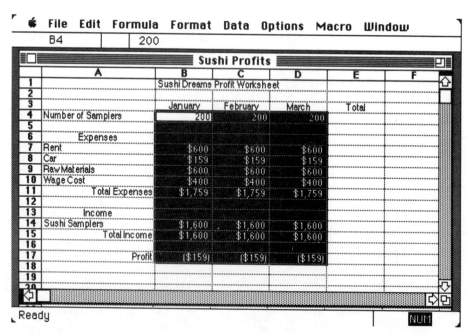

All of the formulas you've defined are copied, turning a one-month projection into a three-month projection. As soon as you change the values for the samplers you expect to sell in February and March, you'll have a three-month profit forecast.

Click on C4 to select it. Then, type "300". Press the right arrow to move to D4. Then, type "400" . Finally, press Enter to accept the number.

Note that when there is something in an Excel cell, you can change it by simply selecting the cell and typing the new information.

Look at your profit now. You see that the profit forecast is very different when you are selling more samplers!

You'll calculate three-month totals for expenses, income, and profit now, but first, you'll define names for columns 2, 3, and 4.

Click on Column B in its column heading (click on the letter B at the top of the column).

The entire column is selected, and should be highlighted.

	File	**Edit**	**Formula**	**Format**	**Data**	**Options**	**Macro**	**Window**

| B1 | | | Sushi Dreams Profit Worksheet | | | |

Sushi Profits

	A	B	C	D	E	F
1		Sushi Dreams	Profit Worksheet			
2						
3		January	February	March	Total	
4	Number of Samplers	200	300	400		
5						
6	Expenses					
7	Rent	$600	$600	$600		
8	Car	$159	$159	$159		
9	Raw Materials	$600	$900	$1,200		
10	Wage Cost	$400	$400	$400		
11	Total Expenses	$1,759	$2,059	$2,359		
12						
13	Income					
14	Sushi Samplers	$1,600	$2,400	$3,200		
15	Total Income	$1,600	$2,400	$3,200		
16						
17	Profit	($159)	$341	$841		
18						
19						
20						

Ready   NUM

Choose Define Name... from the Formula menu. When the dialog box appears, type "January" for the name of column B, then click OK.

You'll also want to define names for columns C and D.

Use the procedure outlined above to define the names "February" and "March" for column C and column D, respectively.

Next, you'll calculate quarterly totals for your expenses, income, and profit. To do this, you'll calculate the three-month sum for Number_of_Samplers, and then use the Fill Down command to copy the formula for each of your expenses, income, and profit. Note that the quarterly total is simply the value for January plus the value for February plus the value for March.

Click on cell E4 to select it. Then, type "=January + February + March". When you are finished, press Enter to accept the formula.

	File	Edit	Formula	Format	Data	Options	Macro	Window
E4			=January+February+March					

Sushi Profits

	A	B	C	D	E	F
1		Sushi Dreams Profit Worksheet				
2						
3		January	February	March	Total	
4	Number of Samplers	200	300	400	900	
5						
6	Expenses					
7	Rent	$600	$600	$600		
8	Car	$159	$159	$159		
9	Raw Materials	$600	$900	$1,200		
10	Wage Cost	$400	$400	$400		
11	Total Expenses	$1,759	$2,059	$2,359		
12						
13	Income					
14	Sushi Samplers	$1,600	$2,400	$3,200		
15	Total Income	$1,600	$2,400	$3,200		
16						
17	Profit	($159)	$341	$841		
18						
19						
20						

Ready

NUM

Using the Fill Down Command

"900" appears in E4. You could go through all of your expenses, and then your income, and finally your profit, and for each one type in this formula, but that would be very tedious. Fortunately, there is a better way.

You can use the **Fill Down** command to copy a formula from one cell to a group of cells directly underneath it. To use the Fill Down command, you select the cell that contains the formula, and the cells in which you'd like to put a copy of the formula. Then, you choose Fill Down from the Edit menu.

In this case, you want to copy the formula in cell E4.

You'll use the Fill Down command now to copy the formula in E4, but first, you'll select the cells which should contain a copy of the formula.

Select the region from cell E4 to cell E17 (by dragging through it).

File Edit Formula Format Data Options Macro Window

E4 | =January+February+March

Sushi Profits

	A	B	C	D	E	F
1		Sushi Dreams Profit Worksheet				
2						
3		January	February	March	Total	
4	Number of Samplers	200	300	400	900	
5						
6	Expenses					
7	Rent	$600	$600	$600		
8	Car	$159	$159	$159		
9	Raw Materials	$600	$900	$1,200		
10	Wage Cost	$400	$400	$400		
11	Total Expenses	$1,759	$2,059	$2,359		
12						
13	Income					
14	Sushi Samplers	$1,600	$2,400	$3,200		
15	Total Income	$1,600	$2,400	$3,200		
16						
17	Profit	($159)	$341	$841		
18						
19						

Ready   NUM

Now, you'll use the Fill Down command to copy the formula in the first cell of the region (E4) to the rest of the cells in the region.

Choose Fill Down from the Edit menu.

Edit	
Undo Entry	⌘Z
Repeat Fill Right	⌘Y
Cut	⌘H
Copy	⌘C
Paste	⌘U
Clear...	⌘B
Paste Special...	
Paste Link	
Delete...	⌘K
Insert...	⌘I
Fill Right	⌘R
Fill Down	⌘D

File Edit Formula Format Data Options Macro Window

E4 | =January+February+March

Sushi Profits

	A	B	C	D	E	F
1		Sushi Dreams Profit Worksheet				
2						
3		January	February	March	Total	
4	Number of Samplers	200	300	400	900	
5					0	
6	Expenses				0	
7	Rent	$600	$600	$600	1800	
8	Car	$159	$159	$159	476.450036	
9	Raw Materials	$600	$900	$1,200	2700	
10	Wage Cost	$400	$400	$400	1200	
11	Total Expenses	$1,759	$2,059	$2,359	6176.45004	
12					0	
13	Income				0	
14	Sushi Samplers	$1,600	$2,400	$3,200	7200	
15	Total Income	$1,600	$2,400	$3,200	7200	
16					0	
17	Profit	($159)	$341	$841	1023.54996	
18						
19						

Ready   NUM

The formula is copied, and the correct monthly total appears in all of the cells of the region. Note, however, that for each row that has blank cells in the second, third, and fourth columns, a "0" appears in column 6. You'll remove the un-wanted zeros now.

Clear each of the cells in column E which contain "0".

To clear a cell you must:

- Select the cell.
- Press Delete.

You'll want to use a dollar format with all of the cells in column E except E4. You'll format all of these cells at once now by first selecting the region that contains them, and then using the Number... command from the Format menu.

Select the region from E7 to E17 (by dragging through it).

	🍎	File	Edit	Formula	Format	Data	Options	Macro	Window		
	E7			=January+February+March							

Sushi Profits

	A	B	C	D	E	F
1		Sushi Dreams Profit Worksheet				
2						
3		January	February	March	Total	
4	Number of Samplers	200	300	400	900	
5						
6	Expenses					
7	Rent	$600	$600	$600	1800	
8	Car	$159	$159	$159	476.450036	
9	Raw Materials	$600	$900	$1,200	2700	
10	Wage Cost	$400	$400	$400	1200	
11	Total Expenses	$1,759	$2,059	$2,359	6176.45004	
12						
13	Income					
14	Sushi Samplers	$1,600	$2,400	$3,200	7200	
15	Total Income	$1,600	$2,400	$3,200	7200	
16						
17	Profit	($159)	$341	$841	1023.54996	
18						
19						

Ready

Choose Number... from the Format menu. Select the $#,##0;($#,##0) format by clicking on it. Then, click OK.

Using "What If?" Analysis

According to your projections, you'll make $1024 in the first three months that you sell sushi. But what if your projections are wrong? You'll use "What If?" analysis now to see how much your profit projection changes if some of your estimates are not accurate.

First, you'll see what happens if you only sell 300 samplers in March.

Select cell D4. Then, type "300" and press Enter to accept the change.

Your quarterly profit plummets to $524!

Let's try another. What if you can buy that rusty old Buick for $2000 instead of $5000? You'll see how this would affect your profit forecast now by bringing the "Car Costs" document to the front, changing the value, and then looking at how that change is reflected on the "Sushi Profits" worksheet.

Choose Car Costs from the Window menu.

```
 🍎  File  Edit  Formula  Format  Data  Options  Macro  Window
        B20              =Car_Payment+Insurance+Gasoline
```

	A	B	C	D	E	F
1	Item	Amount				
2	Car Payments					
3	Price of Car	$5,000				
4	Down Payment	$1,250				
5	Principal	$3,750				
6	Number of Payments	60				
7	Interest Rate	1%				
8	Subtotal	$83				
9	Insurance					
10	Liability	$50				
11	Collision	$0				
12	Comprehensive	$1				
13	Subtotal	$51				
14	Gasoline					
15	MPG	25				
16	Price/gallon	$1.22				
17	Miles/month	$500				
18	Subtotal	$24				
19						
20	Grand Total	$159				

Ready   NUM

The "Car Costs" document appears. Next, you'll change the cost of the car to $2000.

Select cell B3 by clicking on it. Then, type "2000". Finally, press Enter to accept the change.

Notice that the monthly cost of operating the car has declined from $159 to $109. Now, you'll see how this change has affected your profits.

Choose Sushi Profits from the Window menu.

Excel automatically updated the linked values. Your quarterly profit has increased to $674. Now you understand the power of spreadsheet linking. It allows you to combine information from multiple documents and to update the information automatically when the values on any document change.

Finishing Up

You're finished now, but before quitting, you'll print and save your worksheet.

Printing

Make sure that your printer is chosen correctly, turned on, and ready to print.

Choose Print... from the File menu.

You are presented with the Print dialog box. If you'd like multiple copies, type the number.

When you're ready to print your spreadsheet, click OK.

You'll also print a copy of your worksheet with the formulas displayed. First you'll set Excel to display formulas.

Choose Display... from the Options menu. When the dialog box appears, click in the box labeled "Formulas". Then, click OK.

Now you'll print a second copy of your worksheet with the formulas displayed.

Choose Print... from the File menu. If you want more than one copy of your worksheet, type the number. Then, click OK.

Because formulas take up more room, they'll print on two pages.

Quitting

Now, you'll save your final document and return to the desktop.

Choose Save from the file menu. Then, choose Quit from the File menu.

Excel asks if you want to save changes in the "Car Costs" document. You certainly want to do that.

Click Yes.

You are returned safely to the Macintosh desktop.

Review

You've now finished the Advanced Excel module, in which you've learned:

- How to link spreadsheets so they will share information
- How to name rows and columns and use names for rows and columns in formulas
- How to format a group of cells by changing their alignment
- How to insert rows into the worksheet
- How to "Fill" formulas to avoid typing the same formulas many times

What to Turn In

Turn in a copy of both of your spreadsheets: "Car Costs" and "Sushi Profits." Also turn in a copy of the formulas that you printed for the "Sushi Profits" document.

Checkbook Register

	Balance:	2,522.84				
No.	Date	Desc. of transaction	(-) pymnt.	√	(+) deposit	Balance
		Start		√	2,000.00	2000.00
201	6/28/90	Pacific Bell	25.00	√		1975.00
202	6/28/90	Toys "R" Us	15.00			1960.00
203	6/29/90	Marie Thornton (rent)	300.00	√		1660.00
-	7/9/90	Deposit		√	162.68	1822.68
204	7/11/90	Parking ticket (ugh)	10.00	√		1812.68
205	7/13/90	Donut King	15.00	√		1797.68
206	7/13/90	Kairos House	15.00	√		1782.68
207	7/18/90	Parking ticket	10.00			1772.68
-	7/18/90	Interest			4.40	1777.08
208	7/23/90	The Tofu Times	88.60			1688.48
-	7/22/90	Deposit			369.36	2057.84
209	7/23/90	Parking ticket	10.00			2047.84
210	7/24/90	Pacific Bell	30.00			2017.84
211	7/29/90	Marie Thornton (rent)	300.00			1717.84
212	8/2/90	Super Donuts	25.00			1692.84
-	8/3/90	Withdrawal	40.00			1652.84
-	8/3/90	Deposit			1,005.00	2657.84
213	8/15/90	Pizza Hut	25.00			2632.84
214	8/16/90	Parking ticket	10.00			2622.84
217	8/20/90	Haagen-Daz	100.00			2522.84

Description

Using Microsoft Excel, this spreadsheet was created to replace the checkbook register found in every checkbook.

The SUM( ) function was used to calculate the balance and display it at the top of the spreadsheet.

Fill Down was used to copy the same formula into all of the cells in the "Balance" column. The IF( ) function was used to display a number in the "Balance" column only when something had been entered in the "No." column.

Grade Sheet

Grades for History 101: "The History of Pine Valley"

Name	Test 1	Test 2	Test 3	Final Grade
Bogart, Kent	67	87	84	79.3
Bogart, Lars	93	98	99	96.7
Colby, Liza	100	34	90	74.7
Cortlandt, Daisy	99	80	76	85.0
Cortlandt, Nina	50	52	100	67.3
Cortlandt, Palmer	100	100	100	100.0
Cudahy, Tom	80	75	72	75.7
Dalton, Mark	90	87	88	88.3
Gardner, Jenny	99	89	100	96.0
Gardner, Opal	10	12	15	12.3
Hubbard, Angie	100	100	99	99.7
Hubbard, Jessie	90	80	70	80.0
Kane, Erica	75	80	84	79.7
Kincaid, Rick	80	79	80	79.7
Martin, Joe	100	98	95	97.7
Martin, Ruth	70	72	75	72.3
Martin, Tad	50	60	70	60.0
Nelson, Enid	56	87	99	80.7
Nelson, Greg	89	88	80	85.7
Sago, Benny	89	78	76	81.0
Sago, Estelle	50	80	79	69.7
Sloan, Jasper	100	100	100	100.0
Tyler, Phoebe	80	84	83	82.3
Wallingford, Langley	0	12	5	5.7
Average	75.7	75.5	80.0	77.1
Standard Deviation	27.7	24.9	24.0	23.6

Lowest Final Grade	5.7
Highest Final Grade	100.0
Number of Students	24.0

There was at least one perfect score.

At least one person failed.

Description

This spreadsheet uses several Excel functions to calculate statistical information for a group of students who are in the same class. To make creating functions easier, names were given to the four regions in the columns which contain test scores and final grades.

The AVERAGE( ) and STDDEV( ) functions were used to calculate the average and the standard deviation for each of the tests and the final grade. The highest and lowest grades in the class were calculated using the functions MAX( ) and MIN( ). Finally, the COUNT( ) function was used to count the number of students in the class, and the conditional function IF( ) was used to print out a message if there were either any perfect scores or if anyone failed.

1. What is a formula? How do formulas make electronic spreadsheets more useful?

2. What is a function, and how do functions make spreadsheets more useful?

3. Explain what it means for a function to require one or more arguments. Give examples of Excel functions that require arguments.

4. What is the difference between an absolute reference and a relative reference? When is one preferred over the other?

5. What is "What If?" analysis? How is it used?

6. In the Introduction to Microsoft Excel module, you created a spreadsheet to calculate the cost of operating a car. One of the expenses you calculated was the monthly payment. The formula you used generated a single number for the payment. However, you might want to know how much of each payment is interest on the loan balance, and how much is reducing the loan balance. A table that contains this information is called an **amortization schedule.** Amortization schedules are useful for preparing taxes because interest payments are often deductible expenses.

Create an amortization schedule for your car loan. The amortization schedule should include five columns. Column 1 will contain the payment number—0 through 60—with 0 signifying the original loan balance. Column 2 should include the amount of the payment from the "Car Costs" document. Column 3 should include the amount that is interest on the previous loan balance, Column 4 contains the amount of the payment that is applied to the loan balance, and Column 5 contains the new loan balance.

When you are finished, the first two rows of your spreadsheet should look like the one shown below. Be sure to use links to the "Car Costs" document wherever possible.

	A	B	C	D	E
			Amortization Schedule		
1		Interest Rate:	1.0%		
2	#	PMT	Interest	Principal	Balance
3	0				1,500
4	1	33	15	18	1,482
5					
6					
7					

7. Do a "What If?" analysis with your amortization schedule to see how your interest payments change when the cost of the car climbs from $2000 to $5000. Then, try the same "What If?" with a car cost of $10,000.

8. The NOW( ) function gives the current date and time. (The NOW( ) function takes no arguments.) Use the NOW( ) function to update the "Checkbook Register" gallery document so that it displays the current date underneath the current balance.

Hint: Be sure to choose the correct number format for the cell that contains the NOW( ) function.

9. Create a spreadsheet to calculate grade point averages. The spreadsheet should contain the following information for each class: the class name, the grade received, and the total units. From this, you can calculate the grade points for each class by multiplying the grade received by the number of units. Then, calculate the grade point average by summing the grade points for all classes, and dividing by the total number of units.

10. Create a spreadsheet to calculate the cost of enrolling in school for one year.

11. Create a spreadsheet to calculate the costs of throwing a party. Include expenses for refreshments, live entertainment (we can dream, can't we), and clean up. Do a "What If?" analysis on the spreadsheet to see how your total cost changes if you don't have live entertainment.

12. Create a spreadsheet to calculate the costs of traveling to Europe. Be sure to include costs in the currency of the local country. Use "What If?" analysis to figure your total cost in dollars based on several different exchange rates.

13. Generally, interest rates for car loans, mortgages, and so on are quoted at an annualized percentage rate (APR). If the payments are made more frequently than once a year, however, the effective annual yield is higher. For example, $100 invested at 12% compounded annually grows to $112 at the end of one year. Compounded monthly, you would have more than $112 because, for every month after the first, you'd be earning interest on the interest you earned in previous months.

Use Excel to create a spreadsheet that calculates the growth of a $1000 investment over one year if the APR is 10%, but interest is compounded monthly. When you are finished, your spreadsheet should look like the one shown on the next page.

Interest		
	A	B
1	APR:	10%
2	Period	Amount
3	0	$1,000
4	1	$1,008
5	2	$1,017
6	3	$1,025
7	4	$1,034
8	5	$1,042
9	6	$1,051
10	7	$1,060
11	8	$1,069
12	9	$1,078
13	10	$1,087
14	11	$1,096
15	12	$1,105

Hint: If you use the Fill Down command, be sure to use an absolute reference for the interest rate.

14. To calculate the yield on an investment, you use the formula:

Yield = (Beginning Value + Increase in Value)/Beginning Value

Add a formula to calculate the yield on the investment described in the last exercise.

15. In the previous exercise, you used Excel to calculate the effective annual yield on a one year, $1000, investment with an annual percentage rate (APR) of 10%. Use Excel to create an "effective interest rate calculator." That will work for any interest rate and any frequency of compounding. When you are finished, your spreadsheet should look like the one shown here:

Annualized Interest Rates		
	A	B
1	Initial Amount:	$1,000
2	Annual Percentage Rate:	10.0%
3	#Times Interest Compounded/Year	365
4	Future Value:	$1,105
5	Effective Annual Yield:	10.52%
6		

You should use the FV( ) function in your spreadsheet. The FV( ) function computes the **future value** of an investment; that is, it computes the growth in value of an investment over a period of time at a given interest rate. The FV( ) function takes four arguments: the interest rate per period, the number of periods, the payment paid per period (in this example, 0), and the **present value** (the amount you start with).

5 Charts

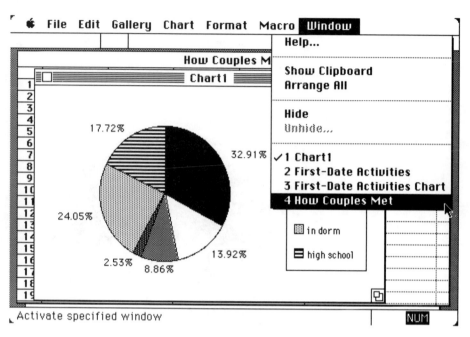

About Charts

Because spreadsheets make numerical calculations fast and easy, computer users have the power to generate huge tables of numbers in the time it would originally have taken to complete a single calculation. But generating numbers is one thing, and understanding what they mean is quite another. With all these numbers available, it becomes important to be able to present them in a way that can be quickly and clearly understood.

Chart-making applications are designed to take a mountain of numbers and create charts and graphs that convey the information in a clearer, more easily understood way. When a group of numbers is presented graphically using a bar or line chart, for example, it's often easier to spot trends and summarize the overall situation quickly. Charts can clarify meaning and add impact to an otherwise confusing set of numbers. In short, chart-making applications can make a picture that's worth a thousand words (or numbers).

Of course you could use a graphics application like MacPaint to create a chart or graph. But the magic of a chart-making application is that it makes the artwork easy. In many cases, you simply enter the numbers you want to plot and choose the type of graph you'd like. The application does the rest.

What's more, chart-making applications make it easy to update your graphs with updated data. If the numbers that you're graphing change, you can change your chart just as quickly. Try that when you're graphing with a pencil and paper.

Also, in many cases, chart-making applications are integrated with spreadsheets so that changing a number in the spreadsheet updates the graph instantly.

About Microsoft Excel

Microsoft Excel can be used to create charts as well as spreadsheets. Excel's charting functions are completely integrated with its spreadsheet functions. When you create a chart in Excel, it's automatically linked to the underlying spreadsheet. That way, if you change any of the numbers in the spreadsheet, Excel will update the chart automatically.

Once you create the chart, you can use Excel to format it in many different ways. You can choose from several chart types, including bar graphs, pie charts, and scatter diagrams. You can add a legend to make the chart more easy to understand, and you can even add a title or a label for one of the axes.

Once you've formatted the chart the way you want, you can copy it and paste it into another document, such as a term paper, to help make your point more forcefully.

Microsoft Excel

The Task

For your Social Psychology project on interpersonal relations, your group has just finished its survey on dating patterns at your school. The results are in, and now they need to be summarized graphically for your final presentation. You'll need two different charts. But rather than laboriously drawing them by hand, you decide to let Microsoft Excel be your graphic artist.

In the first chart you create, you'll learn the basics of creating charts with Microsoft Excel. You'll use the techniques you learned in the spreadsheet chapter to enter data, and you'll learn how to plot it in a number of different chart types.

In the second chart, you'll compare two sets of data by plotting them both on the same set of axes. You'll also use Excel's creative formatting capabilities to customize your chart.

When you are finished, your charts should look like those shown on the next two pages.

How Couples Met Chart

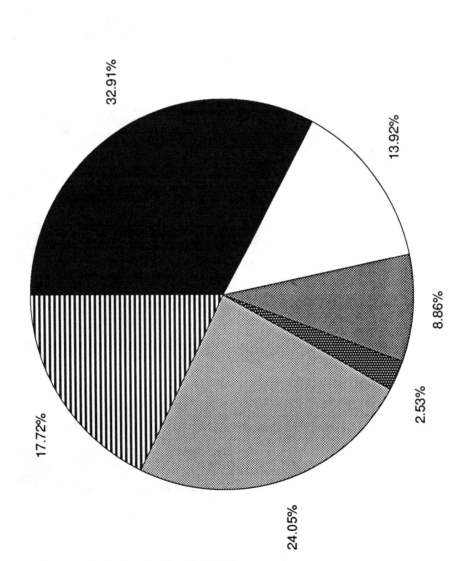

32.91%

13.92%

8.86%

2.53%

24.05%

17.72%

Through friends
In classes
At parties
Blind date
In dorm
High school

Page 1

First Date Chart

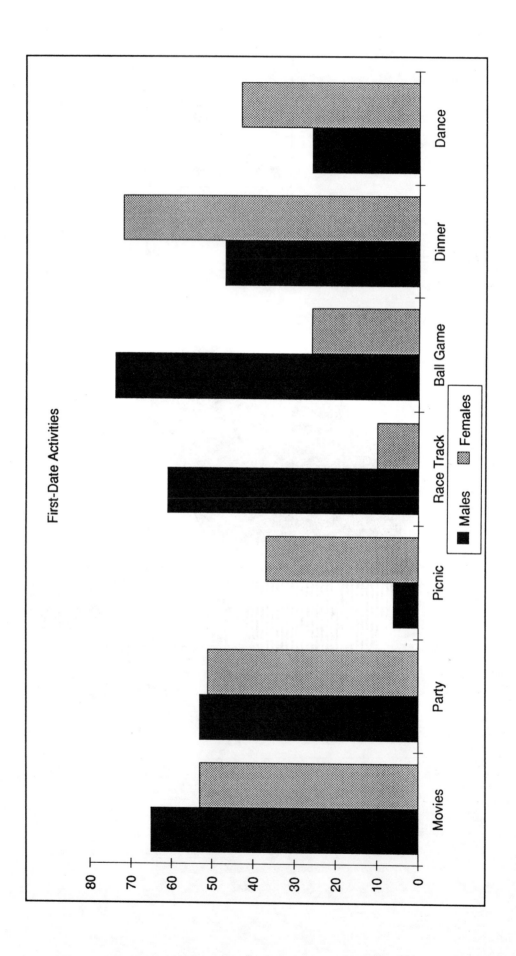

First-Date Activities

Getting Started

Microsoft Excel

Categories, Values And Series

Complete both of the spreadsheet modules in Chapter 4.

Many of the concepts explained in the spreadsheet modules will also be used to complete this chart module.

First, you'll start from the Macintosh Desktop.

Turn on the Macintosh. If you are not using a hard disk, insert the startup diskette in the internal diskette drive.

Soon, you'll see the Macintosh desktop.

Next, you'll open Excel.

If you are using a hard disk, find the Excel icon and double-click on it to open Excel.

If you do not have a hard disk, insert the Excel program disk, wait for the disk icon to appear, and double-click on the Excel icon to open the application.

Excel creates a new, untitled document for you.

You will use Full Menus in this module.

If necessary, choose Full Menus from the Options menu.

Remember that if Excel is already displaying full menus, the Full Menus command will not appear in the Options menu. Instead, the Short Menus command will appear, and you don't need to do anything.

There are three steps you'll use to create each of your charts, they are:

- Enter the data into an Excel spreadsheet.
- Use the New... command to create a chart.
- Format the chart.

You'll enter the data for your first chart now, but first a few words about chart components.

A **data point** is a piece of information that consists of a **category** and a **value.** For example, if you were collecting data on how couples first meet, then the number of couples who met through friends would be a data point. In this case, the category is "through friends" and the value is the number of couples who met that way.

A **data series** is a group of data points. When you create a chart with Excel, the categories are plotted along the horizontal or X-axis, while the values are plotted along the vertical or Y-axis. Excel takes a data series and plots it.

The population of the United States over ten years is an example of a data series. In this case, each data point would be made up of a year (the category) and the population in that year (the value).

The first chart you create will plot the number of couples who first met each other in various places. In this case, each data point consists of a place (the category) and a number of couples who met there (the value). Together, these data points make a data series.

You'll enter your first data series in a moment, but first you'll increase the size of column A to hold your text labels.

Double the width of column A.

Remember that to change the width of a column, you

- Move the pointer over the border of the column; the pointer will change shape to show a double arrow.
- Click and drag the column to the right or left to change its width.

Entering Data

The first step to creating any chart in Excel is entering the data in a spreadsheet.

You'll enter the data for your first chart now by listing each of the possible categories in column A and each of the associated values in column B.

Type in the data shown in the following window.

```
 ┌ ──────────────────────────────────────────────────────────────┐
 │  ⌘  File  Edit  Formula  Format  Data  Options  Macro  Window  │
 │     ┌───────────┬──────┐                                        │
 │     │ B7        │      │                                        │
```

	A	B	C	D	E
1	Through friends	26			
2	In classes	11			
3	At parties	7			
4	Blind date	2			
5	In dorm	19			
6	High school	14			
7					
8					
9					
10					
11					
12					
13					
14					
15					
16					
17					
18					

Worksheet1

Ready — NUM

If you make a mistake while entering the data, use the editing techniques you learned in the Excel spreadsheet modules to correct the mistake.

You'll create your first chart in a moment, but first you'll save the data you've entered.

Choose Save from the File menu.

You are presented with a dialog box asking you to name your document.

Type "How Couples Met" to name your document. Then, click Save.

Creating a Chart

You've entered all the data. Next you're ready to create the chart. You create a chart in Excel by first selecting the data you want to chart, and then choosing New... from the File menu.

Select the data you just entered by clicking on cell A1 and dragging down and to the right to cell B6. Then, release the mouse button.

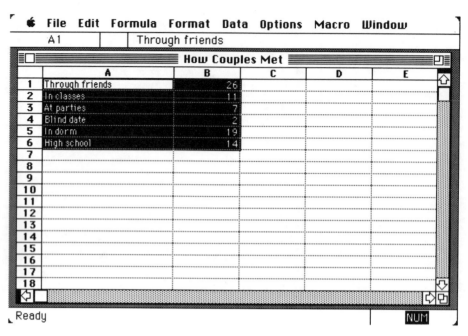

The data is selected and should be highlighted.

Choose New... from the File menu.

You are presented with a dialog box asking you what kind of new document you want to create. You worked with worksheets in the two previous Excel modules, and you're about to work with charts in this one.

Select chart. Then, click OK.

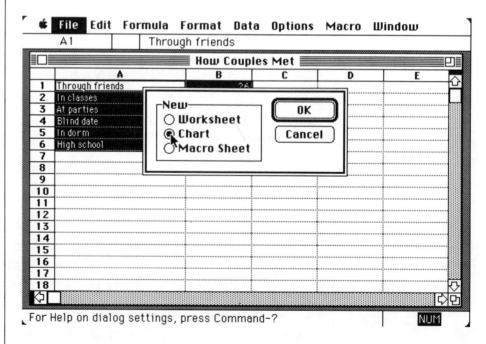

In a few seconds, a column chart appears in the chart window. Wasn't that easy?

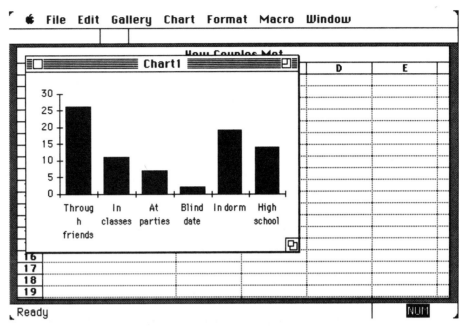

There are many types of charts, and each type conveys information in a different way. In fact, determining the best type of chart for a particular data series depends on the type of data and the intended audience.

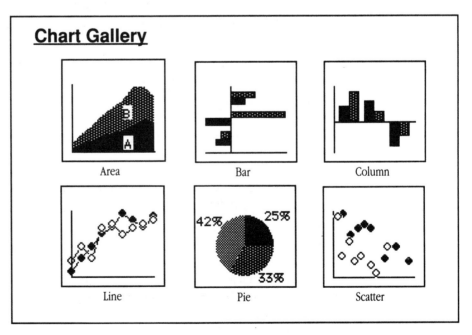

Excel can create six types of charts: **area, bar, column, line, pie, and scatter.** If you are plotting more than one data series, Excel can also create a combination chart.

Each of these chart types has a number of variations available. In a moment, you'll work with some of these variations.

The Gallery Menu

Excel's preselected, or **default** chart type is a column chart. If you don't specify a chart type, Excel will automatically choose a column format.

Take a look at the chart you've created. As a column chart, it gives you an idea of which types of meetings were more popular than others. But it doesn't give a very good picture of what percentage of couples met in the various ways. To determine which type of chart expresses your data best, you'll experiment with some different types.

The Gallery menu shows the available chart types and allows you to change types with a simple click of the mouse.

Choose Bar... from the Gallery menu.

The Bar Chart Gallery appears with one variation preselected.

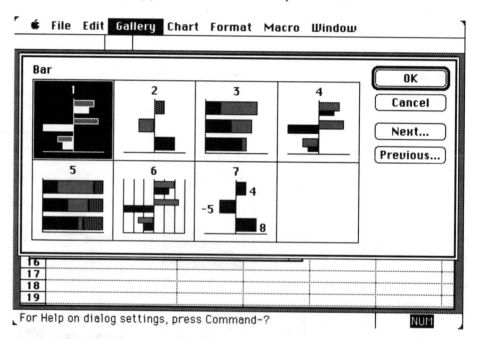

Each Chart Gallery gives you a choice of several variations on a chosen chart type. The differences (some are subtle) are reflected in the numbered pictures.

The column and bar chart formats are quite similar in how they present data, so perhaps the bar chart isn't the best choice for this data either.

Click Cancel.

Because the pie chart calculates percentages for you, it is probably best suited to showing what proportion of couples met in the various ways.

Choose Pie... from the Gallery menu.

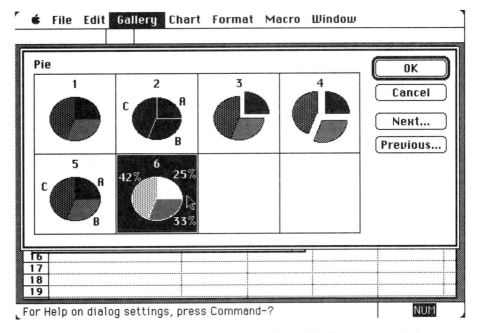

The Pie Chart Gallery appears with a number of possible formats. You'll choose the format that displays the percentages next to each pie wedge. You choose a format by clicking in the picture of the chart with the desired format.

Select the #6 variation by clicking on it. Then, click OK.

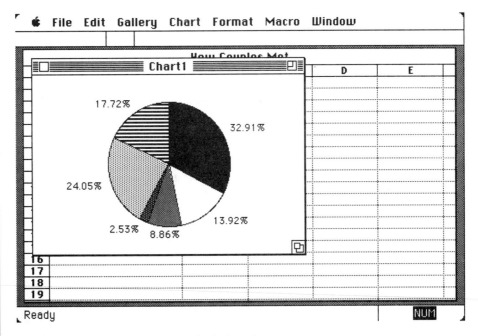

Now you have a pie chart instead of a bar chart.

Formatting Charts

Now that you've created the type of chart that you want, you can use some of Excel's formatting functions to make it look better and present information more effectively.

Using Legends

Though Excel calculated and displayed the percentages for the data, it's impossible to tell which pie wedge represents which category without referring to the spreadsheet. Don't worry, Excel allows you to add a chart guide, called a **legend**, that matches each pie wedge with its corresponding category label.

Choose Add Legend from the Chart menu.

The legend is added automatically.

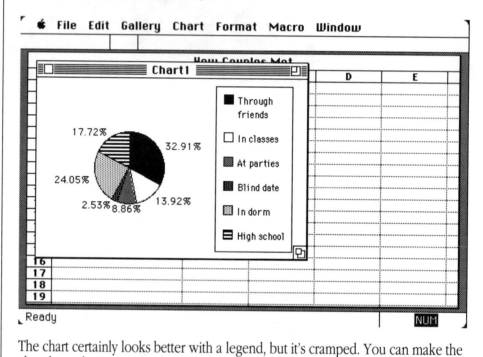

Resizing

The chart certainly looks better with a legend, but it's cramped. You can make the chart larger by increasing the size of the window it's in.

You'll increase the size of your chart now.

Click the zoom box of the chart window.

The chart window expands to fill the entire screen, and the chart resizes automatically to fit the window.

Note that you can also change the size of the chart by clicking and dragging the size box.

Changing Fonts

Before you save and print your chart, you'll change the font to Helvetica so that the chart will look good when printed on either an Apple ImageWriter or LaserWriter printer.

First you'll select the entire chart so you can format the whole thing at once.

Choose Select Chart from the Chart menu.

The white boxes outlining the chart indicate that it's selected.

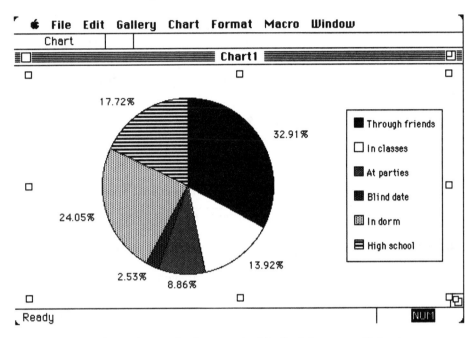

Now you're ready to change the font used with all of the text to Helvetica.

Choose Font... from the Format menu.

A dialog box appears.

Click on Helvetica to select that font. Then, click OK.

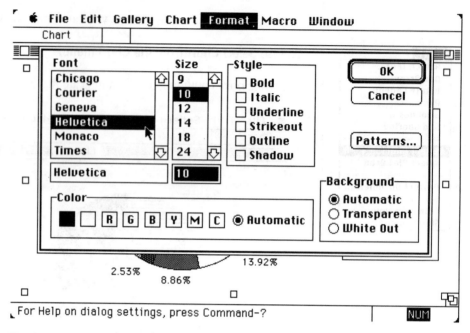

Congratulations!

You've now created your first chart. You'll print it, save it, and move on.

Page Setup

Before printing a chart, you can set up a special format for the page. By choosing a wide orientation, you can make the chart fill the entire page. You can also add special headers or footers—text that will appear on the top or bottom of the page.

Choose Page Setup... from the File menu.

The Page Setup dialog box appears, displaying various options. If you are using an ImageWriter printer, your screen will look slightly different.

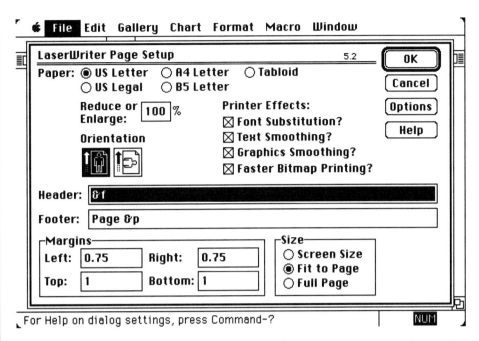

 File Edit Gallery Chart Format Macro Window

LaserWriter Page Setup   5.2   [OK]

Paper: ⦿ US Letter   ○ A4 Letter   ○ Tabloid   [Cancel]
       ○ US Legal   ○ B5 Letter
                                                              [Options]
Reduce or [100] %   **Printer Effects:**
Enlarge: ⊠ Font Substitution?   [Help]
                      ⊠ Text Smoothing?
Orientation   ⊠ Graphics Smoothing?
                      ⊠ Faster Bitmap Printing?

Header: &f

Footer: Page &p

┌─Margins─────────────────────────┐ ┌─Size───────────┐
│ Left: [0.75]   Right: [0.75]   │ │ ○ Screen Size │
│   │ │ ⦿ Fit to Page │
│ Top: [1]   Bottom: [1]   │ │ ○ Full Page   │
└─────────────────────────────────┘ └────────────────┘

For Help on dialog settings, press Command-?   [NUM]

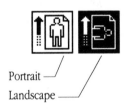

Portrait ——
Landscape ——

This Page Setup dialog box is similar to the one that you saw in the Excel spreadsheet modules. Because the chart is wider than it is tall, you'll select landscape orientation.

Saving

Select Landscape orientation. Then, click OK.

Now, you're ready to save this chart, print it, and move on.

Choose Save from the File menu.

A dialog box appears asking you to name your chart.

Type "How Couples Met Chart" and click Save.

Remember that you named the spreadsheet for this chart "How Couples Met". By using a similar name for the chart, you'll be able to remember which documents are linked.

In a few seconds, your chart will be saved on your disk.

You'll print your chart and then move on.

Printing

Make sure your printer is chosen correctly, turned on, and ready to print.

Choose Print... from the File menu.

The Print dialog box appears.

If you'd like multiple copies, type the number of copies you want.

Click OK to confirm your print settings.

In a few seconds, your document will begin to print.

Closing

You won't need your first chart again, so you can close it.

Choose Close from the File menu.

Your chart disappears, and the "How Couples Met Data" spreadsheet comes to the front. You'll close it too.

Choose Close from the File menu.

If you have inadvertantly made any changes to the document, Excel will ask if you want to save changes. Click No.

Rest

This is a natural stopping place in the module, so you may want to take a break.

Using Multiple Data Series

Now that you're familiar with the basics of Excel charts, you're ready to do some more advanced work. Your second chart will be a comparison between males' and females' responses for which activities they prefer for a first date. You'll have two data series. The categories will be the activity and the values will be the percentage of favorable responses to the activity.

Entering Data

First, you'll create a worksheet, then you'll type in the data, and finally you'll create and format the chart.

You'll create a new worksheet now.

Choose New... from the File menu.

A dialog box appears asking you what kind of document you want to create.

Select Worksheet. Then, click OK.

A new, untitled worksheet appears. You're ready to type your data.

Using the techniques that you learned in the Excel spreadsheet modules, type in the data so it appears as shown in the following window.

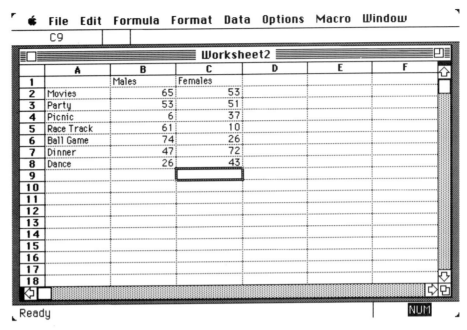

You're almost ready to create your chart, but first you'll save the data.

Choose Save from the File menu.

A dialog box appears asking you to name the worksheet.

Type "First Date" to name your worksheet. Then, click Save.

Now, you're ready to create your chart.

Select the data by clicking on cell A1 and dragging down and right to cell C8.

The region is selected, and should be highlighted.

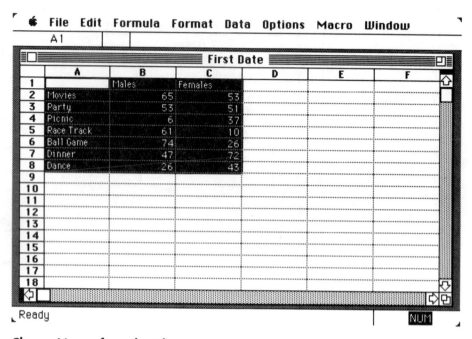

Choose New... from the File menu.

You are presented with a dialog box asking what type of document you want to create.

Select Chart. Then, click OK.

Excel creates a new chart, with two columns for each category.

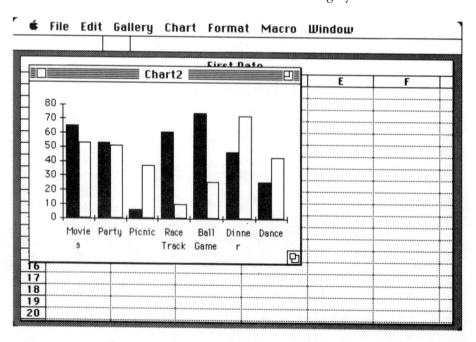

Advanced Formatting

Unfortunately, it is impossible at this stage to tell which column represents which series without referring to the actual data.

Before you do any advanced formatting, you'll resize your chart and add a legend so you can see what's going on.

Resizing

Click the zoom box to make your chart fill the entire screen.

Adding a Legend

A legend makes it possible to plot several graphs on the same set of axes without getting them confused.

Choose Add Legend from the Chart menu.

A legend is added automatically.

Moving a Legend

You could make your chart look even less cramped if you could have the legend appear below the chart. Fortunately, this is easy to do.

You can select almost anything in the chart window simply by clicking on it. This is true for text, legends, patterns, axes, and so on. Once you've selected an item, you can change it in a variety of ways.

Select the legend by clicking anywhere on it.

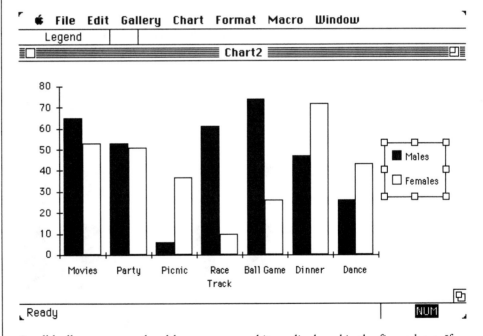

Small hollow squares should appear around it, as displayed in the figure here. If your chart doesn't look like this, try reselecting the legend.

Now you're ready to move the legend to the bottom of the screen.

Choose Legend... from the Format menu.

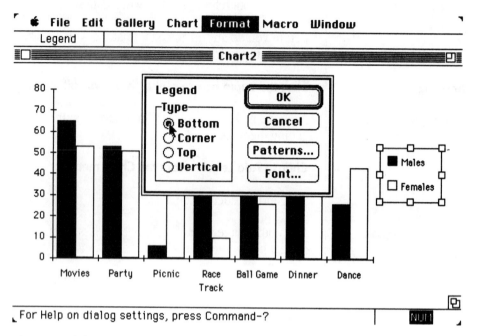

The Legend dialog box appears. Here you can specify the position of the legend on the page.

Select Bottom for Type. Then, click OK.

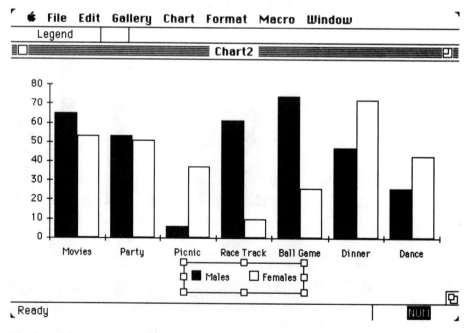

The legend moves beneath the chart, and the columns are no longer cramped.

Using Patterns

The Patterns... option is very useful in the creative formatting of your chart. It allows you to alter the appearance and pattern of the selected object. You'll use the Patterns... option now to change the pattern of the columns for the Females data series from white to gray.

Select the females data series by clicking on any one of the white columns.

The data series is selected when small squares appear in some of the columns.

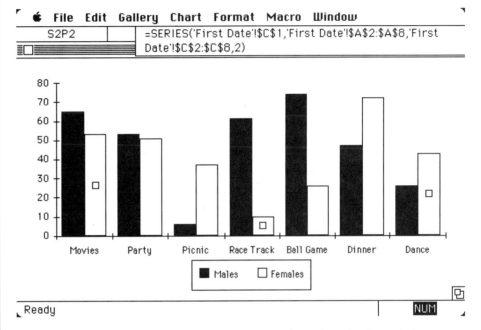

By the way, don't be alarmed by the complicated formula in the formula bar; that's Excel's way of referencing the data on your spreadsheet.

Choose Patterns... from the Format menu.

A dialog box appears, allowing you to change the appearance of the selected series. You can specify various characteristics for both the borders and the interiors of the columns. For example, you can make the borders either solid or dotted, and specify a line weight.

You can also specify the pattern and, if you have a color monitor, the color of the area inside the columns. Automatic is the default setting. It means that Excel selects the pattern for you. You'll select a pleasing light gray pattern instead.

In the Area section of the dialog box, choose light gray for pattern (the fourth selection from the left).

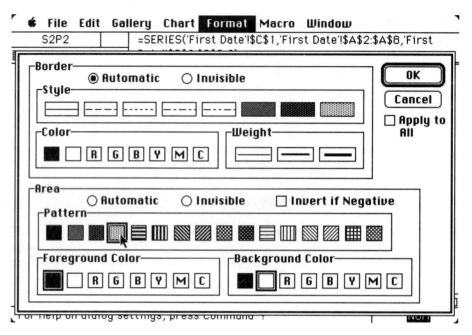

Click OK.

The color of the white columns changes to gray.

Adding Text Labels

Your chart would be more informative if it had a title. With Excel, you can easily add text, such as a title, with the Attach Text... command. You'll use the Attach Text... command to add a title now.

Choose Attach Text... from the Chart menu.

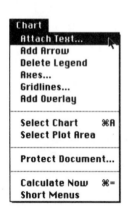

A dialog box appears, asking you what type of text you want to select.

You can attach a title, a label for the value axis, a label for the category axis, or a label for one of the columns. You attach a label to one of the columns by specifying the series (1 or 2 for males and females) and a data point (1 through 7 for movies through dances).

You'll attach a chart title.

Make sure that Chart Title is selected. Then, click OK.

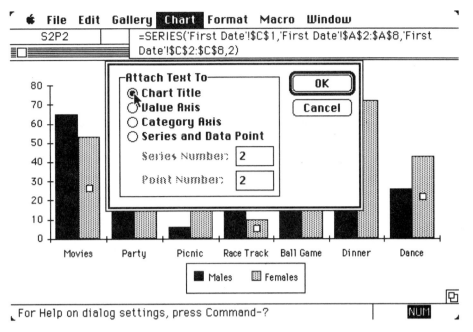

Excel creates a default title, and gives it the name "Title", which is probably no surprise to you.

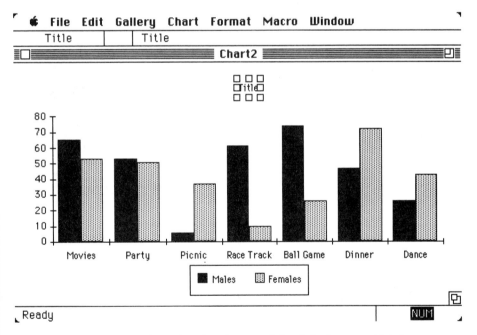

Notice that the Title is selected in the chart, and the default name "Title" appears in the formula bar. Excel lets you format the Title almost any way you want. You can change the name of the title itself, the font size, the style, and so on.

You'll change the name of the title to something more meaningful now. To change text in a chart, you select the text item you want to change, and you type in the formula bar.

Make sure that the chart title is selected (it should have white squares around it, as shown above). Then, type "First Date Activities" as the new title. When you are finished, press Enter to accept the new title.

The new title appears at the top of your chart.

More Patterns

You're just about finished, but you'd like to put a border around your chart to make it more professional looking. To do this, you need to select the entire chart, and then add a border using the Patterns... command. You may select the contents of the entire chart, including the legend, the title, and the plot area, by using the Select Chart command.

Choose Select Chart from the Chart menu.

Now, you can add a border with the Patterns... command.

Choose Patterns... from the Format menu.

The Patterns dialog box reappears. You can add a border for the entire chart by selecting a line weight for the border.

Select the medium border weight icon (the one in the center).

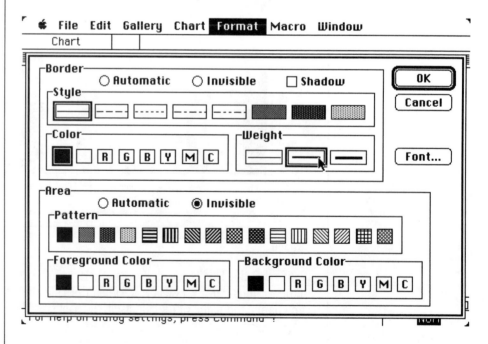

As you might expect, you do this by simply clicking on the border weight you desire. A dark outline is drawn around the chosen border weight to indicate that it has been selected.

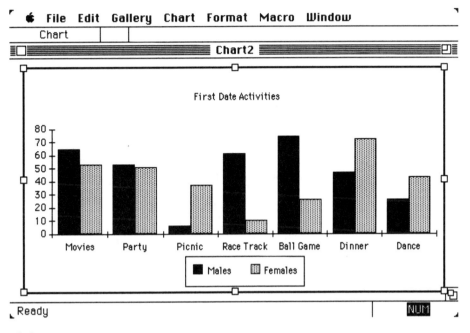

Click OK.

A border appears around your chart.

Finally, you'll change all of your text to Helvetica.

Choose Font... from the Format menu. When the dialog box appears, click Helvetica to select it. Then, click OK.

Finishing Up

You've now created a very professional-looking chart.

Page Setup

Because your chart is wider than it is tall, you'll choose landscape orientation before printing.

Choose Page Setup... from the File menu. When the dialog box appears, select landscape orientation. Finally, click OK.

Now, you'll save your document and then print it.

Choose Save from the File menu.

You are presented with a dialog box asking you to name your chart.

Type "First Date Chart" for a name, then click Save.

Now, you're ready to print.

Make sure your printer is chosen correctly, turned on, and ready to print.

Choose Print... from the File menu.

If you'd like multiple copies, type the number of copies you want.

Click OK to confirm your print settings.

In a few seconds, your document will begin to print.

Quitting

You're ready to return to the desktop.

Choose Quit from the File menu.

If you have made any changes to your chart, you will be asked if you want to save them. Click No.

Review

In this module, you've learned:

- How to enter data in a spreadsheet and then chart it.
- How to use different chart types.
- How to add a legend to a chart.
- How to resize a chart.
- How to create and format a chart title.
- How to format with patterns.
- How to use the Page Setup command to control printing options.

What to Turn In

Turn in a copy of both of your charts.

Cheating with Charts

Microsoft Excel gives you a number of formatting options that give you a lot of control over the way your chart presents its data. The impression your chart makes has a great deal to do with how you format it, as the two examples that follow illustrate.

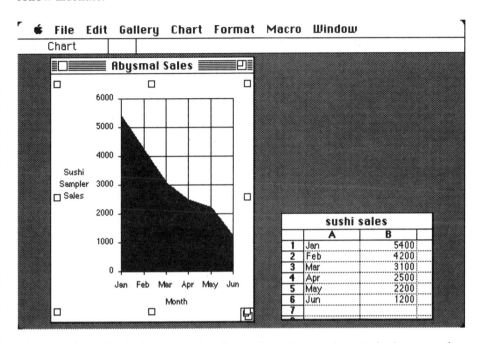

The area chart above illustrates sales figures for a six-month period. Elements of its format were chosen specifically to accentuate what appears to be a very steep downaward trend. Using the Patterns… command from the Format menu, a black fill pattern was selected to provide maximum contrast. The chart was also sized so that it is tall and not very wide. This shape makes the decline appear more drastic

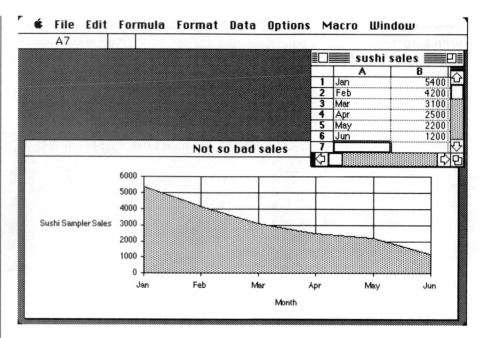

This second chart is the same type of area chart using the same data as the first. In this case, however, formatting commands were used to make the decline appear more gradual. A gray fill pattern was chosen to provide less contrast with the white background. The chart has been elongated to make the decline appear shallower.

Exercises

1. Add a title and a border to the first chart you created.

2. Create a chart that shows your GPA over the last year two years. If you haven't been in school for two years, use projected data. Choose whatever chart type you want, but be prepared to explain your choice.

3. After three months, your sushi business is wildly successful. Some students have requested that you broaden your product line, so you add pizza in the second quarter of the year (Q2), and burritos in Q3. After one year, you have revenues from the three product lines as shown in the chart below.

	1	2	3	4	5
		Q1	Q2	Q3	Q4
1					
2	Sushi	$6,000	$5,500	$6,500	$8,000
3	Pizza	$0	$1,500	$2,000	$3,500
4	Burritos	$0	$0	$1,500	$2,500
5					
6					

Yearly Revenues (data)

Create an area chart to display your revenues for the first year. When you are finished, your chart should look like the one shown below.

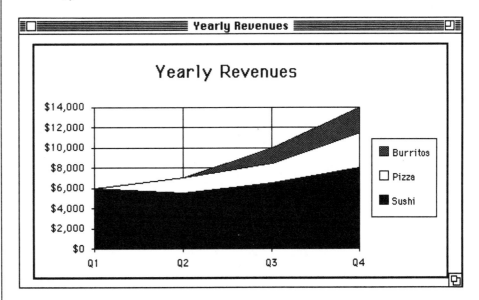

4. Format the chart from exercise 3 as a pie chart. What relationship between the data does a pie chart show better than an area chart?

6 Database Management

About Database Management
Introduction to Claris FileMaker Pro
Advanced Claris FileMaker Pro
Galleries
Exercises

About Database Management

Data bases are large, organized collections of related information, or data. A simple example of a data base is the telephone directory. The telephone directory is a collection of people who have phone numbers, with the listings organized alphabetically by last name.

Database management is the storing, sorting, updating, retrieving, and summarizing of the information stored in a data base.

A data base is made up of groups of information called **records.** In the phone book example, each listing is a record. A typical listing would include pieces of information like last name, first name, address, and telephone number. Each of these pieces of information is called a **field.**

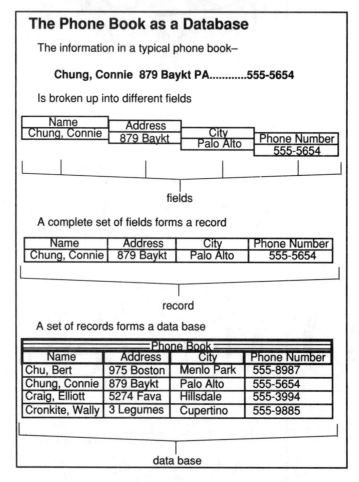

The Phone Book as a Database

The information in a typical phone book–

Chung, Connie 879 Baykt PA............555-5654

Is broken up into different fields

Name	Address	City	Phone Number
Chung, Connie	879 Baykt	Palo Alto	555-5654

fields

A complete set of fields forms a record

Name	Address	City	Phone Number
Chung, Connie	879 Baykt	Palo Alto	555-5654

record

A set of records forms a data base

Phone Book

Name	Address	City	Phone Number
Chu, Bert	975 Boston	Menlo Park	555-8987
Chung, Connie	879 Baykt	Palo Alto	555-5654
Craig, Elliott	5274 Fava	Hillsdale	555-3994
Cronkite, Wally	3 Legumes	Cupertino	555-9885

data base

For example, a record in the phone book data base might look like this:

Chung, Connie, 879 Baykt PA............555-5654

In this example, the number "555-5654" would be the number stored in the phone number field, "Chung, Connie" would be stored in the name field, and so on.

Data bases are used virtually anywhere information needs to be organized, stored, or reported. Schools often use data bases to keep track of students and their grades, and businesses can use them to keep track of inventory and personnel information.

Traditional data bases can present some problems, however. Suppose, for example, that you want a list of everyone whose first name is Bertha who lives in San Francisco. If you got out your trusty copy of the telephone directory, you could go through the listings one by one checking each entry for a Bertha from San Francisco. But because your telephone directory is organized only by last name, not by first name or city, your search would be long and tedious.

Not too long ago, people who constantly do this sort of thing got understandably tired of it and turned to computers for help. With computer database managers, you can quickly and easily enter, update, sort, and find the information in your data base. You could organize a computerized phone book not only by last name, but also by city or first name, allowing you to find the Berthas from San Francisco in seconds, not hours (perhaps a mixed blessing).

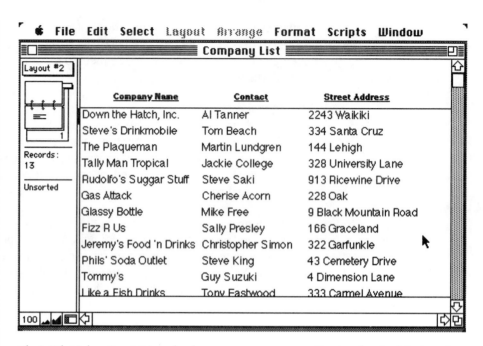

About Claris FileMaker Pro 1.0

Claris FileMaker Pro 1.0 is a database management application for the Macintosh. Taking advantage of the graphic capabilities of the Macintosh, FileMaker lets you easily design the way your data base or **datafile** will appear. Fields in the datafile may consist of text (for instance, a name), number (a price), a date, or even a picture from MacPaint or other graphic applications. FileMaker also lets you view and print the information in the datafile in a variety of layouts. Different layouts can make analyzing and presenting information easier.

Introduction to FileMaker Pro

The Task

It's time once again to decide which classes to take. This is, unfortunately, no easy task, since you have to schedule classes that don't conflict with each other while making sure your work load isn't too hard. You also need to take classes that fulfill distribution requirements in the humanities, the natural sciences, and the social science areas. But how to do it? Traditional class listings are organized by department, not by meeting times or by credits given. To go through the listings in search of classes to take, even skipping over departments you're not interested in, could take a long time.

Fortunately, there does exist a FileMaker data base of many of the classes available to help students in your situation. You will use it to select the right courses to take—and to learn a little about how data bases are used.

You'll begin by organizing the data base or **datafile**. First, you'll sort the list of classes by department and course name, and then you'll find all the classes that fulfill the social sciences distribution requirement.

Next, you'll generate a report on the different classes that fulfill the humanities and natural sciences distribution requirements. The report will be in the form of a table. You'll use it to compare the courses that fulfill the distribution requirements.

Finally, in the Advanced FileMaker Pro module, you'll actually create you own datafile to store information about classes you've already taken.

Course	Credits	Time	Distribution Area	Final?
Introduction to Psychology	5	10:00	Social Sciences	Yes
The Hero in Modern Literature	4	2:15	Social Sciences	Yes
America 1938-1948	5	9:00	Social Sciences	Yes
Human Prehistory	5	9:00	Social Sciences	Yes
The Death Penalty	5	11:00	Social Sciences	Yes
Yorkist and Tudor England	5	1:15	Social Sciences	No

Getting Started

This module assumes that you are familiar with the basics of using the Macintosh, how to work with a hard disk and/or diskettes, how to choose menu commands, and so on. If these concepts are not familiar to you, please review the Approaching Macintosh module.

First, you'll start from the Macintosh desktop.

Turn on the Macintosh. If you are not using a hard disk, insert the system diskette in the internal diskette drive.

Soon, you'll see the Macintosh desktop.

Class Listing

In this module, you'll need to use the "Class Listings" document that has been created and stored on the **Approaching Macintosh Documents Diskette**. You will need to copy the "Class Listings" document onto your hard drive or where your instructor tells you.

Copy the "Class Listings" document to your hard drive.

If you're unsure of how to do this, please see the Approaching Macintosh module.

Now you'll open "Class Listings" by double-clicking on the "Class Listings" icon. Note that opening the "Class Listings" document will automatically open File-Maker Pro.

Locate and double-click on the "Class Listings" document.

The "Class Listings" datafile window appears, displaying the first record of the datafile.

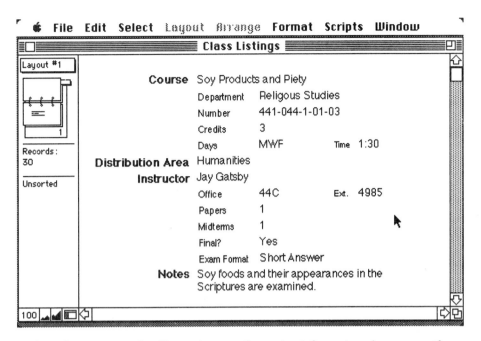

In the "Class Listings" datafile, each **record** contains information about a specific class. The individual pieces of information about each class—its name, department, instructor, and so on—are the **fields** for each record.

For example, in the record for the Soy Products and Piety course, Religious Studies appears in the Department field, Jay Gatsby in the Instructor field, 1:30 in the Time field, and so on.

The Datafile Window

The information you work with is stored in a **datafile.** FileMaker displays this information to you in the **datafile window.** Like any other window, you can move the window by dragging its title bar or resize the window using the size box at the lower right of the window. You can scroll through the window using the scroll bars at the right and bottom of the window, and view information not on the screen. Consult the Approaching Macintosh module if you're unfamiliar with windows and scrolling.

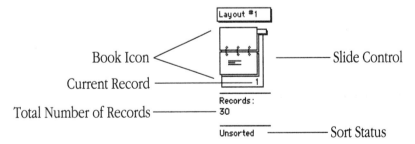

The **Book icon** is used to move between records of the datafile, much like turning the pages of a book. You can click the pages of the Book icon any number of times to turn pages forward or backward. The current record number is shown in at the bottom of the Book icon. The **Slide Control** allows you to move quickly to any record. Just below the Book icon and the Slide Control, the total number of records in the datafile is shown. It indicates that there are 30 records in the "Class Listing" datafile.

Click on the bottom page of the Book icon twice.

FileMaker now displays the third record of the datafile.

Grab the Slide Control and drag it up and down slowly.

Notice the current record indicator at the bottom of the book icon changes as you move the Slide Control down. Now you'll move to the sixth record of the datafile using the Slide Control and return to the first record by paging with the Book icon.

Stop moving the Slide Control when the current record indicator is at 6 and let go of the mouse button. Click on the top page of the Book icon five times to return to the first record.

Organizing the Data

As you might have noticed as you scrolled through some of the records, they are in no particular order. That makes this class listing even less useful than the listings that are organized by department. Fortunately, FileMaker allows you to organize the records of a datafile in many different ways.

The Sort... Command

The first step toward making the datafile more organized is to sort the records, making it easier to pick useful classes. You can perform sort on any field in the datafile (with the exception of picture fields, of course).

Choose Sort... from the Select menu.

You will be presented with the Sort dialog box.

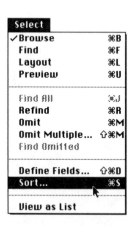

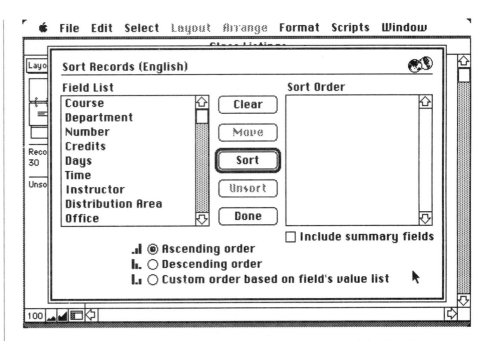

The sort dialog box contains a list of all the fields contained in the datafile. To make this class list at least as good as the others available, you should begin the organization of the datafile by sorting the courses by department.

Click on Department in the Field List, and then click Move.

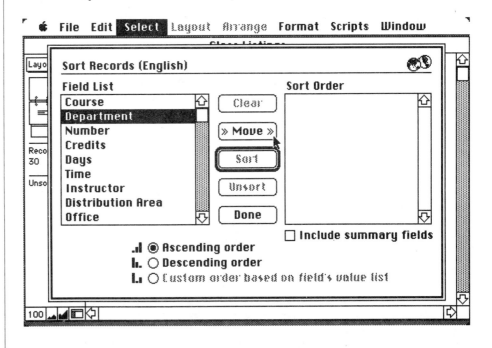

The Department field is now in the Sort Order box with an ascending order icon. This way, all the courses in the English department will appear in the datafile before the courses in the Math department, which will be before the courses in the Religious Studies department (E before M before R, at least in the English alphabet). If you select the Department field in the Sort Order box and choose Descending Order, the datafile will be sorted in descending alphabetical order and the icon will reverse. Leave it in ascending order for now.

You can clear the Sort window by clicking **Clear.** You need to do this if you ever change the fields on which you want to sort. If you mistakenly choose a field on which you don't want to sort, click on the field in the Sort Order box, and the arrows in the Move button will change direction, allowing you to remove that field.

Now that you've specified the field you want sorted, you can begin the sort.

Click Sort to sort the records.

By clicking on the bottom page of the Book icon, scroll through the sorted records in the datafile window.

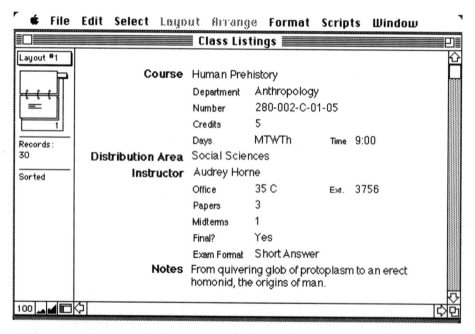

All the courses are sorted in ascending alphabetical order according to their department. Notice, however, that courses in the same department are in no particular order. It would be nice to have all the courses in one department sorted by course name. A second sort should be performed.

Choose Sort from the Select menu.

The sort box appears again. Notice that the first sort, ascending according to the Department field, is still chosen.

To specify a second sort, simply click on the field you on which you wish to perform the second sort and then on the Move button. In this case, you'd like to perform a second sort on the Course field.

Click on Course in the Field List. Then, click Move.

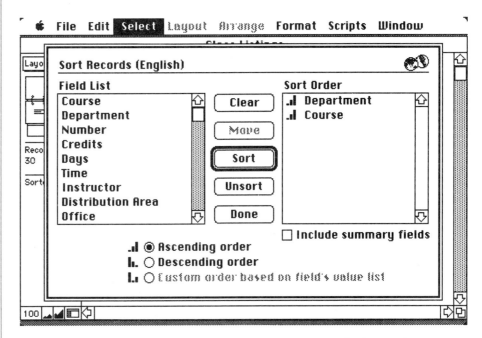

The fields are sorted in the order they appear in the Sort Order list. In this case, they will be first sorted alphabetically by department and then by course.

Click Sort to sort the records.

The records are now sorted by course name within each department.

Click on the Book icon to browse through the records.

Notice the effect of the sort.

Searching the Datafile

Besides allowing you to sort your records according to a field value, File-Maker allows you to find records in the datafile that meet any requirements you choose. For example, you could find all the courses that are worth three credits, or that are in the English department, or that don't have a final. You can even combine all of these requirements, and find all the three-credit English courses that don't have a final.

Choose Find from the Select menu.

The Find window appears on your screen.

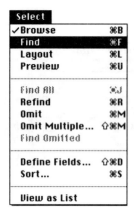
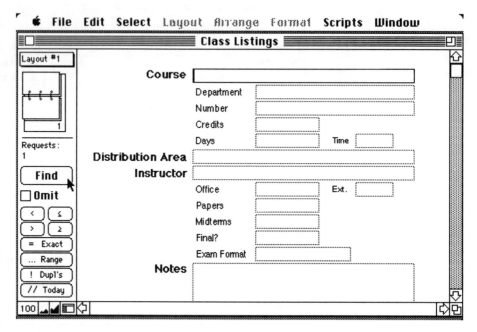

To specify values you want to find, simply type your requirements in the appropriate field. FileMaker finds all records with fields that match exactly or begin with your requirements. For example, if you typed "Art" in the department field, you will get all classes in the Art department as well as any in the Art History department.

In order to choose the class we'd like to take, it might be handy to find which courses don't have finals.

To select the field you want to search on, click in the box to the right of the field name.

Click in the box to the right of the field name Final?.

Type "No" in the Final? field. Then, click Find.

All classes that don't have finals have been found.

You can find information based on multiple criteria by using the **New Request** command. For example, say you want to find all the courses in the English or the Art departments.

Type "English" in the Department field. Choose New Request from the Edit menu.

Type "Art" in the Department field. Click Find.

Use the Book icon to scroll through the six selected records.

All the classes in both the English and the Art departments are selected.

Find Operators

There are several operators you can use when performing a find. The operators allow you to specify in greater detail exactly the criteria you are looking for. You can either type them in, or click on the icons on the left of the screen that appear when Find is chosen from the Select menu. For text fields, the operators work alphabetically, and for number and date fields, they work numerically.

Here's a list of operators you can use:

<>	Does not equal what you type
>, <	Match with values greater than, less than what you type
>=	Match with values greater than or equal to what you type
<=	Match with values less than or equal to what you type
=	Finds the exact match (not necessary with numbers)
...	Match with values between values you type
!	Finds duplicate records with duplicate entries
//	Finds today's date (in date fields only)

For example, "3...5" in the Credits field will find all courses worth between 3 and 5 units of credit, while "< =3" in the Credits field finds all courses worth 3 or fewer credits.

Empty Fields

FileMaker considers a text field to be empty if it contains no letters or numbers, and a number field to be empty if it contains only text other than Y or N (no numbers). To find a record that contains an empty field, type an equal sign alone in the field.

Omit

If you would like to omit a certain set of records from a request, you fill in the fields the exact same way as when finding a record, but now you check the Omit box. All records that match the selection criteria will be omitted and those that are left will be "found".

For example, since you have fulfilled all your English requirements, you would now like to find all the non-English department courses.

Choose Find from the Select menu.

Type "English" in the Department field, and click the Omit box.

Click Find.

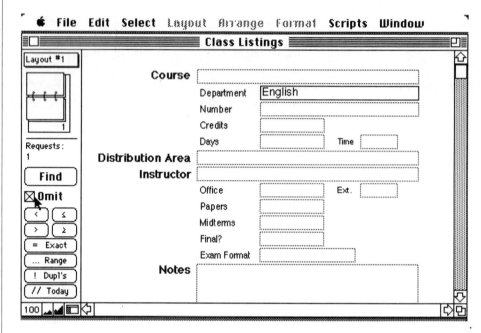

All records that aren't offered by the English department will remain.

Since one of your goals is to get a list of classes that satisfy the social sciences distribution requirement, you should use the Find command to locate all these classes. First, we must make all the records available to be searched.

Choose Find All from the Select menu.

Choose Find from the Select menu.

Type "Social Sciences" in the Distribution Area field.

You also need to find a class that is more than three credits in order to fulfill your social science requirement.

Type ">3" in the Credits field. Then, click Find.

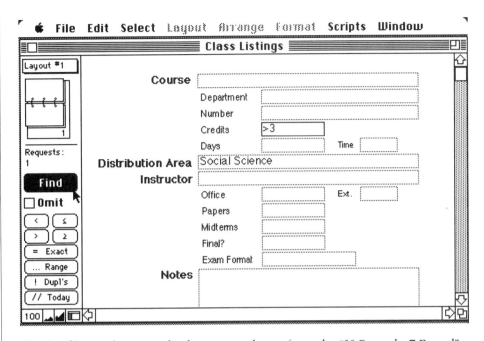

The datafile window now displays seven classes (note the "30 Records, 7 Found" beneath the Book icon) that satisfy the Find requirements you specified.

Omit Records

There may be some records which match the conditions you specified, but which you'd still rather not have visible in the datafile window.

Using the Book icon, page through the records until the class "Soy Foods and Nuclear Disarmament" is visible.

Notice that Professor Marlow's class requires several field trips. Since you like to spend your afternoons playing ultimate frisbee, you aren't going to sign up for this course. Therefore, you should **Omit** this record from view.

Choose Omit from the Select menu.

The record chosen is now omitted. Note that the numbers in the upper left corner now say "30 Records, 6 Found".

To see all 30 records again, you would use the **Find All Records** command from the Select menu. Don't choose this yet, though; you haven't printed a list of the classes.

Notice that there is no Save command in FileMaker. This is because FileMaker automatically saves whatever changes you make to the datafile. You can't open a datafile, change the values, and then quit without saving—changes are always saved.

If you want to alter the values of a datafile, but still have the datafile keep its original data after you're through, you need to first duplicate the datafile and make changes to the duplicate datafile.

Since you haven't altered any values, you really haven't changed this datafile. All the records are still intact, even those you can't access in the datafile window.

Preview

You're probably anxious to print your report, but being an ecologically-aware person of the '90s, there is a better solution than randomly printing.

Choose Preview from the Select menu.

By using the scroll bars you can see what your new layout will look like when printed out.

Click on the small box to the right of the number 50 in the lower left corner of the window.

This is the Zoom Out box. The box to the right of it (with the larger picture) is the Zoom In box. The present view is indicated by the number to the left. 25 means the view is 25% of the actual size.

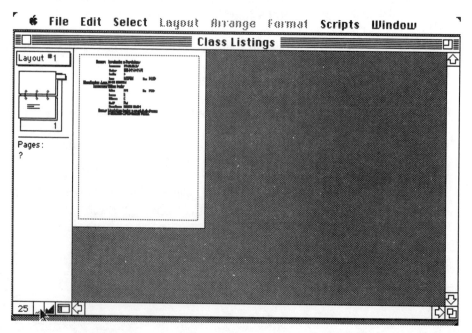

The page is reduced to fit on the screen.

Click on the lower page of the Book icon.

The information for each class is printed on its own page. This may be a good solution for some reports, but a definite tree-waster.

Alternate Layout

FileMaker gives you the ability to have multiple layouts for the same information. For example, you find it helpful to look at the key factors when choosing a class in columns. That way each of the attributes can be easily compared and the important information printed on one handy page.

Choose Layout from the Select menu.

Choose New Layout from the Edit menu.

This will allow you to look at the same data in a different format.

Select Columnar report layout and click OK.

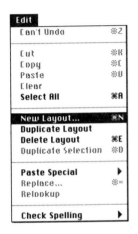

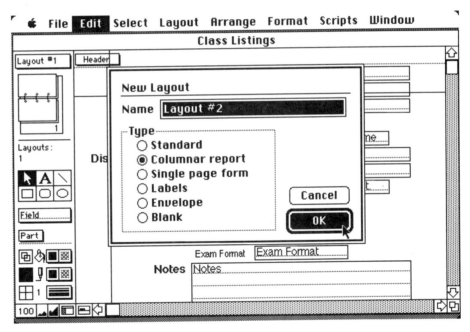

The dialog box (very similar to the one used to sort) allows you to choose which field you'd like to have appear in the layout.

To most effectively compare the classes, you tell FileMaker to take the most pertinent information (like whether or not there is a final) and align it in a column format.

Select Course from the Field List, then click Move. Use the same method to move Credits, Time, Distribution Area, and Final? to the Field Order box.

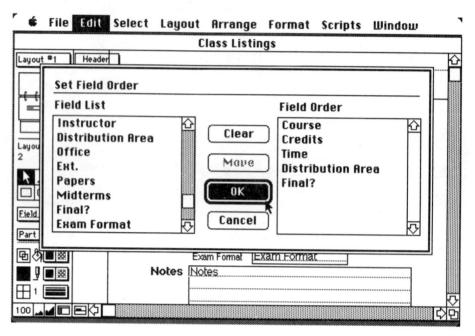

Finally, click OK.

The new layout is shown in a columnar fashion. You may need to use the scroll bar to see the fields off the right end of the screen. Also, notice that under the Book icon you see the words "Layout #2". This indicates that there are now two different layouts available for this datafile. Just as you used the Book icon to move between records, you may page up or down to select which layout you would like to use to view the datafile.

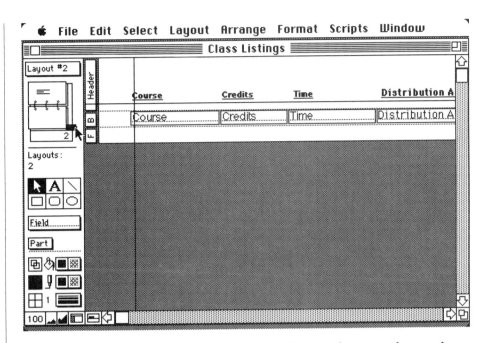

Choose Browse from the Select menu to view the new layout with records included.

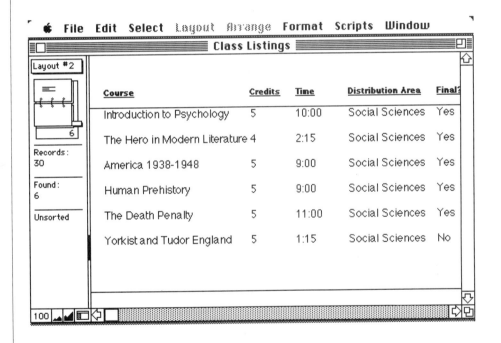

Previewing Reports

Once again you'll use preview to see how your report will look before you print it.

Choose Preview from the Select menu.

Use the scroll bars to see the entire report.

Printing Records

Now that you've made the list of classes into a more manageable size, you should print the list out to better view the information.

Select Print from the File menu. Click OK to begin printing.

You now have a printed the classes you have to choose from.

Select Quit from the File menu.

Review

In this module, you've learned:

- What a data base is and how an electronic data base helps you organize information
- How to sort the records of a datafile
- How to find records in a datafile that meet the requirements you set
- How to print the records of a datafile
- How to create an alternate layout
- How data bases can be organized in any manner you choose
- How to find particular records in a datafile
- How to sort the records

What to Turn In

Turn in the printed report.

Advanced
FileMaker Pro

The Task

In the Introduction to FileMaker module, you learned how to organize the records of a datafile and how to generate a report from the information stored in a datafile. Now, you'd like to create your own datafile to store information about the different classes you've taken during your college career.

To do this, you'll design a form to structure the information in your datafile. First, you'll create text, number, and computed number fields in which to store course information: the course name, credit value, instructor's name, and fields to store the results of your test scores, your course score, and your total number of credits to date. You'll also include fields for the weights of these different scores, allowing you to calculate your total course score. You'll then arrange the field locations so your datafile will be more readable. You'll also format the various fields to make the datafile more presentable. When the form is complete, you'll enter your data into the datafile.

My Classes

Course Name Applied Nuclear Botany   **Grade**   A-

Credits 4

Instructor Audrey Horne

	Scores	Weight
Homework	75	20%
Midterm	88	20%
Final	75	50%
Other	91	10%

Course Score 79.2

Description   Lab project: Fusion properties of ferns

Getting Started

FileMaker Pro

The first step in creating a new datafile is to open the FileMaker application.

Turn on your Macintosh. If you are not using a hard disk, insert the system diskette in the internal diskette drive.

Double-click on the FileMaker icon to open the application.

When you open FileMaker, you are immediately presented with a dialog box asking whether you wish to open an existing datafile or create a new one. If you wanted to open an existing datafile, you would use the scroll box arrows to find the name of the file you wanted, and then double-click it.

In this case, you want to create a new datafile.

Click on the New button in the dialog box.

Type "My Courses" as the name of the new datafile, and click New to continue.

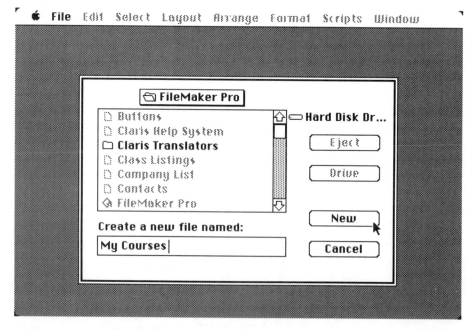

Adding Data Fields

Since your database is new and has no fields, FileMaker automatically opens the Field Definition window.

The first piece of information you want to store is the course name, so you should now create a field to store the course name.

Type "Course Name" in the Field Name box to name the new field.

Notice below the Field Name box is a list of Field types. The Field type defaults to Text—leave it that way for the Course Name field.

Click Create when you finish typing the name.

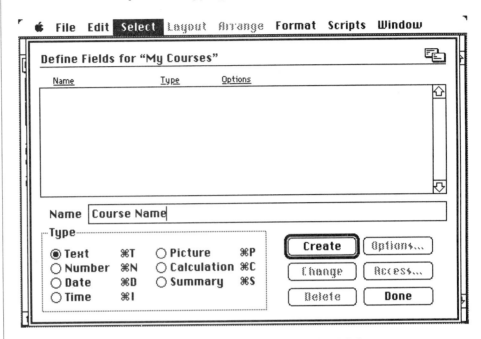

The Field Name box is highlighted, ready for the next field definition.

Type in "Grade" and click Create.

Remember that the default field type is text, so you can simply click Create after naming a field to create a text field.

The Field Name box should be highlighted again.

Type in "Instructor" and click Create.

The fields you have defined and the field types are listed in the window.

Number Fields

The next field you'll create will be to store the score you received on the final. This will be a number field.

Type "Final Score" as the name for the new field.

Click Number in the Field Type column and click Create to make the Final Score field a number field.

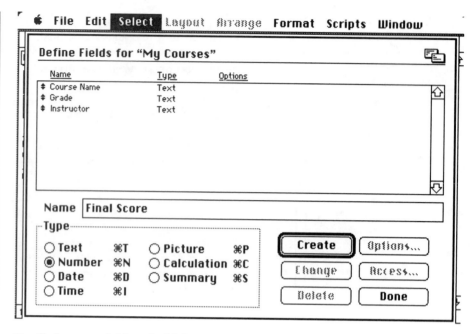

You'll also want fields to hold the score you received on the midterm, as well your homework score. An additional field would also be useful in case there were two midterms, a project, or papers which also contributed to your grade.

Type "Midterm Score" as the name for the new field.

When entering data, it is often more convenient to keep your hands on the keyboard. You can press the Return key here and it will have the same effect as clicking Create.

Press Return when finished.

The Midterm Score field, like the Final Score field, should be a number field.

Create the following fields by typing their names into the new field one at a time. After typing each name, press Return, and make sure that number remains selected in the Field Type column.

> **Homework Score**
> **Other Score**
> **Final Weight**
> **Midterm Weight**
> **Homework Weight**
> **Other Weight**
> **Course Score**

If you had a score stored in the Other Score field, it would be nice to know what the score referred to (a project, a paper, etc.). So, you'll need another field to hold a description of that score.

Type "Description" to name the field. Click on "Text" in the Field Type column to make the Description field a text field.

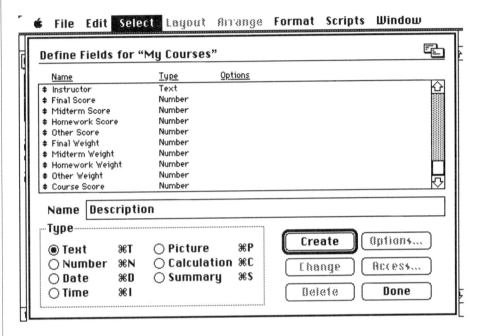

Click Create.

Designing a Layout

You have defined all the fields in your data base and their types. Now we will leave the Field Definition window and organize the information on the screen.

Click Done.

A window appears with your fields in the order you created them.

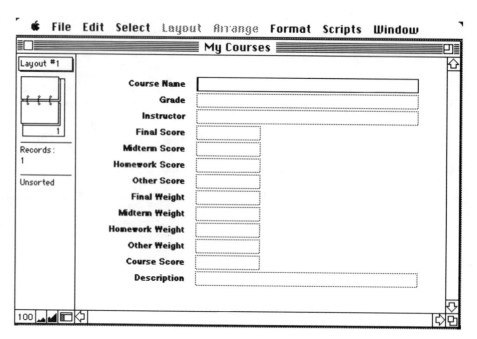

Information in this data base can be viewed in a variety of different ways. Each different view of the data is called a **layout.**

The field titles you've defined are listed on the screen in a single line with an associated box (the field itself where information will later be entered). This is known as the **standard layout.**

This is a good start, but a new layout that repositions the fields will help make the data base more organized and legible.

Choose Layout from the Select menu.

The layout also displays the **header,** which controls the top margin; the **body,** which controls what is displayed and printed for each record; and the **footer,** which controls the bottom margin.

You could now modify the present layout by moving fields, adding graphics, and adding additional fields. Instead, you will duplicate the present layout and modify it, leaving the original intact.

Select Duplicate Layout from the Edit menu.

This layout, as you might guess, looks exactly like the first. The Book icon now indicates that there are two layouts to choose from—the standard layout and the one you're working on.

Moving Fields

You're now ready to arrange the fields in the layout window. You can move field titles and the fields themselves wherever you like by clicking and dragging them anywhere you like.

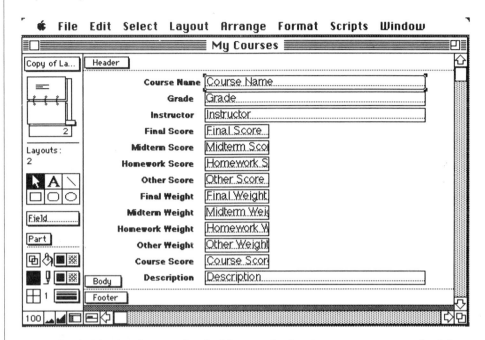

Drag the field title (the word in bold—not the box) Course Name to the left edge of the window.

Drag the field itself (the box with the words "Course Name" inside) just to the right of the field title Course Name.

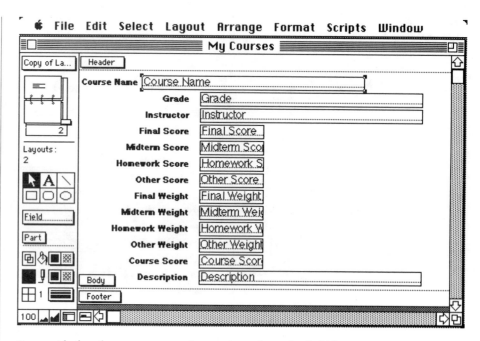

Resizing Fields

Even with the obscure courses that you've taken, the field box Course Name is probably larger than is necessary. FileMaker will display as much of the information that's in a field as will fit in the box. The rest of the information that is entered won't be lost, it just won't be visible. To make the Course Name field larger or smaller, you use the small black handles in the lower, right corner of the field.

Grab the handles of the field Course Name and move it about one inch straight to the left.

If you accidentally move the handles up or down, you will increase or decrease the height of the field. Use the handles to make sure your screen looks like the screen above.

Resize the Grade field so the box is approximately the size of the word Grade that appears inside it.

Moving Multiple Fields

You're ready to start arranging the fields as they appear in the print out at the beginning of this module. You can move each of the fields individually, but it may be easier to move more than one field at a time. Now, you'll move the Grade field and Grade field title together.

Click on the Grade field title.

The corners of the Grade field title will turn black.

While holding down the Shift key, click on the Grade field box.

Now, both fields will be highlighted.

Drag the Grade field and field title just to the right of the Course Name field box.

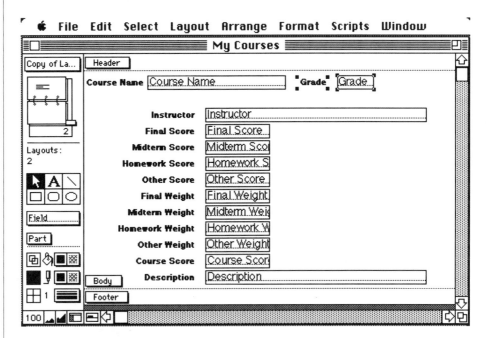

By using the Shift key, you were able to move both fields at the same time and maintain the original alignment.

Layout Tools

The basic movement of the fields and their titles is very easy in FileMaker, but making sure that fields are properly aligned can be a challenge. FileMaker provides tools that makes this job easier.

Select T-Squares from the Layout menu.

A horizontal line and a vertical line now appear on the layout window. These lines can be grabbed and moved on the screen as tools to help you align fields and field titles as you move them. By using the T-Squares in conjunction with the rulers, accurate alignment and measuring of fields can take place.

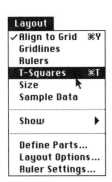

Choose Rulers from the Layout menu.

For example, if you wanted the T-Squares to cross at the center of a letter-size page (8-1/2 by 11 inches), you would move the vertical T-Square to 4.250" and the horizontal to 5.500".

Drag the horizontal line to the bottom of the Course Name field box.

Also in the Layout menu is an item called Align to Grid. When this item is selected, a check mark appears to the left of it in the menu. Fields and field titles jump in small increments (12 per inch) as they are moved, instead of moving smoothly. This usually makes them much easier to line up. In most circumstances it is better to leave it on. Occasionally, it can be a hindrance when doing detailed work. If you seem to be having trouble aligning objects and they tend to jump away from where you'd like to place them, try turning Align to Grid off by selecting it again from the Layout menu.

Editing Field Titles

Some of the field titles will be unnecessary and should be removed.

Click on the field title Final Weight.

Be sure you've selected the field title and not the field box itself.

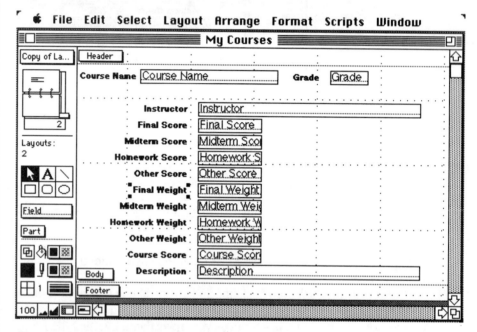

Choose Clear from the Edit menu.

To remove more than one item at a time, you can use the Shift key to select multiple items at once.

Hold down the Shift key and click on field titles Midterm Weight, Homework Weight, and Other Weight.

Choose Clear from the Edit menu.

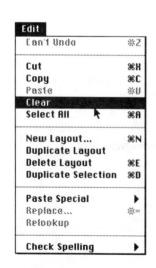

FileMaker's automatic field title generating feature saves time, but the field titles you use aren't always exactly what you'd like to see on the screen. The field titles for Homework Score, Midterm Score, Final Score, and Other Score are a little redundant and would look better with a single column heading.

The tool palette, located on the left side of the Layout window, contains tools for drawing lines, circles, and rectangles, as well as the text tool.

Select the letter "A" text tool from the tool palette.

Position and use the crossbar cursor to select and delete the word "Score" from each of the field titles.

You'll add the column heading a little later.

Adding Fields

Whoops! You forgot to make a field for the number of credits the course was worth! What do you do?

Don't panic. If you forget to create a field, or decide to add one later, just create a field and move it to the desired position.

Choose Define Fields from the Select menu.

You are now back to the same window that you originally created the fields in.

Create a number field called "Credits".

Remember: To do this, type "Credits" into the Field Name box, click on Number in the Field Type box, and press Return.

Click Done.

Using the techniques you have learned, resize and arrange the rest of the fields to match the following screen. Don't forget to use the horizontal and vertical T-Squares to align the field titles and fields.

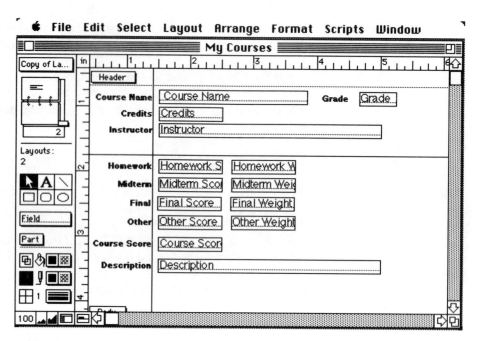

Adding Titles

Adding headings will help your layout be more understandable.

Select the "A" from the tool palette. Then, choose Align Text and Center from the Format menu.

Choose Font and Helvetica from the Format menu.

Choose Size and 14 from the Format menu.

Click over the center of the column of scores and type "Scores".

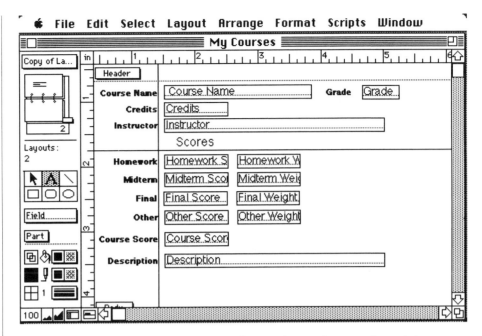

Use the exact same technique to center the word "Weight" over the weight column. (FileMaker will remember the Alignment and FontSize you used last time, so you shouldn't have to reselect it.)

Use the arrow from the tool palette and the T-Square to align the two column titles.

Headers and Footers

FileMaker may print multiple records per page depending on the length, but the items contained in the Header and Footer sections of the layout will only be printed at the top and bottom of the page, respectively.

Use the "A" text tool to type "My Classes" in the Header section.

Change the Font Size to 14 in the Format menu under Size.

"My Classes" will appear at the top of each page printed.

Now you will add some new field types to the Footer area. You may have to scroll down to see the Footer.

Choose Define from the Select menu.

Field Types

You will now create new type of field that will calculate the total number of credits you've taken to date.

Type "Total Credits to Date" in the Field Name box.

Click on the Summary Field Type and click Create.

By selecting Summary as the field type, you can perform a variety of mathematical functions on a single field for all the records. In this case, you would like to total the Credit field and place the answer in the field you just created, "Total Credits to Date".

Make sure that Total is selected, then scroll down and select Credits, and click OK.

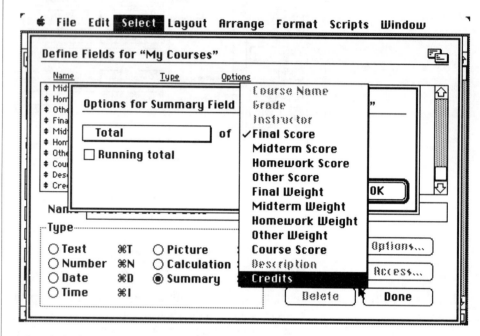

The total of all the numbers entered in the credit field will now be added up and placed in the "Total Credits to Date" field.

It might be nice to have a field in the Footer that shows the date the data base was modified. FileMaker can automatically fill in fields when requested. In this case, whenever a change is made to the data base, the date will automatically be updated.

Type "Modified date" in the Field Name box, click on the date Field Type, and press Return.

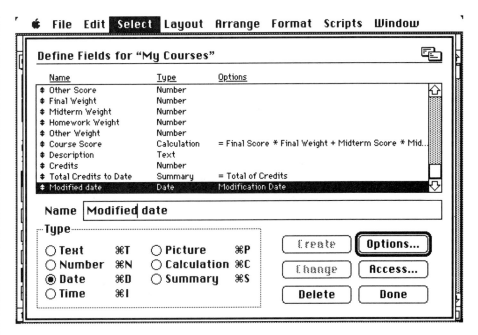

Define Fields for "My Courses"

Name	Type	Options
⬍ Other Score	Number	
⬍ Final Weight	Number	
⬍ Midterm Weight	Number	
⬍ Homework Weight	Number	
⬍ Other Weight	Number	
⬍ Course Score	Calculation	= Final Score * Final Weight + Midterm Score * Mid...
⬍ Description	Text	
⬍ Credits	Number	
⬍ Total Credits to Date	Summary	= Total of Credits
⬍ Modified date	Date	Modification Date

Name `Modified date`

Type

- ○ Text ⌘T
- ○ Number ⌘N
- ● Date ⌘D
- ○ Time ⌘I
- ○ Picture ⌘P
- ○ Calculation ⌘C
- ○ Summary ⌘S

[Create] [**Options...**]
[Change] [Access...]
[**Delete**] [**Done**]

Select the field you just created from the Field Definition box. You may need to scroll down.

Click Options.

FileMaker has the ability to automatically enter a default value in any field, display a list of values you can choose from, look up a value in another FileMaker data base, or check to see if the information entered in a field fits certain requirements. For this example FileMaker will enter today's date in the field whenever a modification to the data base is made.

Click on the check box next to Creation Date.

The Creation Date menu will now be active.

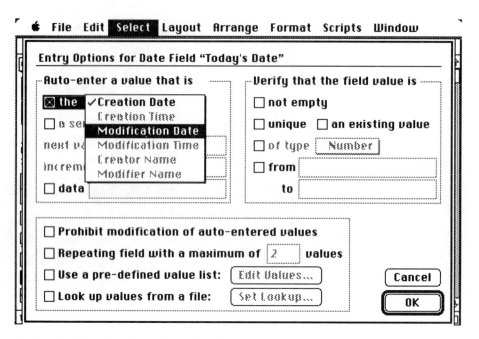

Select Modification Date from the Creation Date menu.

Click OK.

Click Done.

Now you can position the two new fields in the Footer.

Move the Modified Date field box to the bottom right corner of the Footer. Using the Shift key and the arrow tool, select both the field and field title for Total Credits to Date. Move them down to the left corner of the footer.

Formatting Fields

FileMaker has the ability to automatically display information with additional attributes. For instance, the weights of the scores would be most accurately displayed in a percentage format.

Hold down the Shift key and click on each of the four weight fields to select them all.

Choose Number Format... from the Format menu.

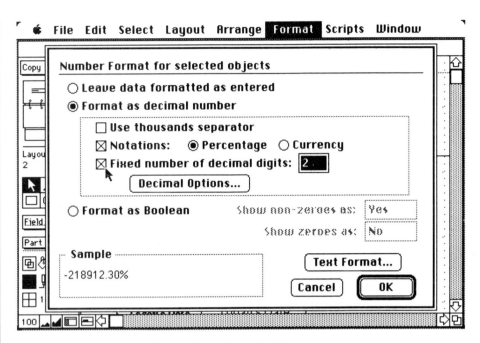

Click on the Format as decimal number check box.

Click the Notations check box.

Click on Percentage and click OK.

Now when you enter this information as a decimal part of one, it will be displayed as a percentage (.25 will be 25%).

Calculations

When you created the Course Score field, you gave it a field type of number. You could figure it out manually and enter the answer in this field, but FileMaker's calculation ability will make it much easier than that.

Choose Define from the Select menu, scroll down, and select Course Score.

Change the Field Type from number to calculation and click OK.

FileMaker warns you that if you had already entered data in this field, the new calculation you are about to enter would replace that data. You haven't entered any data yet, so there is no problem.

Click OK.

You could type the formula to calculate the average, but FileMaker provides the tools so you can use the mouse and avoid errors.

Click on the field names and the keypad to enter the following formula:

= Final Score * Final Weight + Midterm Score * Midterm Weight + Other Score * Other Weight + Homework Score * Homework Weight

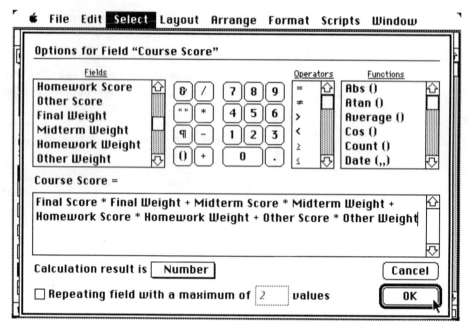

Click OK to return to the layout.

There! Now all the fields have been formatted, and the form is ready for use. You can now start entering data into your datafile.

Entering Data

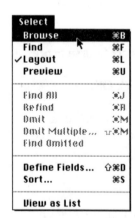

Data is always entered and displayed in the Browse window.

Choose Browse from the Select menu. Scroll to the top of the window so that the title "My Classes" can be seen.

Click just to the right of the field title Course Name.

The field boxes appear to show where you will enter data. The Book icon shows only one record in the datafile, the empty one before you. To enter data, you simply start typing.

Since the insertion point is inside the Course Name field, you can start typing in the name of the first course.

Type in "Applied Nuclear Botanics" as the name for the first course.

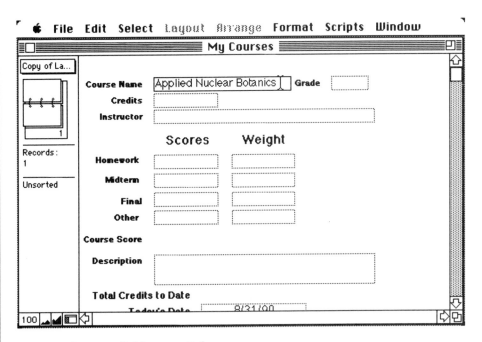

To go to the next field, press Tab.

Type in "A-" and press Tab.

Editing Information

You can also edit the information you've entered as if it were normal text. If the name of this course is actually "Applied Nuclear Botany", you should click to position an insertion point after the "s" in "Botanics". Then edit as if you were in Microsoft Word.

Click to position the insertion point after the word "Botanics" in the Course Name field.

Backspace over the "ics".

Type in the letter "y".

You've just edited the name of the course. You should now finish entering the information for this record.

Click to position the insertion point inside the Credits field.

Type "4" and press Tab.

Type "Audrey Horne" for the Instructor's name. Press Tab.

Type "75" as the Homework Score and press Tab.

Type ".2" as the Homework Weight and press Tab.

Notice now that the Course Score is 15, which is 75 x .2.

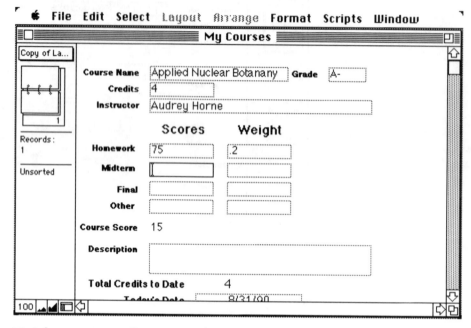

Finishing Up

Finish entering information for this record. Use the following values:

Midterm:	Score 88, Weight .2
Homework:	Score 75, Weight .2
Final	Score 75, Weight .5
Other:	Score 91, Weight .1
Description:	Lab project: Fusion properties of ferns

You're all finished. Now, print the record. Consult the section on printing records from the Introduction to FileMaker Pro module if necessary.

Choose Print... from the File menu.

Select your desired options and click OK.

Select Quit from the File menu.

Review

In this module, you've learned:

- How to create a datafile
- How to design a form by creating and formatting fields and labels
- How field types differ—text, number, calculated, etc.
- How to calculate fields
- How to format information entered in fields

What to Turn In

Turn in the printed record.

The Authors

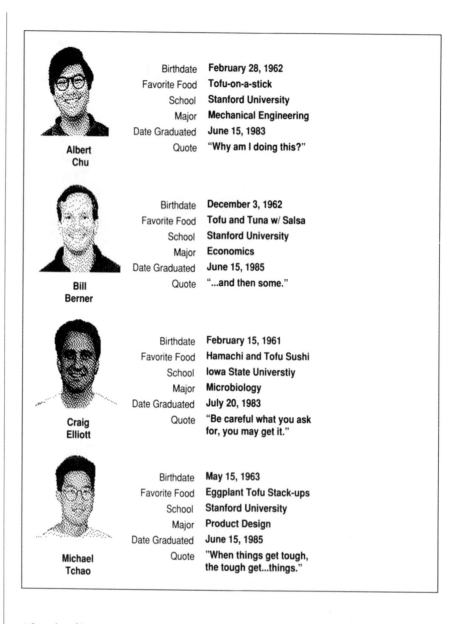

	Birthdate	February 28, 1962
	Favorite Food	Tofu-on-a-stick
	School	Stanford University
	Major	Mechanical Engineering
	Date Graduated	June 15, 1983
Albert Chu	Quote	"Why am I doing this?"

	Birthdate	December 3, 1962
	Favorite Food	Tofu and Tuna w/ Salsa
	School	Stanford University
	Major	Economics
	Date Graduated	June 15, 1985
Bill Berner	Quote	"...and then some."

	Birthdate	February 15, 1961
	Favorite Food	Hamachi and Tofu Sushi
	School	Iowa State Universtiy
	Major	Microbiology
	Date Graduated	July 20, 1983
Craig Elliott	Quote	"Be careful what you ask for, you may get it."

	Birthdate	May 15, 1963
	Favorite Food	Eggplant Tofu Stack-ups
	School	Stanford University
	Major	Product Design
	Date Graduated	June 15, 1985
Michael Tchao	Quote	"When things get tough, the tough get...things."

Description

This datafile contains information about the authors of *Approaching Macintosh*. One difference between this datafile and those in the modules is the inclusion of picture and date fields.

Photographs were digitized using an Apple Scanner, converted to MacPaint images, copied to the Clipboard, and pasted into the fields. The pasted image is scaled to fit the size of the field and can be distorted. It's best to make the field large enough to store the image unscaled.

Exercises

1. If you were designing the Course Listings datafile for the FileMaker Pro Introduction module, what type of field (text, date, number, picture) would you make the time field (the field that stores the time the course meets)? Why? Hint: It's not a picture field.

2. FileMaker Pro automatically saves any changes you make to a datafile. How then can you open a datafile, change some of the entries, and be able to quit without altering the datafile?

3. Imagine you're designing a datafile that stores names and birthdays. Accidentally, however, you make the birthday field a text field instead of a date field. How can you fix this, assuming

    a) You haven't closed the layout window yet?

    b) You've closed the layout window and already entered two records into the datafile?

4. What fields would you use when creating a datafile to store:

    a) A list of your albums, tapes, and compact discs?

    b) A list of books you used in writing a research paper? (Note that you can use this list to create a bibliography.)

    c) A list of important historical battles from the Civil War?

Justify your answers.

5. Using FileMaker Pro, create a dorm datafile that will keep information about the different people in your dorm. You can have as many fields as you like, but be sure to include fields for the first and last names, home and school telephone numbers, home and school addresses, and birth date. How could you adapt this datafile to print a mailing list of each student and their home address?

6. Adapt the datafile you created in Exercise 5 so that you can print mailing labels from the datafile. Use FileMaker's ability to have two views of the same form. Turn in a copy of the mailing list.

HOWDY DO.!

7 HyperCard

About HyperCard 2.0

HyperCard has been defined in many ways, but is probably best summed up as a personal programming and information management system. HyperCard allows information to be accessed and presented in a way that would be impossible by noncomputerized means. When information is presented in traditional written form, such as a book, it is usually accessed in a linear fashion. You start at the beginning and move toward the end. The amount of information that is delivered is set by the author, not the interest level of the reader.

HyperCard gives you the tools to present and access information in a much more flexible way. By creating links between pieces of information, you can move through data in the order and at the depth that is appropriate for you as the requester of the information. You can access information as you wish, exploring additional areas where you're interested and viewing only highlights where you're not.

HyperCard allows you to connect pieces of information by association. For instance, a time line might be drawn with several key dates in the history of soy foods highlighted. For an amateur soy history buff, this may be all the information required. A serious student of bean by-products, however, would need more information. With HyperCard each date on the time line could be linked to a complete account of the historical event. By clicking on the date on the time line, the additional information would appear, and the additional knowledge requested would be available.

The ability to establish these links between pieces of graphical and text information gives HyperCard its power and flexibility.

HyperCard Terms

Before you can get too far with HyperCard, there are some terms and concepts you must be familiar with.

Cards

HyperCard deals with a unit of information called a **card**. You can think of a HyperCard card as an electronic version of an index card. HyperCard cards come in different shapes and sizes, which you specify when you create them.

Stacks

A collection of related cards is a called a **stack**. Cards in a stack typically all contain information about one subject, and all the cards of a same stack are the same size. A stack of cards might be graphically represented by individual cards placed one on top of another.

Fields

In true Macintosh fashion, each card in a HyperCard stack contains text and graphics, or any combination of the two. The areas where text is located and changes from card to card are called **fields**.

Buttons

A HyperCard card can also contain **buttons**. When you click on a button, something happens. Exactly what happens is up to the programmer. Often, clicking a button takes you to another card, but buttons can also start sounds sounding, animations animating, or other exciting things.

Getting Started

Home

Addresses

HyperCard

This module assumes you are familiar with the basic use of the Macintosh. HyperCard is a sophisticated program and requires a hard disk to run effectively. The stacks that will be used in this module also require the font Palatino. Make sure your hard disk has this font loaded. If you're unfamiliar with how to load fonts, consult your Macintosh owner's manual.

You'll also need to check to make sure you have the necessary files to run HyperCard and to complete the exercises. Besides the HyperCard application itself, you'll always need a Home stack. HyperCard needs the Home stack to start so you'll need to copy that stack to your hard disk as well.

Also make sure that a new copy of the Addresses stack provided with HyperCard is available on your hard drive. If your Addresses stack is a modified copy, you'll still be able to complete the module, but you may see different information on the cards than is in this module's screens.

The second half of the module will use the Soy Stack from your Approaching Macintosh Diskette. Now would be a good time to copy that stack to your hard disk.

Double click on the HyperCard icon.

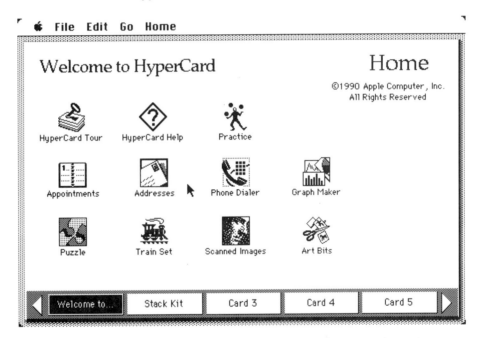

HyperCard automatically opens the **Home stack** first. There must always be a Home stack present to open HyperCard. If HyperCard is unable to find your Home stack, a dialog box will come up and require you to find it.

The Home stack is a directory for your most important HyperCard information. Each of the small pictures is a button that represents a link to a stack of information. To open a stack, you can click on one of the buttons on the Home card.

Only the most frequently used stacks have buttons on the Home stack, so if there isn't a button for the stack you want, you can use the Open Stack in the File menu to choose the stack directly.

The best way to understand the concepts behind HyperCard is to use it. In this module, you will use the Addresses stack to explore some of the most common elements of HyperCard.

As you move the mouse, you'll see the cursor shaped as a small hand. Position the extended index finger of the hand over the Addresses button and click.

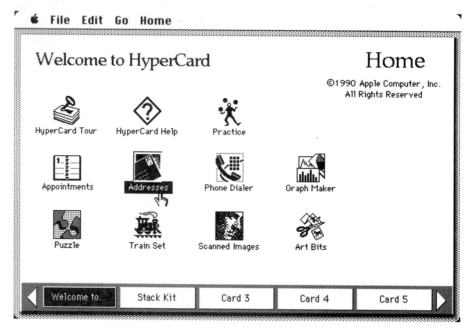

The first card of the Addresses stack will appear.

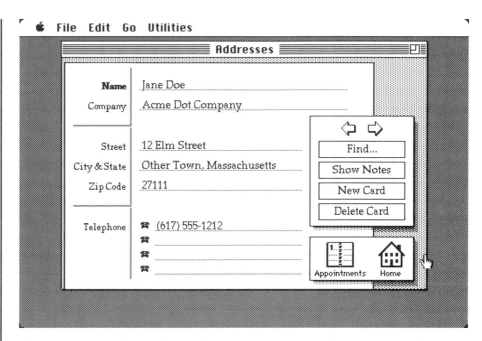

The Addresses stack is really an electronic rolodex. You'll use it to learn about HyperCard browsing techniques and the parts of a stack.

In order to make sure you have enough cards in the Addresses stack to practice browsing techniques, you'll start out by adding new cards to this stack.

Click the New Card button to add a blank card to the stack.

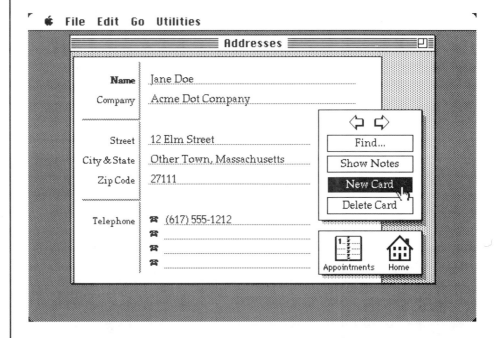

The New Card button creates a new, blank card that you can use to enter information. The **labels** are the titles for information in the stack. They remain the same. The **fields** are the areas where you enter text information. HyperCard uses information in the fields to search for cards—not in the labels.

Type "Connie Chung" in the Name field and press Return.

Type "Tofu for You, Inc." in the Company field.

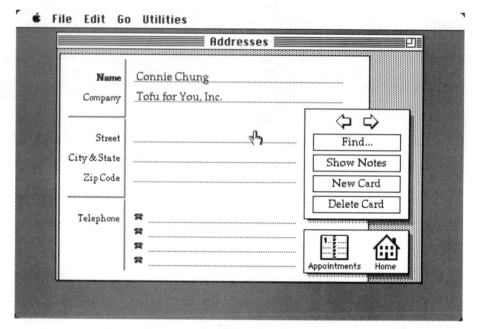

Press Tab to jump to the Address field and type "2030 Stevens Creek".

Press Return and type "Computertino, CA".

Press Return and type "95014".

Press Tab to jump to the Telephone field and type "408-555-3904".

You've just entered the information for a new card that should look like the one on the next page.

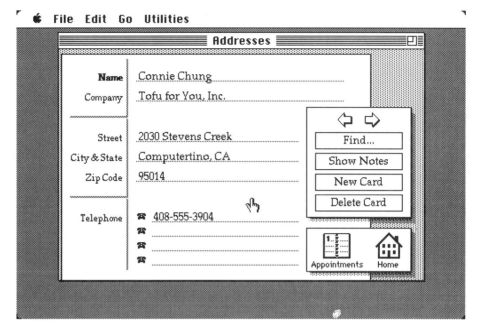

You'll need to create one more card.

Click the New Card button.

Enter the following information.

Type "Lisa Sprocket" in the Name field.

Press Return and type "Gearheads, Inc.".

Press Tab to jump to the Address field and type "Suite 479B, Route #1".

Press Return and type "Tempe, AZ".

Press Return and type "85224".

Press Tab to jump to the Telephone field and type "602-555-7580".

If you press Tab instead of Return and end up in the wrong field, click the mouse next to the field where you would like to enter information.

The card you just created should look like this:

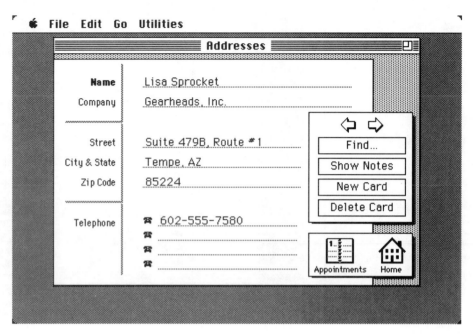

Browsing

Browsing is merely HyperCard's term for moving around among cards and stacks. When you move from one card to the next, HyperCard moves the front card on the back of the stack. You'll never come to the end of a HyperCard stack.

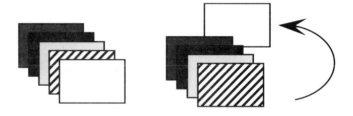

There should be at least three cards in the Addresses stack—Jane Doe, Connie Chung, and Lisa Sprocket. If the Addresses stack contained other cards, the actual card you see when browsing may be different than the one pictured. The important point to remember is how you move through the cards in the stack.

Click the Next Card button.

The right arrow takes you to the next card in the stack.

The second card is now at the top.

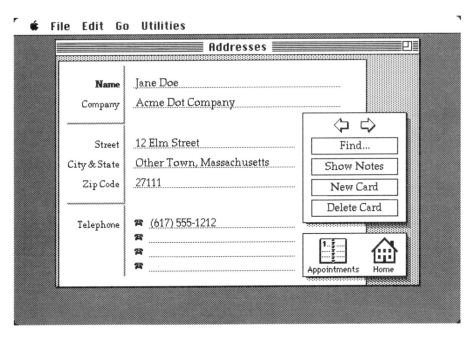

As you might imagine, the left arrow button takes you to the previous card of the stack and moves it to the top, just the opposite effect of the right arrow.

The top card is now at the bottom of the stack and the second card is now on top and visible. The left arrow key brings the bottom card of the stack back to the top.

Click the Previous Card button.

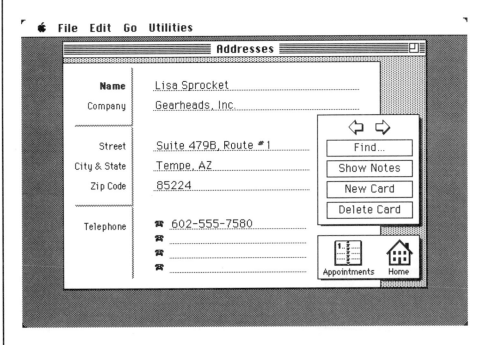

It's important to remember that cards are just placed on the bottom of the stack—not removed. For instance, if the right arrow key is hit enough times, each card in the stack will be shown, moved to the bottom of the stack, and then reappear on the top when all the other cards have been viewed.

HyperCard also has other methods besides the arrow buttons to move through the cards in a stack. In the Go menu, the first eight commands give you a series of options to help move through the cards.

Back	Takes you to the last card you were at
Home	Takes you to the first card of the Home stack
Help	Takes you directly to the HyperCard help stack
Recent	Shows you small pictures of the last 42 cards you have accessed. By clicking on any of the pictures of these cards you go directly to that card
First, Last	Takes you to the first or last card in the stack
Prev, Next	Moves you backward or forward one card at a time

Choose First from the Go menu.

You return to the first card in the stack.

Find

The arrow buttons and other browsing commands work well to move through cards one at a time, but in a large stack, this could become incredibly tedious. The Find command allows you to search all the cards in a stack for the words or parts of words contained in the fields. Remember, the Find command does not search HyperCard labels, just the fields where information is entered. In this stack, a button has been created called Find, but this may not always be the case. The Find command can also be chosen from the Go menu if a Find button isn't present.

Select the Find command in the Go menu.

Choosing Find brings up the **message box.** The flashing cursor comes up between the quotation marks. This is where you type the word you would like to find. It's very important that you type between the quotation marks for Hyper-Card.

Type "sprocket" and press Return.

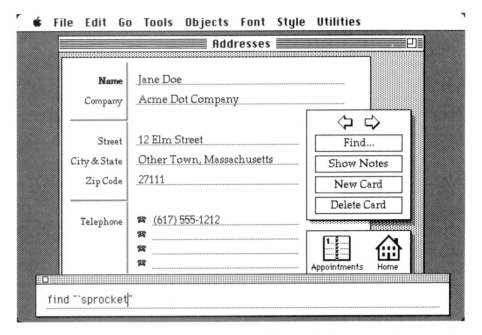

HyperCard finds the word "sprocket" in one of the cards, brings it to the top, and highlights the word. By pressing Return again, HyperCard will display the next card that contains that word. If HyperCard can't find the text, the Macintosh will beep.

You've used a few of the buttons in the Addresses stack, but sometimes it can be difficult to tell what is a button and what is just a graphic on a card. To find all the buttons on a card, hold down the Command and Option keys at the same time.

Hold down the Command and Option keys.

All the buttons will be outlined in gray.

Let go of the keys.

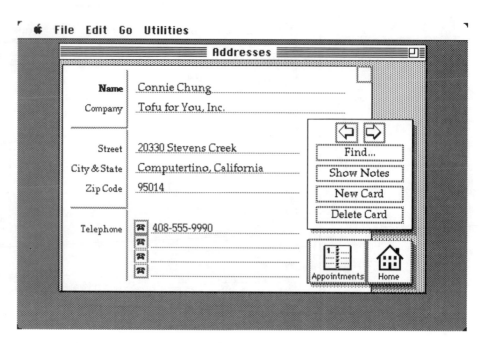

You may also want to return to a card you've seen recently. HyperCard keeps track of the last 42 cards that you've seen in reduced form, accessed by the Recent command in the Go menu.

Choose Recent from the Go menu.

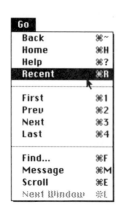

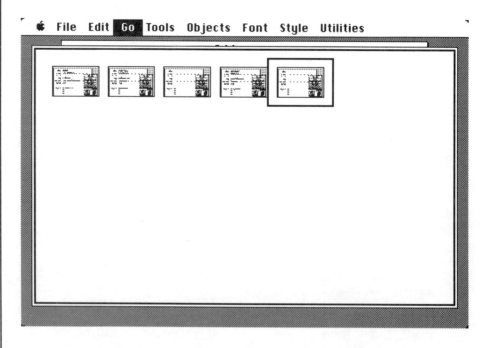

The small pictures represent the last cards you've seen. If you have been to one card more than once, it still only appears one time. Clicking on any of the small pictures takes you immediately to that card.

Click on one of the small pictures to jump directly to that card.

Choose Home from the Go menu.

Modifying a Stack

There are thousands of stacks created in HyperCard for a multitude of applications, but the real power resides in the ability to make your own. Up to this point, you have been browsing and entering data in the fields provided, but not making any changes to the cards or stacks themselves. In fact, you couldn't have made any changes if you had tried.

HyperCard has five **user levels** that allow you various abilities—from just exploring stacks and making no changes at all in level 1, to the complete ability to change everything in level 5. Each level contains all the abilities of the previous levels plus new abilities.

Choose Preferences from the Home menu.

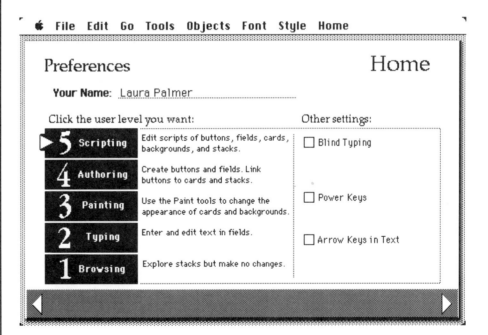

Click on level 5, Scripting, and type your name in the field provided.

Two new menu items now appear in the menu bar: Tools and Objects. These menus will be used in the creation and modification of stacks and cards.

You're ready to learn how to modify stacks, the first step toward creating your own.

Choose Open Stack... from the File Menu.

A dialog box with the options for opening a stack appears.

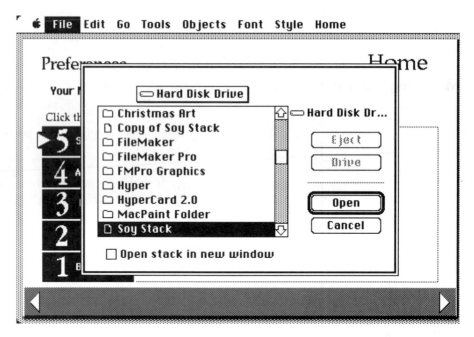

Find and select "Soy Stack", the stack you copied from your Approaching Macintosh Diskette in the beginning of this module.

Click Open.

The first card of the Soy Stack will appear. This stack contains some of the elements that you will need for the remainder of the module. You'll create the rest of the elements.

The stack you create will demonstrate HyperCard's ability to link information. You will link the diagram of the soybean to cards with more detailed text of its various parts. HyperCard also supports sound. You will link sound files with the buttons so the parts of the soybean are spoken as well as written.

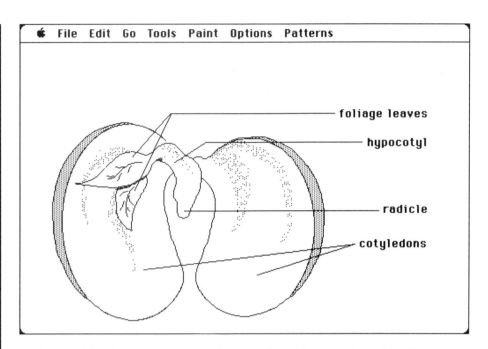

Background is where the common elements shared by a number of cards are stored. For instance, in the Addresses stack, the labels, buttons, and graphics remained the same in each of the cards. Each time a new card was created, those elements appeared.

In your new Soy Stack, you will have some common background elements that all the cards will share. The drawing of the bean and the titles of its parts will be contained in all of the cards you'll create. You'll add different elements to each card, but the basic drawing will remain.

Anything that you want to appear on every card in a stack and that you won't want to modify should be placed in the background. You'll need to add a title to all of the cards, so that will go in the background.

Choose Background from the Edit menu.

Notice the Menu bar now has dashed line around it. This lets you know that you're working on the background of a card.

Pull down the Tools menu and select the capital "A" Text tool.

The title of each of the cards will be the same, so you'll add that to the background.

Select Text Style... from the Edit menu.

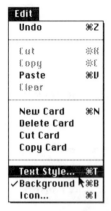

Choose Helvetica and 18. Click OK.

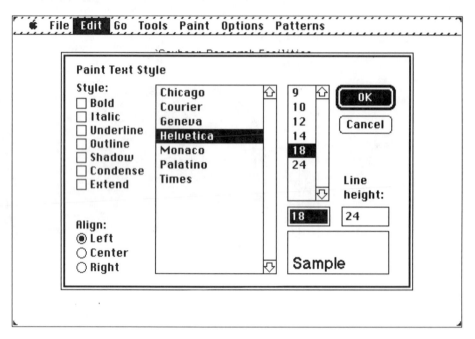

Click about half an inch down from the top of the card. Type "Soybean Anatomy".

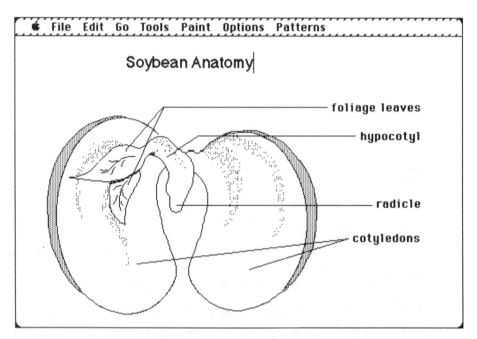

Since we are typing in the background (notice the dashed menu bar), this will become the title for all of the cards in this stack.

Use the lasso from the Tools menu to circle and move the title so it's in the top left corner of the card.

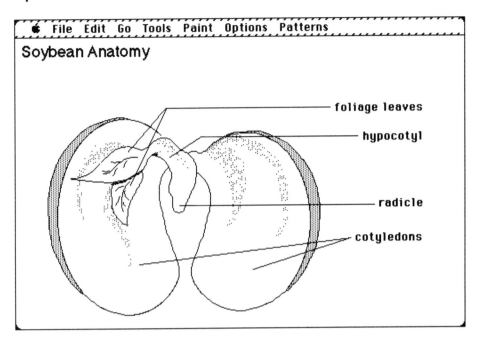

The diagram of the soybean and the title you just created will make up the background of each card in this stack. Since the background is now complete, you'll select Background again from the Edit menu to return to the foreground.

Select Background from the Edit menu.

Notice the dashed lines disappear from the menu bar.

Some people might be very well served by the diagram showing the main parts of the soybean. Others would want more information. By creating a new card with more detailed information and creating a link between it and the main card, you can provide more in-depth information. The reader can determine how much information he or she wants.

Now you are ready to create buttons and cards that will provide more detailed information about the diagram.

Choose New Card from the Edit Menu.

Creating a New Card

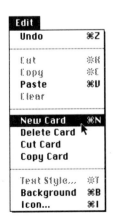

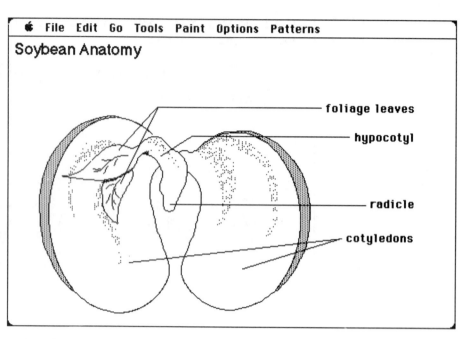

Did anything happen? Yes, an exact copy of the first card and its background was made. Now you'll modify this card to include more information about those ever fascinating foliage leaves.

First, you'll draw a box to type in the in-depth definition.

Select the rectangle tool from the Tools menu.

You'll want the rectangle that you draw to be filled in—not transparent—or the diagram will show through.

Select Draw Filled from the Options menu.

It would look best to have it filled in with white. The text will be easier to read.

Select the white pattern from the top left corner of the Patterns menu.

Now you're ready to draw the box where the text will go.

Draw a rectangular box, about 1 inch by 3 inches over the top of the words "foliage leaves".

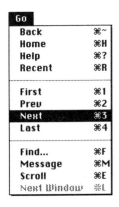

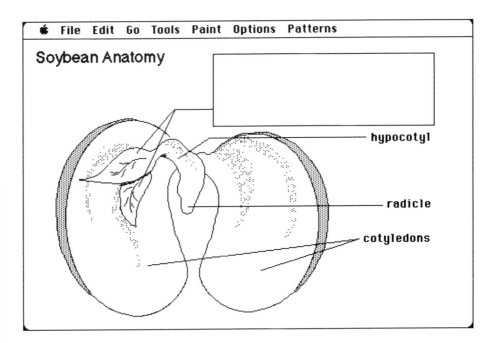

Adding Text

Now, you'll add the definition of foliage leaves to the box you just drew.

Choose the text tool from the Tools menu.

Choose Text Style from the Edit menu and select Helvetica, 12, and Bold.

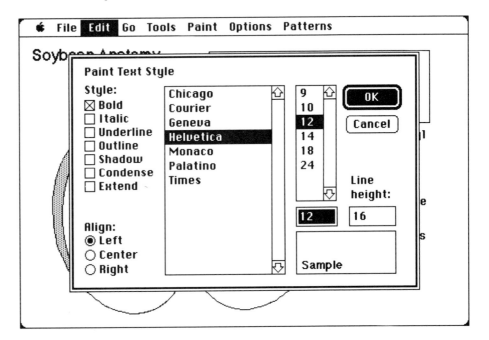

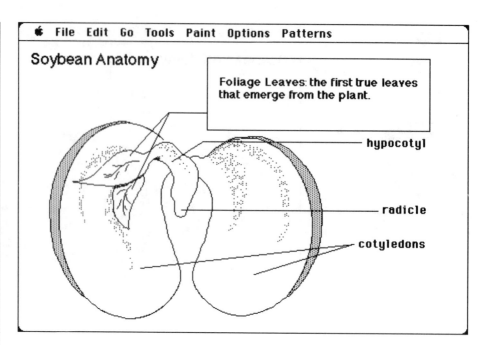

Type the following in the box:

    Foliage Leaves: the first true leaves to emerge from the plant.

Remember to press the Return key as you approach the right border of the box you drew.

Linking Cards

You have completed the card with the definition of foliage leaves. Now you have two cards—one with a broad overview, and one with more specific information. You need to create a way to link the information between the two cards.

Choose First from the Go menu to return to the original card.

You'll now create a button that will link the foliage leaf drawing of this card to the definition card you just created.

The second tool from the left in the Tools menu is the Button tool. When this tool is selected, HyperCard is in a special mode to work with buttons.

Select the Button tool from the Tools menu.

Now, you can create a new button.

Select New Button from the Objects menu.

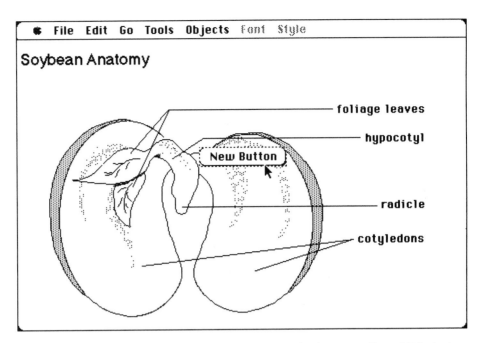

A new button, aptly named New Button, appears. This button will establish the link between this card and the card that you created with the definition of foliage leaves.

Use the pointer to drag the New Button over the top of the foliage leaves.

Once it's in place, drag the bottom right corner and stretch the button to cover the foliage leaves completely.

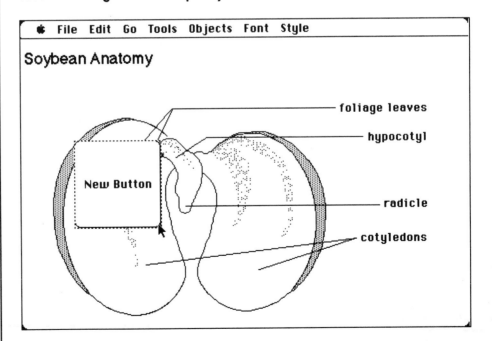

The attributes of buttons (including the name) can be modified by selecting Button info while a button is selected. You can tell a button is selected when its border moves, like a marquis.

If the New Button's border is not moving, click on it.

It's important to remember that when selecting buttons, you must be using the Button tool in the Tools menu (second over from the left, top row).

Select Button Info... from the Objects menu.

Replace the name "New Button" with "Foliage Leaves".

This will be the name used to refer to the button.

Click on Show Name so it is NOT checked.

If Show Name was left selected, the words "Foliage Leaves" would appear in the center of your button.

By making the button transparent, you'll be able to see the diagram underneath.

Under the Style column, click on Transparent.

To make the button flash black when it is selected, you will select Auto Hilite. This is particularly useful with transparent buttons.

Click on Auto Hilite.

The dialog box should look like this:

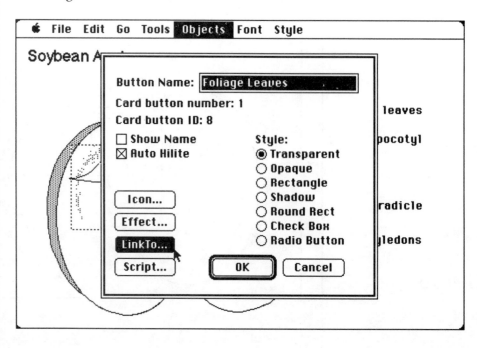

Now you'll create a link between the button you've defined and the card that includes the definition of foliage leaves.

Click Link To...

The Link To dialog box comes up. This is a unique dialog box because it will remain active when you use other menus.

This is the way to establish links between the Foliage Leaves button and the card you created with the definition. In this case the card is the previous card. You'll move back to it to establish the link.

Choose Prev from the Go menu.

The first card appears.

Click on This Card to establish the link.

Clicking on the Foliage Leaves button will take you to the card with the foliage leaves definition. This card is now in front.

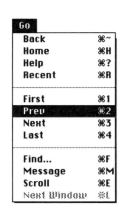

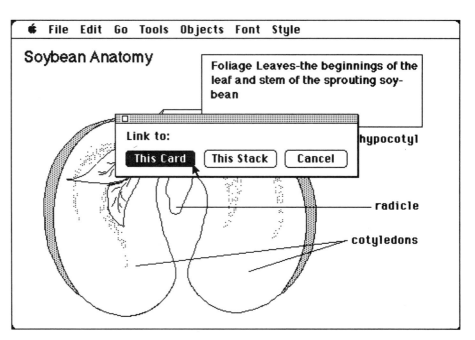

You just performed an exercise in computer programming, HyperCard style. While you were establishing the link between the Foliage Leaves button and the definition card, HyperCard was writing a simple computer program, called a script, to describe the actions.

Click on the Foliage Leaves button you created.

Choose Button Info from the Objects menu and click on Script.

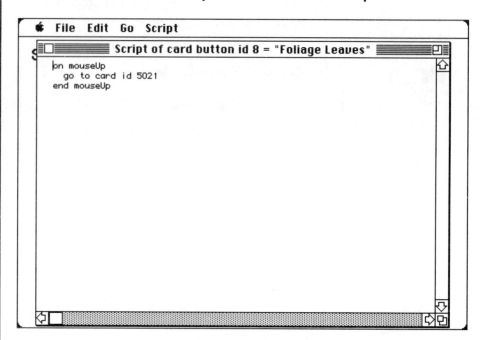

```
on mouseUp
   go to card id 5021
end mouseUp
```

The script is a very simple one. When the mouse is clicked on the Foliage Leaves button, HyperCard goes to the card with the ID of 5021 (your number maybe different, but that's your definition card).

Adding Sounds

These scripts can be edited so you can do your own programming. As mentioned in the beginning of this module, HyperCard can also use sound. Buttons can play sounds that have been recorded and stored in the HyperCard stack. Because the Macintosh system you're using might not have the ability to record sound, we've recorded and stored some sounds for you.

Click just to the right of the card id number in the script and press Return.

This will give you a blank line on which to type.

Type 'play "Foliage Leaves"'.

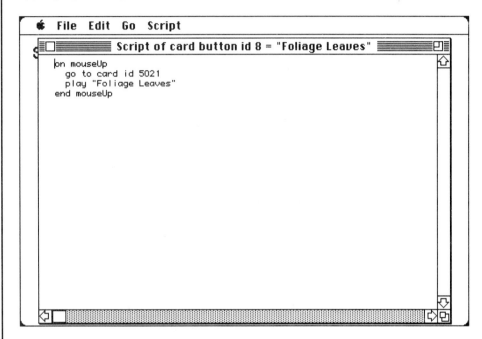

The command "play" followed by the name of the sound file, in this case, "Foliage Leaves", will cause HyperCard to play the sound.

Now, you'll see if it worked.

Click in the close box at the top left corner of the script window.

Click Yes to save your changes.

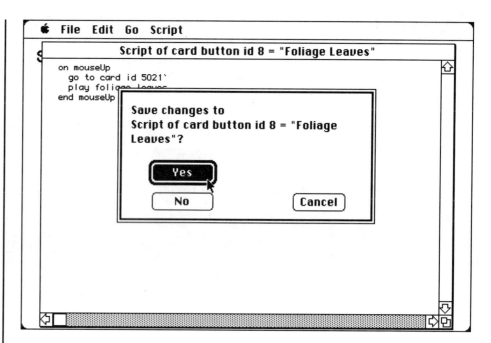

You're still using the button tool. Now, you'll change back to the standard pointer.

Choose the pointer tool from the Tools menu.

Although the outline of the Foliage Leave button disappeared, it's still there.

Click on the foliage leaves in the diagram.

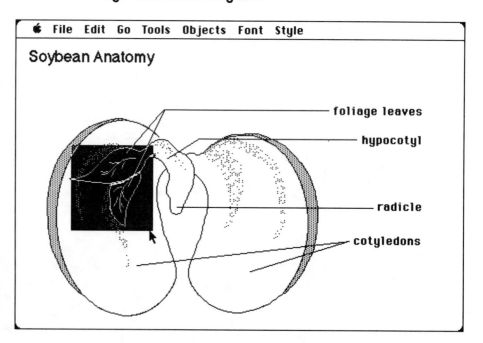

If things went as planned, the Foliage Leaves button should have flashed black (Auto Hilite), the definition should have move to the top of the stack and been displayed, and a sound should have been played.

Pretty neat, huh? And you didn't think you were a programmer.

Choose Prev from the Go menu.

You're back to the main card.

There are three other parts of the soybean diagram that can have exactly the same kind of button as the one you just created for the Foliage Leaves.

Finishing Up

The steps for creating these buttons are exactly the same:

1) Start with the main card, create a new card, and add the definition of the soybean part..
2) Create a new button and place it over the plant part on the main soybean card.
3) Set the attributes for the button.
4) Link the button on the main card to the definition card.
5) Add the "play sound" command with the appropriate sound name to the script for the button you created.
6) Try it.

If the sound doesn't play, check to make sure the spelling is exactly as printed below. The names must match the sound files that were created and saved in the Soy Stack.

The definitions for the other plant parts are as follows:

Hypocotyl: the "first stem" that elongates to push the new plant through the soil.
Sound name: hypocotyl

Radicle: the shoot that initiates root development.
Sound name: radicle

Cotyledons: food source for the new seedlings.
Sound name: cotyledon

Optional

Platypus: a small mammal rarely found in large cities.
Sound name: platypus

Complete the stack by repeating the instructions for the other three parts of the soybean (platypus is optional).

Printing

Your stack is now complete. Now you'll print a copy of all the cards you created.

Make sure your printer is turned on, selected properly in the Chooser, and ready to print.

Choose Print Stack... from the File menu.

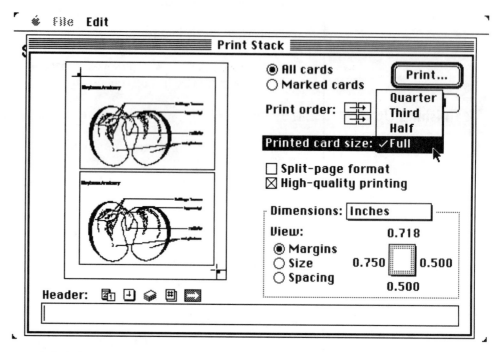

The default for printing a stack is two cards per printed page. By printing out the cards in half, third or quarter size, you can get up to 28 cards (very small ones) per page.

Individual cards may be printed by choosing Print Card from the File menu.

Review

In this module, you've learned:

- The parts of a Hypercard stack and card
- How to add information to a stack
- How to find a card by searching
- How to create and modify a new card
- How to create buttons and use them to link cards
- How to modify scripts
- How to print stacks

What to Turn In

A printed copy of all the cards in your stack.

The Map

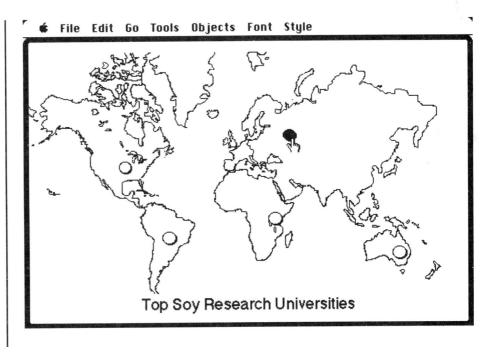

File Edit Go Tools Objects Font Style

Soybean Research Facilities

Annual Production	300 million Metric Tons
Research College	Iowa State University
Director of Legumes	Lisa Lenkaitis
Address	318 Welch Avenue
City	Ames
State/Country	Iowa/ USA
Zip	50212

Return to Map

Home

Description

This HyperCard stack contains a world map with buttons linked with cards that contain detailed information on various universities that carry out soybean research. By linking the map card with the more typical database style card, a user can simply click on a button to find out about a university in a particular area. A standard database might require typing country names to search for until a match was made—very inconvenient.

The map was created in MacPaint, copied to the Clipboard and pasted into HyperCard.

Exercises

1. Define card, stack, background, field, Home card, and label.

2. Why will you never come to the end of a HyperCard stack?

3. Give an example of when you would draw on the background and when you would not. How do you know if you are in the background?

4. How would you move ahead one card in a stack? Move back one card? Jump directly to a card you recently viewed?

5. Name two common elements that cards in the same stack share. Which one of these is absolute and which one just makes sense?

6. How do labels and fields differ? If you wanted to search for information in a stack, would it be better in a label or a field?

7. What would be the fastest way for you to locate the card that you just saw that had an Arizona address in a field? Another way that isn't as fast?

8. How can you check to see where all the buttons are on a card?

9. How could you create a stack that would only allow people to view information, but not change it? Enter information, but not paint or move buttons? Make any changes they wished?

HOWDY DO!

8 Reference

Glossary

Index

Glossary

absolute reference
In a spreadsheet, a reference that always refers to the same cell or group of cells, even if you copy the formula containing the reference. For example, C12.

active window
The frontmost window on the desktop. The title bar of an active window is highlighted with horizontal lines.

Apple menu
The menu found under the  symbol at the far left of the menu bar. The Apple menu contains desk accessories such as the Chooser and Find File.

MacPaint   Word

application program
A tool used to manipulate information. Claris MacPaint and Microsoft Word, for example, are application programs for the Macintosh.

argument
Information needed by a function or an instruction to produce a result.

arrow keys
The arrow keys are used to navigate through a document.

background
In Hypercard, information that is shared by a group of cards. Changes to the group's background affect all of the cards in the group.

bitmap
A graphic image created by selectively turning on and off pixels on a computer screen. A MacPaint document is a bitmap graphic.

browse
To move through a set of information, often used in reference to data bases and HyperCard stacks.

button
Clicking a button designates, confirms, or cancels an action. Buttons are usually found in dialog boxes or HyperCard stacks.

Cancel button
A button which, when clicked, cancels the command that brought up the dialog box.

card
The basic set of information that makes up HyperCard.

cell
The basic unit of a spreadsheet in which you store numbers, labels, and formulas. A cell is the intersection of a row and a column.

choose
To pick a command from a pull-down menu. To choose a command, press the mouse button in the menu title, drag the mouse until the appropriate command is highlighted, and release the mouse button.

Chooser
The Chooser is a desk accessory that you use to select resources (such as a printer or a file server).

click
To quickly press and release the mouse button without moving the mouse.

Clipboard
A temporary holding place for the most recently cut or copied selection. The Clipboard can be used to transfer text, graphics, or other information between documents.

close
To remove a window from the desktop. To close a window, choose the Close command from the File menu, or click in the window's close box at the upper left corner of the title bar.

close box
The small white box on the left side in the title bar of an active window. Clicking in this box closes the window.

command
An action for the Macintosh to perform. Commands are usually found in the menus.

Command key
A special key found just to the left of the space bar on the keyboard. When held down while another key is pressed, the Command key may have the same effect as choosing a command from a menu.

cut
To remove a selection using the Cut command from the Edit menu. The cut selection is stored temporarily on the Clipboard.

data base
An organized collection of related information (data).

datafile

The name given to a Claris FileMaker document. It consists of a collection of records organized into a data base.

Delete key

A key at the upper right-hand corner of the Macintosh keyboard that moves the insertion point one space to the left, removing the last character typed. The Delete key also removes the current selection.

desk accessories

Small applications that can be opened from the Apple menu, at any time—even while you're using another application. The Chooser, Find File, and Note Pad are examples of desk accessories.

desktop

The area of the Macintosh screen where you do your work. The desktop includes the menu bar and the gray area below it.

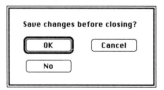

dialog box

A box that appears with a message to request more information from the user. The message can be a warning or error message.

Diet Coke

A basic source of nourishment and caffeine for aspiring authors.

dimmed icon

An icon representing a diskette that has been ejected, or a document, folder, or application on a diskette that has been ejected.

diskette

The magnetic medium on which the Macintosh stores information. Single-sided diskettes store 400 kilobytes (K) of information. Double-sided diskettes store 800K of information. High-density diskettes store 1,400K, or 1.4 megabytes (MB), of information.

diskette drive

The diskette drive (either internal—part of the Macintosh, or external—connected to the Macintosh) retrieves information from the diskette and stores information on it.

document

What you create using a Macintosh application. Macintosh remembers the application you used to create your document, and opens the application automatically when you open your document.

double-click

A mouse technique used to perform a short cut. To double-click, position the pointer on the desired item (for example, an icon) and click the mouse button twice in rapid succession without moving the mouse.

drag

To position the pointer on an item, press and hold the mouse button, and move the mouse to a new location. Releasing the mouse button either confirms a selection or moves the item to a new location.

Enter key

A special key, found at the bottom right of the numeric keypad, that confirms or terminates an entry or a command.

field

In a data base, where one specific piece of information in a record is stored. A field can usually only hold one specific type of information (for example, text, number, boolean, and picture).

file

A collection of information stored on a hard disk or diskette, usually a document.

Finder

An application used to manage hard disks, diskettes, documents, folders, and applications on the Macintosh desktop.

folder

A holder for documents and applications on the desktop. You use folders to organize and group your documents and applications.

font

A collection of typographical symbols, such as letters, numbers, and punctuation marks that are visually related. An example of a Macintosh font is Times.

handles

Small black or white boxes that surround a selection, allowing you to resize or reshape it.

hard disk

A place to store a lot of information, such as applications, documents, and HyperCard stacks. A hard disk is like a very, very large and very, very fast diskette.

highlight

To make something stand out against its background. An item is usually highlighted to indicate that it has been selected or chosen.

Home card
In HyperCard, an index to your important stacks.

I-bar
A special type of pointer used in entering and editing text.

icon
A small picture of an item on the Macintosh desktop, like a hard disk, a folder, and so on.

information window
A window that appears when you choose the Get Info command from the File menu. The information window contains such information as the size, type, and date of the currently selected diskette, application, document, or folder.

initialize
To prepare a diskette to receive information. All diskettes must be initialized before they can be used.

insertion point
The point in a document where something will be added. The insertion point is usually marked by a flashing vertical bar.

lock
Locking a diskette prevents that diskette from being altered. Locking a document prevents it from being discarded. To lock a diskette, set the write protect tab at the upper right corner of the diskette.

memory
The part of the Macintosh that stores information while you work with it. When you turn your Macintosh off, everything stored in memory is lost. Saving transfers a copy of the information in memory onto your hard disk or diskette for safe-keeping.

menu
A list of commands that appears when you press the mouse button while over the menu title in the menu bar. Dragging through the menu highlights each command in order. Releasing the mouse button while a command is highlighted chooses that command.

menu bar
The list of menu titles that runs across the top of the Macintosh desktop.

mouse
A small device that you move to control the pointer on the Macintosh screen. When you move the mouse, the pointer moves correspondingly on the screen.

mouse button
The button on the top of the mouse. In general, pressing the mouse button initiates some action on whatever is under the pointer, and releasing the button confirms the action.

Note Pad
A desk accessory that allows you to enter and edit small amounts of text while working on another document. Use the Note Pad to store phone numbers, messages, and other information that might otherwise get lost when you're working with your Macintosh.

open
Opening a document, application, folder, or hard disk creates a window from its icon

Option key
A key used like the Shift key to give an alternate meaning to another key. You can use the Option key to type foreign characters or special symbols.

palette
A menu that has been "torn off" of the menu bar and is positioned somewhere on the screen.

paste
To reposition the contents of the Clipboard—whatever was last cut or copied.

pattern
A variety of shades, simulated textures, or colors used in computerized painting and drawing applications.

pixel
Stands for *picture element,* the dots that make up the images on the Macintosh screen.

platypus
A small, four-legged mammal not usually found in large cities.

point
A unit of measure often used with text characters. One point is equivalent to 1/72 of an inch.

pointer
A small shape on the screen that follows the movement of the mouse. Most often an arrow that points up and to the left (toward Alaska, for those in the continental United States. Note that if you live in Alaska, the mouse points somewhere else— we're not quite sure where, but most probably still up and to the left).

pop-up menu
A menu that can appear anywhere on the screen.

Power On key
Used to turn on some Macintosh computers (most modular Macintosh computers can be turned on this way).

press
To position the pointer and then hold down the mouse button without moving the mouse.

record
One entry in a data base. A record is made up of fields that store the specific pieces of information.

relative reference
In a spreadsheet, a reference to a cell's position in relation to another cell. For example, if A1 is the current cell, the reference "B3" refers to the cell that is one column to the right and two rows down from the current cell. A relative reference will indicate a different cell each time the formula moves.

report
A presentation of database information in the form of a table. A report allows you to perform mathematical calculations on the information.

Return key
A key that moves the insertion point to the beginning of the next line. It's also, in some cases, used to confirm a command.

save
To store information on a hard disk or diskette. Saving transfers a copy of information in memory to the hard disk or diskette.

Scrapbook
A desk accessory in which you save frequently-used pictures or text.

script
A set of commands written in HyperTalk, HyperCard's programming language.

scroll
To move the contents of a window so that a different part of it is visible.

scroll arrow
An arrow on either end of a scroll bar. Clicking a scroll arrow moves the document or directory one line in the direction of the arrow. Pressing a scroll arrow scrolls the document continuously.

scrollbar
A rectangular bar that appears along the right or bottom edge of a window. Clicking in the gray area of the scroll bar moves the contents of the window a screenful at a time.

scrollbox
A small, white box found in a scroll bar that indicates the position of the window's contents relative to the entire document. For instance, if the scroll box appears at the top of the scroll bar, the current window displays the first part of the document. Dragging the scroll box to a position on the scroll bar moves you to that position in the document.

select
To indicate where the next action will take place. Usually, selected items are highlighted to set them apart.

selection
The information or items affected by the next command. The selection is usually highlighted to make it stand out from its surroundings.

shift-click
To extend a selection by holding down the Shift key while you click or drag to select additional items.

Shift key
A key that, when pressed, causes a typed letter to appear in uppercase. Also causes the upper symbol to be typed when used with a number or symbol key.

size box
A box on the bottom right of some active windows that lets you resize a window.

software
Programs or instructions for the Macintosh to carry out.

soybean
A small legume used, among other things, to produce tofu.

splitbar
In some Macintosh applications, a small box that can be used to divide a window into two or more panes. By dividing a window into panes, you can view more than one part of a document at the same time.

stack
A collection of cards based on the same subject and of the same size. A Hyper-Card document.

startup disk

A hard disk or diskette with the system files necessary to start the Macintosh when it's first switched on. Usually startup disks have a system folder with the System and Finder files on it.

style

A stylistic variation of a font, such as **boldface,** <u>underline</u>, or *italic*.

Tab key

A key that, when pressed, moves the insertion point to the next tab marker. In a dialog box, the Tab key usually moves the insertion point to the next rectangle to enter information.

title bar

The horizontal bar at the top of a window that displays the name of what's inside the window. Dragging the title bar lets you move the window on the desktop.

tofu

A food made from soybeans.

Trash

A place where you can put documents or applications that you want to get rid of. The Trash bloats when something is in it.

window

An area of the desktop that displays information. You view documents through windows that you open on the desktop. Windows can also be moved, over-lapped, resized, scrolled, and closed.

zoom box

A box in the title bar of a window. You click in the zoom box to make the window fill the entire screen.

Index

**About
the Authors**

In the olden days, before 1984, not many Stanford University undergraduates used personal computers—for a very good reason. Not many of them knew how—and not very many of them wanted to learn. After all, in those days it meant sleeping through endless lectures, wading through computer manuals as thick as the Manhattan Yellow Pages, and staying awake all night memorizing cryptic commands and equally cryptic error messages.

Then, on a particularly bright day in Stanford, California, some particularly bright undergraduates had a particularly bright idea: since only students really understood what other students were all about, they could teach each other about personal computers. Not just any personal computer, mind you, but the zippiest, friendliest, most engaging personal computer around—the Apple Macintosh.

So it was that this band of zany undergraduates worked long days, late nights, and a few legal holidays using their Macintoshes to help them get through school, and teaching other students how to do the same. They taught about how to use MacWrite to write home for money, how to use MacPaint to draw maps of Upper Malta, and how to use Microsoft Word to send out customized resumes to perspective employers.

Five years later, on another particularly bright day in Cupertino, California, some particularly bright Apple employees had a particularly obvious idea: the book they had written five years earlier needed a revision.

So, they dusted off the coffee pot, took their phones off the hook, and settled in for another string of sleepless nights, restless weekends, and seemingly endless revisions.

The results of their efforts is this book: *Approaching Macintosh,* Second Edition. And while some said it couldn't be done, no one is more amazed to see it in print than the authors themselves.